The Althouse Press
Faculty of Education, The University of Western Ontario
Sobocan and Groarke, CRITICAL THINKING EDUCATION AND
ASSESSMENT: CAN HIGHER ORDER
THINKING BE TESTED?

Critical Thinking Education and Assessment:

Can Higher Order Thinking Be Tested?

Edited by Jan Sobocan
and Leo Groarke
with Ralph H. Johnson
and Frederick S. Ellett, Jr.

The Althouse Press

First published in Canada in 2009 by
THE ALTHOUSE PRESS
Dean: *Julia O'Sullivan*
Director of Publications: *Greg Dickinson*
Faculty of Education, The University of Western Ontario
1137 Western Road, London, Ontario, Canada N6G 1G7

Editorial Assistants: *Jessie Coffey, Katherine Butson, Lois Armstrong*
Cover Design: *Louise Gadbois*

Library and Archives Canada Cataloguing in Publication

Critical thinking education and assessment : can higher order thinking be tested? / Jan Sobocan, Leo Groarke, editors.

Includes index.
ISBN 978-0-920354-66-7

1. Critical thinking—Study and teaching (Higher). 2. Creative thinking—Study and teaching (Higher). 3. Critical thinking—Testing. 4. Creative thinking—Testing. 5. Educational tests and measurements. I. Sobocan, Jan, 1966- II. Groarke, Leo

LB2395.35.C754 2008   370.15'2   C2008-906248-5

Printed and bound in Canada by Aylmer Express Limited, 390 Talbot Street East, Aylmer, Ontario, N5H 1J5.

Contents

In Memoriam

Chester Potyrak, 1958–2002

This book is dedicated to the memory of Chester Potyrak. Chester was an accomplished physician who loved philosophy—the dedicated son of my dear friend Anastasia (Stella) Potyrak. Chester's professors at the University of Toronto considered him one of the brightest minds they had ever taught. I talked at length with him about ways of thinking and the Socratic method, and he always tested the limits of my thinking. The end of his life was shattering for many, but none more than his mother.

When Stella was fifteen, her family was interned in prison camps under Stalin. She lost three brothers to the sicknesses that spread on overcrowded camp trains. Her father died of starvation, and her mother died shortly after being tortured for stealing frozen potatoes for her children. Stella's journey to Canada was a long and circuitous one that took many years. Once in Canada for some time, she lost her husband to cancer, six years after her only child was born.

Stella and her son Chester spent their lifetimes struggling to face and fight the shadows of those horrific events and deaths. Even in the face of her loss of Chester, Stella has maintained her strength and dignity through to her eighties. My extended and meaningful talks about critical thinking in the Potyrak backyard have ceased, but my and Stella's quiet gardening, bird feeding, and cooking continued for some time.

Stella told me her entire story with sadness, but without complaint. She has continued to love everyone around her with all of her heart despite the silence, despair, and abuse that conditioned much of her living. This silence and her graciousness give me pause for thinking now. This mother and her son expressed to me in many ways that thinking critically assumes a freedom and peace that we take too much for granted. They both believed in the intent behind my work and have provided financial and moral support for it to be realized.

I write this dedication with gratefulness and hope that all of us are inspired to consider our complaints more carefully and, instead, pause every day to appreciate our lives in this beautiful, spacious, and democratic Canada—as least as much as the Potyraks did.

—Jan Sobocan

Acknowledgments

I would like to thank Michael Scriven and Robert H. Ennis for accepting my invitation to be keynote speakers at the conference where the ideas for this book originated. Without their participation, I would not have been able to bring together so many distinguished scholars, government representatives, and teachers. I will always be grateful for their modesty and their willingness to support me as a student—even though I was not *their* student.

For their support, I must thank Ralph H. Johnson and J. Anthony Blair, my former teachers and supervisors, who taught me how to organize, administer, and conceptualize, and who have inspired me with their passionate teaching of critical thinking and argumentation thus impelling me to continue my career in this area. Special thanks to my co-editor Leo Groarke, who, with and apart from this book project, has helped me to remain both sane and confident in all aspects of my career, and who has consistently and unconditionally supported my work in critical thinking education.

Thank you to all of the contributors to this volume, many of whom travelled long distances to spend three relentless, tightly scheduled days sorting through complex issues in a small conference room. The conference was an incredible learning experience that I will not forget. A special acknowledgment goes to Lorna Earl, distinguished speaker, academic, and former director of the EQAO Office, for bringing to the conference invaluable ideas, honest commentary, and good humour. She taught me to better appreciate and understand government officials and the work and dedication they put into improving education.

Key behind-the-scene supporters who worked hard in support of the conference included Dr. Fred Ellett, my PhD co-supervisor, who helped with the organization of the conference, sold it to the administration, and found the perfect conference location when I ran out of options. My other co-supervisor, Suzanne Majhanovich, was another key supporter. I want to thank her for taking time out of her busy schedule to tirelessly send me articles on critical thinking and testing, for preparing and attending the conference in the place of Carol Ann Giancarlo-Gittens, for doing such a wonderful job presenting and arguing the issues on Carol's behalf, and for taking notes of all of the responses. I am very grateful for the work of Fred and Suzanne which extended far beyond normal doctoral supervision.

I want to acknowledge Anne Escrader and Rick Kitto, my fellow PhD students, for giving me their support before, during, and after the workshop and for their enthusiastic participation in it. The support of Western's former Dean of Education, Allen Pearson; Greg Dickinson, Director of The Althouse Press; Research Western; and, Stella Potyrak (who personally helped finance the conference) made this book possible.

Thanks to my friend, Antin Jaremchuk, for his artistic inspiration and Steve Fife for his photographic contribution—both lent significantly to the striking cover created by Louise Gadbois. Many people helped me persevere through technological struggles and more creatively reach my goals. They include Clint Bourdeau, Lois Armstrong, and especially Richard Gilmore.

Without the consistently exceptional, patient, and friendly support of The Althouse Press's team, namely, Greg Dickinson, Katherine Butson, and Jessie Coffey, this book would not be so well organized, both physically and conceptually. This was the most efficient and hardworking team with whom I have ever had the pleasure to work.

Special thanks are due for the financial, mental, and emotional support of the many friends, teachers, and colleagues in my life, who kept me balanced through the whole process, and who listen patiently and endlessly to my critical thinking theories. These people, among others, include my mom, Corinne Trepanier-Sobocan; my sister, Anne-Marie Elliott; Cre and Bogdan Comanita, Wendi Roscoe, Joyce and Duri Dobransky, Patricia Merka, Lois Ward, Maggie Johnson, Maureen O'Dwyer, Derek and Patsy Allison, Dianne Nemcek, Michelle Foster, and Kathy Hibbert (who always shows interest in my work on critical thinking); my first and very influential reasoning skills professor, Dr. Mark Letteri; and Dr. Janet Pope, my rheumatologist, for keeping me optimistic and making it possible for me to physically and mentally work through seemingly endless hours of pain and sleeplessness. I must extend to my family—Steve Fife, Rae-Anne, Vincent, and Holly— thanks for all of the music and laughter, and for putting up with my nuttiness and ever-changing work schedule. I have learned many things in this process, but the most important one is that without any of the people above who share my vision, push me on personally, and, most importantly, mind my children, my success in achieving *any* work in academe as a single parent would not have been possible.

Finally, and most importantly, my ultimate gratitude is to Dr. Ralph H. Johnson (Dr. J.), the teacher who changed my life and who is my mentor. Dr. J. taught me for so many years, when I was barely teachable and when I finally excelled. He always believed in me, and with me, that in teaching critical thinking we might be able make the world a better place. Because of what he taught me and modelled for me, I will always and enthusiastically keep trying to make life better by teaching and exercising critical thinking. I hope that whatever personal, social, and educational obstacles they face, this book will inspire people to do the same.

—Jan Sobocan

⟩⟩⟩⟩⟨⟨⟨

First and foremost, I want to thank Jan Sobocan for the opportunity to help her with this book, and applaud her vision in recognizing the importance of the questions it addresses. Many other people assisted in the assessment of the papers and their preparation for publication. I would, in particular, like to thank Ralph Johnson and Greg Dickinson for their careful reading of the papers it contains. I am grateful for the opportunity to work within an informal logic/critical thinking community which is actively committed to furthering our understanding of the assessment, analysis, and teaching of critical thinking and its ideals. Even as teenagers, my children, Jazz, Scott, and Katie, kept me balanced while I was working on the book.

—Leo Groarke

List of Contributors

J. Anthony Blair is Professor Emeritus of Philosophy and Co-Director of the Centre for Research in Reasoning, Argumentation and Rhetoric at the University of Windsor. He is co-founder and co-editor of the journal *Informal Logic*, the co-author of *Logical Self-Defense*, and *Reasoning: A Practical Guide*. He has published many noted essays on reasoning and argument. He is a founding member and current executive committee member of the Association for Informal Logic and Critical Thinking, and a board member of the International Society for the Study of Argumentation.

Roland Case is Executive Director of The Critical Thinking Consortium, an international association working to support critical thinking from grade school to graduate school. Before retirement, Roland was Professor of Curriculum at Simon Fraser University. He has written various scholarly and professional articles on critical thinking and edits *Critical Challenges Across the Curriculum*, an award-winning series of teaching resources for critical thinking. Roland is the 2006 recipient of CUFA's Distinguished Academics Career Achievement Award.

Frederick S. Ellett, Jr. is Associate Professor of Education at The University of Western Ontario. His areas of interest include theories of rational action and moral-ethical criticism; theories of educational aims; and theories of educational evaluation, research, and policy. He has published papers on the philosophy of education, rationality, and values in education.

Robert H. Ennis is Professor Emeritus of Philosophy of Education at the University of Illinois, Adjunct Professor of Philosophy at

New College, Florida, and former Professor of Philosophy of Education at Cornell University. He has long been interested in the conception and assessment of critical thinking, and in such concepts of research and assessment as causality, explanation, definition, reliability, and validity; often approaching issues from an ordinary-language point of view. He is co-author of three critical thinking tests and a book on evaluating critical thinking, and author of a critical thinking text and approximately fifty published articles.

Bart Garssen is Assistant Professor in the Department of Speech Communication, Argumentation Theory and Rhetoric at the University of Amsterdam. He has published on argumentation schemes and the study and teaching of reasoning from the pragma-dialectical perspective.

Carol Ann Giancarlo-Gittens is an Associate Professor of Education at Santa Clara University. She serves as the University's Director of Assessment as well as the Associate Dean of the School of Education, Counseling Psychology and Pastoral Ministries. In addition to her administrative roles, Dr. Giancarlo-Gittens teaches courses in educational assessment, research methods, instructional technology, critical thinking across the curriculum, psychological foundations of education, developmental psychology, and community health education. Her scholarly works examine the relationship between critical thinking, motivation, and academic achievement in adolescent and young adult samples. She is author of the *California Measure of Mental Motivation* (CM3), a critical thinking disposition assessment instrument for children, adolescents, and adults, and the new Adolescent Reasoning Test (ART), a critical thinking skills test specifically for adolescents.

Leo Groarke is Vice President/Principal of the Brantford Campus of Wilfrid Laurier University and Professor of Philosophy at Wilfrid Laurier University. He is the author of many articles on informal logic, visual argument, fallacies, and competing approaches to argumentation theory. With Christopher Tindale, he has co-authored three editions of the popular Oxford University Press textbook, *Good Reasoning Matters!*

William Hare is Professor Emeritus at Mount Saint Vincent University. In 1995 he received the Distinguished Service Award from the Canadian Association of Foundations of Education, and in 1999, the Mary Anne Raywid Award from the Society of Professors of Education. His books include *Open-mindedness and Education* (1979), *In Defence of Open-mindedness* (1985), and *What Makes a Good Teacher* (1993).

Donald L. Hatcher is Professor of Philosophy at Baker University where he directs its Liberal Arts Program, a three-course requirement that integrates instruction in critical thinking and writing. He is the author of four books, including *Reasoning and Writing: From Critical Thinking to Composition* and *Science, Ethics, and Technological Assessment*. He has also published numerous articles on critical thinking in *Informal Logic and Inquiry: Critical Thinking Across the Disciplines*.

Cornelia Hoogland is a professor in the Faculty of Education at The University of Western Ontario. Her interests include arts-based research as an aesthetic, critical form of inquiry; narrative inquiry; arts education (story, poetry, drama, and online education). Hoogland's four books of poetry include *Cuba Journal* (Black Moss Press, 2003). She is the founder and artistic director of Poetry London (www.poetrylondon.ca), and her work has been published internationally and produced on radio and on stage. In September 2006, she guest edited *Descant's* special issue on Cuban poets (Cuba Inside/Out, www.descant.ca). She can be reached at chooglan@uwo.ca or through her website at http://publish.edu.uwo.ca/cornelia.hoogland/.

Ralph H. Johnson is Professor Emeritus at the University of Windsor and a Fellow of the Royal Society of Canada (2003). He is the co-founder, co-editor, and co-publisher of *Informal Logic*, co-author of *Logical Self Defense* (1977, 1st ed.; 1983, 2d ed.; 1993, 3d ed.; 1994; 1996) and author of *Manifest Rationality* (2000). He has given numerous workshops and papers on critical thinking in a variety of settings for the past 25 years. In 1993, Johnson received a 3M Teaching Fellowship for Outstanding University Teachers, one of ten such awards conferred that year in Canada. That same year he received the Laurel Award for Outstanding Teaching from the Lt. Gov. of Ontario. Johnson was regularly listed in the *Maclean's* University issue as one of the most popular teachers at the University of Windsor.

Linda Kaser is co-developer of the BC Network of Performance-Based Schools, and co-designer of and faculty member in the Certificate Program for School Management and Leadership (a graduate program for new school leaders) at the University of Victoria. She has worked as a teacher, principal, district leader, and senior policy advisor at the provincial level in British Columbia, and is an adjunct professor in the Education Administration Department at UBC. Her research interests include critical thinking in leadership development, networks of inquiry, and forms of shared leadership. Linda is the co-author of *Leadership Mindsets*.

Sharon Murphy is Professor of Education at York University in Toronto, Canada. Her research interests include assessment and literacy learning. She has co-authored or co-edited books on literacy education (*Literacy Education Through Language Arts*), arts education (*Telling Pieces: Art as Literacy in Middle Grade Classes*), literacy assessment (*Fragile Evidence: A Critique of Reading Assessment*), and curricular materials in literacy (*Report Card on Basal Readers*), and has written numerous articles in academic and professional journals and books.

Gerald Nosich is Professor of Philosophy at Buffalo State College. His book *Learning to Think Things Through: A Guide to Critical Thinking across the Curriculum* (Prentice Hall) has recently been translated into Arabic, Chinese, and Spanish. He is also author of *Reasons and Arguments* (Wadsworth), of articles and videotapes on critical thinking, and (with the Foundation for Critical Thinking) has given over 200 workshops on numerous aspects of critical thinking, particularly on teaching for and testing of critical thinking. He is at work on a new book, *Assessing Critical Thinking Across the Curriculum*.

Laura Elizabeth Pinto is a lecturer at the Ontario Institute for Studies in Education of the University of Toronto and past president of the Ontario Business Educators' Association. Her publications include three information technology textbooks and scholarly articles on education policy, critical thinking, and the publishing industry. Her dissertation research is an analysis of the education policy development processes in Ontario.

Allan Pitman is Associate Professor of Education at The University of Western Ontario. His interests include mathematics education; curriculum policy and change; definitions of teacher work; and the interaction of technology and schooling. He has published on globalization, school reform, and professionalism.

John P. Portelli is a Professor of Education, Co-director of the Centre for Leadership and Diversity, and Associate Chair of the Department of Theory and Policy Studies, Ontario Institute for Studies in Education (OISE) of the University of Toronto. He teaches in the philosophy of education, educational administration, and preservice education programs. His publications include *What to Do? Case Studies for Educators* (2003) and *Key Questions in Education* (2005), both co-authored with William Hare.

Michael Scriven is a faculty member at Claremont Graduate University and a Senior Research Associate at Western Michigan University. He has taught in the United States (including twelve years at the University of California/Berkeley), Australia, and New Zealand in departments of mathematics, philosophy, psychology, the history and philosophy of science, and education. He has also held appointments at the Center for Advanced Study in the Behavioral Sciences (Stanford), the Centre for Advanced Study in Theoretical Psychology (University of Alberta), the Educational Testing Service (Princeton), the Center for the Study of Democratic Institutions (Santa Barbara), the Academy of Social Sciences in Australia, the National Science Foundation, and as a Whitehead Fellow at Harvard University. His more than 400 publications are mainly in the fields of his appointments and in the areas of critical thinking, technology studies, computer studies, and evaluation. He is or has been on the editorial boards of forty-two journals in these nine fields and some others, such as psychiatry, and has edited several of them, including *University MicroNews* and the *Journal of MultiDisciplinary Evaluation*. Scriven is a former President of the American Educational Research Association and of the American Evaluation Association, and the recipient of the American Evaluation Association's Lazarsfeld Medal for contributions to evaluation theory.

Jan Sobocan is a PhD candidate and Social Foundations Lecturer at the Faculty of Education at The University of Western Ontario. She specializes in the areas of critical thinking and testing, literacy, and citizenship education. She has conducted many workshops and short courses with teacher candidates in the area of assessment and evaluation of critical thinking skills. She has reviewed high school post-secondary curricula and written critical thinking curriculum for UWO continuing education courses. Her PhD dissertation, in curriculum studies, analyzes the revised Ontario curriculum for the presence of critical thinking with respect to its role in national and global citizenship education.

Frans H. van Eemeren is Professor of Speech Communication, Argumentation Theory and Rhetoric in the University of Amsterdam. With Rob Grootendorst, he is the founder of pragma-dialectics, a theory that has become one of today's most influential approaches to the study of argument and critical discussion. His many books include *Speech Acts in Argumentative Discussions*; *The Study of Argumentation*; *Handbook of Argumentation Theory*; *Argumentation, Communication, and Fallacies*; and *Argumentative Indicators in Discourse*.

Foreword

Michael Scriven

Critical thinking is one of that elite group of educational values that everyone agrees should be promoted, and also agrees that they are not adequately taught at the moment. Today, they are often stressed as increasingly important as we move into a globalized knowledge economy. But interestingly, they are all extremely elusive when one gets down to the practical business of defining them and testing their occurrence, whether natural or allegedly consequent upon some educational intervention. Besides critical thinking, the fellowship of that Parthenon surely includes cultural sensitivity, ethical insight and motivation, technological literacy, and then of course, that ethereal complement (or is it rather a competitor?) of criticality—creativity. It would hardly be an exaggeration to say that these educational desiderata are almost as remarkable not only for their universally accepted value, but for their very limited explicit presence in the regular curriculum: the most important, but scarcely deserving of their own courses? Surely this is a paradox worth considering.

Now this elusiveness is a little mysterious in itself, for everyone thinks they "know these things when they see them," and they believe they do see them from time to time—not indeed as often as they would like—unmistakably present in this speech or article, that student assignment (oh, happy day!), and even the occasional television program. And unmistakably absent, we are equally confident, in an even wider range of daily examples of speeches, essays, and of course—fortunately for authors of texts on how to improve critical thinking—advertisements. With such clarity of recognition, how can the task of specification be so difficult?

The root of the problem is the contextual nature of the cases we are so confident about. We all know a great deal about many particular areas within the vast realms of current knowledge, be they matters of everyday life and domestic finance or scholarly specialties, and as we have struggled to master these domains to some reasonable level of adequacy, we have become familiar with the many pitfalls and distractions that lie in the way of developing a clear vision of these complex structures. We have learned to understand many of these tricky phenomena, and learning how to understand an area means that we have learned to distinguish insights from hasty generalizations or superficial prejudices. And that is exactly the distinction that enables us to identify critical thinking, for critical thinking is essentially the laser beam of insight in contrast to the flashy neon of fuzzy thinking and false advertising. But it's a tough challenge to summarize what it is that characterizes all insights, in all fields of knowledge, and distinguishes them from all fuzzy thinking. No less a problem than to identify all creative thoughts by contrast with all ideas that appear original and valuable but fail on one of those two necessary conditions of creativity.

This contextual embeddedness of our paradigms of critical thinking means there has always been one good answer to the question of how to teach critical thinking, and for some distinguished contributors to our field, as well as many specialized scholars outside the field, it has seemed to be the only answer: teach any disciplined area of inquiry to a high level of competence and you have taught critical thinking. But for many of us, more seemed possible—and very important. It seemed to us that there were certain features of critical thinking that could be identified as common across fields, could be spelled out—at least to a useful degree of approximation—and exemplified, could be contrasted with false substitutes, and could thereby be instilled in learners in a way that would benefit their thinking in all subjects they approached, *including new subjects*. The last clause is very important, since new subjects are springing up at an unprecedented rate, just as new political and ethical dilemmas are appearing every few years, and providing some help in dealing with these is of the greatest importance. It cannot be provided by critical thinking that is limited to previous subjects.

This is hardly a novel view: 2,500 years ago, a distinguished group of thinkers and teachers, referred to as the Seven Sages of Greece, made their living by doing exactly that. And the long history of the fallacies, whose names—for example, *argumentum ad hominem*, and equivocation—are part of our language today, memorialize that approach. But a small group of scholars has continued to work away at refining the earlier approaches, as often by critically rejecting part of them as by adding more, and it seems reasonable to say that despite the very limited support from the mainline academies (much more in Canada than in the United States, by the way) we are now the workers in a very substantial and valuable field. We are at a point in the history of the study of critical thinking when we can at last point to really solid evidence, by scientific standards, that shows critical thinking can be improved by direct pedagogical attention. And we are at a point when small but excellent scholarly journals and a couple of good professional associations now exist to support and promulgate the newly matured discipline.

In this volume there is good evidence for this view. It contains a good answer to the problem of definition, and many excellent points are made about the subtle and difficult task of testing critical thinking. It is an honour to be able to introduce readers to an important book on this most important subject.

Introduction

Jan Sobocan and Leo Groarke

> *…even as more provinces bring in new rosters of tests for children, the critics are growing louder. Is standardized testing the best way to educate children, or are we producing kids who know how to pass a test but don't know how to think for themselves?*
> (Anne Marie Owens, *National Post*, 16 November 2002)

*I*n a world that spends billions—possibly trillions—of dollars on public education annually, governments and citizens demand educational accountability. In an enterprise as crucial, diverse, and expensive as education, they demand that public money be spent wisely. Standardized tests (data gathering instruments now more commonly referred to as achievement indicators, surveys, and assessments) have become the preferred way to evaluate not only students, but also teachers, schools, courses, colleges, programs, and provincial, state, and even national systems of education.

It is difficult to deny that education should be scrutinized and that teachers and administrators should be held accountable in some way for the effectiveness of their teaching and programs. More importantly, students struggling in the system should be identified and offered the proper educational support long before reaching university where the financial and emotional stakes for students and their families are much higher. Common sense dictates that scarce resources should be devoted to teaching that works, and to programs that help struggling learners achieve more than they would if they were not identified.

Standardized tests are attractive because they seem to be the most convenient and inexpensive way to measure the quality of public education, and because they can be used to identify at-risk students as well as to compare alternative approaches to teaching. In these ways, good testing may help in sorting through some difficult questions about teaching and learning. But it is easy to overestimate what testing can accomplish, particularly when the ultimate goal is the development of critical or higher-order thinking.

Standardized tests aim, across educational contexts and over time, to assess student knowledge and understanding of a subject in a consistent way. Despite this lofty goal, such tests are more often than not criticized for being the crudest of assessment instruments (Moll 2004). Among other things, they are criticized as instruments that measure only basic (rote) or minimum competency skills, and not what most would consider high-level learning. Consequently, they do not allow for conclusions that can concretely help administrators or teachers address the intricate problems associated with the individual mind, not to mention educational policy and practice.

In many cases, standardized tests are attractive for precisely the wrong reason: because they can be used to reduce inherently complex questions and information to simplistic arithmetical comparisons. Such assumptions about the tests and the data they produce ignore key aspects of teaching, learning, and test validity questions, as well as the ethical issues arising from misinterpretation, misrepresentation, or misuse of data.

In light of both the popularity of accountability-through-testing and the problems associated with it, many commentators have criticized a growing commitment to standardized or performance tests as a means of measuring student, teacher, school, board, and program success (see Darling-Hammond 1999; Apple 2001; Gorrie 2004; Ricci 2004). According to Chomsky (2000), the widespread push for educational accountability through testing has produced an "antipolitical" malaise among educators and academics, who increasingly share a "disdain for political parties and the whole democratic process" (55). The careless ways in which "high stakes" tests have been administered and graded, and test results often been employed, have been roundly criticized both in Canada (see Moll's *Passing the Test: The False Promises of Standardized Testing* [2004]) and in the United States (see Popham's *The Truth About Testing* [2001]).

The critiques of North American commentators who oppose large-scale testing can be summarized in terms of three general objections to the trends in testing. First, they argue that accountability measures do not improve education. Rather than manifesting some level of instructional performance, standardized tests instead promote a robotic "teaching to the rote test" (Popham 2001). The competition in learning rote information and question types that is encouraged by such uninspiring teaching is quite antithetical to the goal of producing independent or deep thinkers.

Second, commentators claim that large-scale tests and teacher testing compromise the professional autonomy and freedom of teachers, who are intimidated by the need to teach to tests (Runte 1998; Popham 2001). According to Popham, the public belief that standardized tests measure instructional quality puts great pressure on teachers and principals, who are judged by their ability to improve their students' scores.[1] Initiatives like the "No Child Left Behind" program in the United States and the quasi-governmental Education Quality and Accountability Office (EQAO) in Ontario are, on this account, counterproductive, because they make it difficult for teachers to focus on broader and more important, but less testable, goals like intellectual development.

The third broad objection to testing raises the concern that the use of test scores can discriminate in a way that penalizes at-risk students, creative thinkers, or a diverse student body (Moll 2004). Students outside the mainstream are, this line of argument suggests, more likely to fare poorly on tests that are designed for general use, and not with their individualized needs in mind.

Testing has not been as zealously pursued in Canada as it has in the United States, but an increased emphasis on testing has characterized Canadian public education over the last two decades and has raised the same concerns voiced as a result of the American experience. According to Moll, "large-scale provincial, national, and international testing is not designed to improve learning. It is designed to collect data from the system, and to catalogue, classify and rank that data" (2004, 13). Objections to the reporting of data by various institutions (among them, the Fraser Institute and the *National Post*) have increased, but testing results and rankings based upon them remain a matter of intense interest to governments and the general public alike.

It is ironic that the increased use of standardized testing that characterizes the current educational climate has emerged during a period in which educators and systems of education have embraced "critical thinking" as a fundamental goal of education. The model of education proposed by the critical thinking movement suggests that education should aim to endow all citizens with higher-order thinking skills that will make them critical, self-reflective, and creative. So conceived, education should not aim to produce students who possess circumscribed knowledge and information just so they can be tested more easily and cheaply. Instead, its goal should be to produce students who have more life-relevant (though much more difficult to define) abilities, skills, and dispositions—i.e., students who are disposed to ask questions, to reason through issues and problems, and to self-evaluate. Such students will be more able to acquire and assess new knowledge and information, but it is difficult to see how their abilities can be tested with instruments as undeveloped as those containing only multiple-choice and short-answer items accompanied by rigid, inside-the-box (correct or incorrect) scoring criteria.

The chapters of this book examine topics at the intersection of what is becoming a widespread commitment to the idea that critical thinking should be the central goal of education and international debates about testing and educational accountability. They consider, among many others, the following topics and issues:

❖ different accounts of critical thinking and different approaches to its testing and assessment;

❖ the criteria for judging the validity of test instruments and testing contexts;

❖ the role of critical thinking in education and its assessment within a democracy;

❖ the validity (or invalidity) of particular, widely used performance or standardized achievement tests that claim, in part or whole, to measure critical thinking;

❖ the policy issues around the testing of higher-order thinking; and

❖ the relationship between critical and creative thinking, and how we might assess creativity.

As the authors of these chapters demonstrate, a commitment to critical thinking as a central goal of education makes testing and assessment issues particularly acute.

A critical scrutiny of attempts to teach and assess critical thinking is especially important given the apparently limited progress in this area. As Kuhn (1991) wrote in the introduction to her groundbreaking study of informal reasoning, "Seldom has there been such a widespread agreement about a significant social issue as there is reflected in the view that education is failing in its most central mission—to teach students to think" (5). More recently, the same sentiment has been expressed not only about the lack of critical dialogue in college and distance education but with respect to the connection between the lack of critical thinking education and the failure of liberal reforms (see Bullen 1998; Nixon 1999; van Gelder 2005). These alarming claims, and the comprehensive evidence Kuhn assembles in her book and current research, strongly support the view that higher-order thinking skills (mainly informal logic or everyday reasoning skills) need to be taught better in schools. Yet it is much less clear how this instructional goal and the curriculum that would aim to deliver it can be developed and accomplished. In a testing and assessment era, the essential question is whether and how we can know what works if we do not have some ways to measure our successes and, equally importantly, our failures.

The issues that critical thinking teaching and testing raise are, it should be noted, not limited to K–12 education. Colleges and universities often declare a strong commitment to critical thinking and its development in their courses and programs, but few institutions turn this rhetoric into a concerted attempt to ensure that critical thinking shapes their curriculum. More frequently, those supporting traditional programs protect themselves from change by claiming that their program already embodies the spirit and goal of critical thinking. Such claims are ironic given that they are made without any attempt to marshal evidence in their favour, i.e., in a manner that fundamentally violates the major canons of critical thinking.[2]

Critical thinking courses have become a staple of undergraduate education in the arts. Although we believe that this is a very positive development, others have raised serious questions about the efficacy of such courses. Theirs is a legitimate concern because it cannot be said that the efficacy of the courses has been proven or backed by extensive research and testing. To make matters worse, the content of the critical thinking courses taught in universities varies widely, reflecting fundamental disagreements about the best way to teach critical thinking. Instead of consensus among the experts, one finds conflicting approaches that represent the particular biases of the individual instructors (some emphasizing traditional formal logic, some focusing on fallacies, some employing rhetorical techniques, and so on).

From this point of view, it is somewhat paradoxical that the claimed value of university courses in critical thinking is backed by vague truisms about the value of critical thinking rather than by critical reflection that genuinely demonstrates either the relevance of such courses for learners or the effectiveness of the teaching.

These considerations suggest that it is important to examine more closely different attempts to assess higher-level thinking. In the course of that examination, and especially in a context that concerns passing and failing, and the attempt to assay the human mind for its strengths and weaknesses, it is important to consider questions raised by both theorists of critical thinking and experts in assessment. What parts of a critical thinking process need to be tested to evince that a person is thinking at a higher level? How can teaching and assessment incorporate critical thinking? How can assessment be done in a way that is fair but reaches beyond the mere measurement of students' basic abilities to reinforce and promote the different components of critical thinking? What are the best kinds of assessment tools for doing this? What role, if any, can standardized testing play? And, is formal testing even necessary to deciding how teachers, disciplines, schools, colleges, universities, and whole systems of education can best embrace critical thinking as a true goal rather than a mere platitude?

The issues raised in this book reflect the complexity of the testing of critical thinking. It is fraught with difficulties in relation to the very nature and definition of critical thinking, the ethics of assessment policy and practice, and the impact of assessment on teaching critical thinking. Such issues are so complicated that many commentators (including several authors in this volume) believe that the skills and/ or dispositions that make up critical thinking are too complex to be captured and quantified in a standardized format. It is quite difficult, then, to find ways to validly test critical thinking and especially difficult to test the system as standardized formats require simplified scoring keys and come at great cost to taxpayers.

Many of the authors who have contributed to this book have responded to the need to try to find a way to test more accurately for critical thinking skills and dispositions—skills and dispositions that, we believe, are essential for the maintenance of democracy. Considerations of this sort give rise to many questions.[3] The one that best captures the issues discussed in this book is how negative conclusions about testing programs might be reconciled with the recognition that concerns about educational accountability are legitimate. Many specific questions of validity are spawned by this general query.

❖ How can we establish whether students are acquiring the traits that characterize the critical thinker?

❖ How can we establish the extent to which critical thinking is taught in the K–12 and post-secondary curricula?

❖ How can we ensure some consistency between instruction/student learning and critical thinking as an educational goal?

❖ How can we use multiple-choice instruments more effectively to measure critical thinking?

❖ What is to be said about existing tests?

❖ What happens to teaching when tests become the measure of successful teaching in the classroom?

❖ What other kinds of classroom assessments and evaluations can be used to measure critical thinking, and are they better measures of it?

❖ On what basis should we choose between different approaches to critical thinking programs and courses?

❖ How can we ensure that the comparative gains data we use to inform curriculum development are reliable?

❖ How can we ensure that the data we collect is used democratically, to improve student learning?

The contributors to this volume have addressed these and related questions from a variety of perspectives. Different authors have focused on different components of education as professors, educational theorists, philosophers, evaluation experts, and policy and program developers. Many of them have taught and/or administered (and continue to teach and/or administer) critical thinking instruction in K–12 or at university.

In putting this book together we have tried to situate it within the extensive research literature that has spurred the development of critical thinking and cognate disciplines (informal logic, argumentation theory, rhetoric, dialectics, etc.). In the last twenty years, they have made the study of such thinking a promising intellectual exercise focused on the ways in which we think and reason, the ways in which we should think and reason, and the ways in which we can best teach students to be stronger thinkers. The book is designed to foster a discussion of educational theory and practice that will better integrate both with the study and teaching of critical thinking. We hope that this discussion will motivate educators, governments, and theorists to work together to redress some of the disappointments that have attended earlier efforts to understand and promote critical thinking and educational accountability.

A notable obstacle to progress in this area has been the debate over the definition of "critical thinking"—a debate joined by the authors of many of the essays to follow. In some ways, issues of definition, and the debates they produce, can enrich understanding of the nature and the teaching of critical thinking. For example, they have contributed to a growing recognition that the notion of critical thinking should be expanded to incorporate literacy in general, and media literacy in particular. The recognition of the latter importantly includes an ongoing critique of technology, with an emphasis on the images and Internet advertisements that bombard us every day. This broader understanding of the content of critical thinking can usefully promote a still more significant mandate for critical thinking education, one that many of the contributors here have passionately pursued.

In dealing with the issue of defining critical thinking, we stress that one should not expect a consensus on some exact definition of critical thinking (least of all from those of us who work as philosophers, who are prone to disagree about definitions). Complete agreement is not a prerequisite for a better understanding and assessment of critical thinking and its pedagogy. However one defines critical thinking, everyone agrees that it encompasses certain core abilities and practices—the ability to evaluate evidence, to recognize and deal fairly with opposing points of view, to ask key questions, to self-reflect. Understanding critical thinking in these general terms allows us to study it from both theoretical and pedagogical points of view.

After exploring definitional issues, and dealing with disagreements thereon, we might ultimately rely on the understanding of critical thinking that has gained currency in common parlance. Limiting ourselves to one example, we cite the following comment by Hans Blix, the former United Nations weapons inspector in Iraq, who was responding to questions in an interview about the mistakes made by the American administration when they claimed that Iraq had amassed weapons of mass destruction before the Iraq war.

> **HANS BLIX**: You see, there were lots of things that were unaccounted for. We knew that they had quantities of mustard gas and anthrax and other things, and they could not tell us with any evidence of where it had gone. Therefore, it was labeled unaccounted for. However, there was a tendency on both the U.S. side and the U.K. side to equate unaccounted for with existing. And that was an error.

> **JIM LEHRER**: Was it an intentional error? Or what is your interpretation of what they were doing? Why would they look at the same information you were looking at and come to a different conclusion?

> **BLIX**: Well, I think there was not enough *critical thinking* [emphasis added], neither in the Intelligence agencies nor at the governmental level. (Lehrer 2004)[4]

Everyone who has contributed to this book would recognize Blix's statement as an appeal to the notion of critical thinking as it should be understood, but many of our contributors would unpack what this means in different ways. To this extent, the contributors to this volume share a common conception of critical thinking, but one that can be accounted for in theoretically different ways.

The chapters included in this book have been organized in Parts that represent key issues and themes that arise when one considers critical thinking and its assessment. In Part One the validity of various popular standardized tests is examined. In Part Two, the authors discuss often overlooked issues with respect to the relationship between critical thinking and creative thinking (because critical thinking, in the proper sense of the term, implies something more than the ability to be critical of others' points of view). In Part Three, particular approaches to critical thinking teaching and assessment are offered. Here, the authors discuss different programs and related evaluations of their success to teacher education, classroom instruction, and to non-standardized informal assessments of critical thinking. Part Four includes attempts to answer broad questions about critical thinking education policy or accountability, and how such policy supports (or does not support) critical thinking education and testing to the extent that it supports the goals of a pluralistic, democratic society. In the final Part of the book, Sharon Murphy comments on all of the essays in the book, and suggests a way to further our thinking on issues of critical thinking and assessment.

We envision this book as a volume that does something more than criticize (though criticism is an essential and a healthy component of critical thinking). As educators, we want to move beyond negative criticism, toward critical decision-making. We have tried to develop the book in a way that will allow its readers—philosophers, administrators, educational theorists, teachers, students, policy-makers, and others—to emerge with a better understanding of critical thinking and its relationship to issues of testing and assessment. And we hope for something more: that this book becomes an important step toward a shared understanding of how critical thinking might be better taught and tested. In the future, this might include the design of better and more reliable tests that could have an impact on curriculum and policy to an extent that motivates us all to promote critical thinking education. If our tests were valid measures of critical thinking, then teaching to them would not be a bad idea.

Notes

1. In the United States standardized testing initiatives unduly pressure teachers and principals by offering financial incentives for passing the test

and by threatening to close schools who fail them. In this context, the attraction of testing is its ability to produce rankings that tell us who has won the competition and, more commonly, who has failed: "Americans love contests—and while we derive modest gratification from applauding a winner, we appear to get more fundamental joy from identifying losers. Yes, the sports pages are the natural home for score-based school rankings" (Popham 2001, 11).

2. It may be useful to mention a case in point. One of Canada's best liberal arts institutions publishes a recruitment "viewbook," a website and a calendar that repeatedly tout the ability to think critically as one of the benefits of its degrees. In its calendar, for example, one reads that its programs shape "leaders who are critical thinkers, problem solvers and creative participants in society." These are laudable ideals but it is difficult to see how they have, in any conscious way, shaped the programs in question. There is, for example, no explicit program of the sort that Don Hatcher describes in his contribution to this book (i.e., Baker University's adoption of a liberal arts program with critical thinking as its goal). And there is nothing that someone who has studied critical thinking (which has been an area of research and scholarship for over thirty years) would recognize as a concerted effort to infuse critical thinking into the curriculum. Rather, the university simply assumes (in a manner quite inconsistent with the critical reflection that is the heart of critical thinking) that its programs fulfill this ideal. And not because the university is more negligent than other universities in this regard. It can better be said that a rhetorical, but not substantive, commitment to critical thinking is the norm in most liberal arts programs in North American universities.

3. The questions raised here and most of the ideas and opinions expressed in this book were first developed, presented, and discussed at a workshop that Jan Sobocan organized through the Faculty of Education at The University of Western Ontario. In the current "high stakes" climate for testing—in which critical thinking and testing are central topics on the educational agenda—she brought together philosophers, teachers, critical thinking and education scholars, testing experts, and government representatives. The goal was to discuss how well we teach and test critical thinking; how and if we should develop critical thinking curriculum (which includes tests for it); and what might be done to establish tests and testing programs that reliably reflect the standards that critical thinking requires.

4. This excerpt was taken from an interview done on Jan. 29, 2004, in which the former chief U.N. weapons inspector talks to Jim Lehrer about his assertion that pre-Iraq war intelligence was "almost all wrong" (Lehrer 2004).

References

Apple, M. 2001. *Educating the "right" way: Markets, standards, God and inequality*. New York: Routledge Falmer.

Bullen, M. 1998. Participation and critical thinking in online university distance education. *Journal of Distance Education* 13(2): 1–32.

Chomsky, N. 2000. Democracy and education. In *Chomsky on miseducation*, ed. D. Macedo, 37–55. Oxford: Rowman & Littlefield.

Darling-Hammond, L. 1999. *Teacher quality and student achievement: A review of state policy evidence*. Seattle: Center for the Study of Teaching and Policy.

Gorrie, P. 2004. Literacy test a write-off? *The Toronto Star*, Sunday, February 15.

Kuhn, D. 1991. *The skills of argument*. Cambridge: Cambridge University Press.

Lehrer, J. 2004. A newshour with Jim Lehrer transcript. Online focus. Newsmaker: Hans Blix March 17, 2004. http://www.pbs.org/newshour/bb/international/jan-june04/blix_3-17.html.

Moll, M. 2004. *Passing the test: The false promises of standardized testing*. Ottawa: Canadian Centre for Policy Alternatives.

Nixon, G. 1999. Whatever happened to 'heightened consciousness'? *Journal of Curriculum Studies* 31(6): 625–33.

Owens, A. 2002. Putting schools to the test: How standardized exams are changing education in Canada. *National Post*, Saturday, November 16.

Popham, W. 2001. *The truth about testing*. Alexandria, VA: Association for Supervision and Curriculum Development.

Runte, R. 1998. The impact of centralized examinations on teacher professionalism. *Canadian Journal of Education* 23: 166–81.

Ricci, C. 2004. Breaking the silence: An EQAO marker speaks out against standardized testing. *Our Schools, Our Selves* Winter: 75–88.

van Gelder, T. 2005. Teaching critical thinking: Some lessons from cognitive science. *College Teaching* 53(1): 41–6.

PART ONE

Testing the Test

Introduction

Standardized testing can be understood, generally, as testing "designed to assess the knowledge and understanding a student has acquired of a school subject" and, more specifically, as testing that has to be administered and "scored in the same way, whenever and wherever it is used" (Traub 1994, 5). In this part of the book, Carol Ann Giancarlo-Gittens, Leo Groarke, Ralph H. Johnson, Robert H. Ennis, Frederick S. Ellett, Jr., and Allan Pitman explore answers to questions about how different standardized and non-standardized tests of critical thinking can be valid to the extent that they accurately measure an adequate range of critical thinking dispositions or critical thinking skills.

In the first chapter, Giancarlo-Gittens introduces the problems standardized testing creates for teachers and students of critical thinking. She then discusses critical thinking dispositions testing as one way to address some common problems. In Chapter Two, Groarke argues in favour of accountability and supports the attempt to design and administer adequate tests of critical thinking skills. Groarke believes that such tests are required to judge the effectiveness of the many competing approaches to critical thinking education. However, Groarke nevertheless argues that one of the most popular critical thinking tests—the *California Critical Thinking Skills Test*—does not validly measure critical thinking skills. In criticizing the test, he enumerates a range of skills belonging to the exercise of critical thinking, a skills set that would need to be incorporated for adequate testing (and so teaching) of critical thinking to occur.

In Chapter Three, Johnson builds upon the work he has done elsewhere on "the dialectical tier" (Johnson 2000). The "dialectical tier" comprises the notion not only that arguments must be judged in terms of their logical cogency but that arguers must also be judged on how well they recognize and anticipate objections to their views. In keeping with his broader point that studies of argument have not paid enough attention to the dialectical tier, Johnson contends that the

15

same can be said of critical thinking tests.

Despite their concerns about existing tests, Groarke and Johnson—like Giancarlo-Gittens—remain optimistic about the possibility of developing valid critical thinking tests that will work toward improving critical thinking education. These authors stress the importance of thinking about ways to improve current tests and to create new instruments that more adequately cover the different facets of critical thinking. In Chapter Four, Ennis discusses the series of tests that he thinks may be the best available measures of critical thinking—*The Cornell Critical Thinking Test (Levels X and Z)*. He explains not only how this series of tests has been consistently evaluated for their validity but, more generally, he provides a methodology for testing the validity of any critical thinking measure of the X and Z sort. It can be plausibly said that Ennis outlines a methodology that should be applied if and when others attempt to develop new standardized tests, especially alternative kinds of assessment that purport to support critical thinking as the main goal of instruction.

In Chapter Five, Ellett and Pitman broaden the discussion to include an account of the proper goals of critical thinking education in a pluralistic democracy. They contend that education emphasizing critical thinking is particularly important within the context of a society that attempts to uphold the ideals of rationality. They explain the difficulties in trying to achieve education that promotes and maintains democracy, and how and whether such achievement can be reliably tested. Ellett and Pitman criticize standardized testing but propose a constructive approach to assessment that may allow what might be considered an important part of a citizenship skills set: respect.

References

Johnson, R. 2000. *Manifest rationality*. Pittsburgh: Erlbaum.

Traub, R. 1994. *Standardized testing in Canada: A survey of standardized achievement testing by ministries of education and school boards.* Toronto: Canadian Education Association.

Chapter One

Assessing Critical Thinking Dispositions in an Era of High-Stakes Standardized Testing

Carol Ann Giancarlo-Gittens

On the first day of school, fifth-grade teacher Erica Bradley waits with anxious anticipation to greet her students and to begin what she has dreamed of for years—a career of helping children to learn about amazing new subjects while becoming skilled and knowledgeable about the world around them. At the secondary school down the street, Jerome Harris, a mathematics teacher fresh from his teacher preparation program, enthusiastically describes to his students how they will be experiencing a technique called *problem-based learning* this semester (Duch 2001). Trained in social constructivist teaching methods, Mr. Harris is eager to guide his students through a collaborative process of meaning-making regarding real-world problems as they master the standards-based mathematics content.

It is not long into the school year, though, before Ms. Bradley is told by her principal to spend more time on reading and math because those are the subjects on the state-mandated standardized test. At the high school, Mr. Harris is approached in the break room by his mentor teacher, who conveys her concern that Mr. Harris's teaching, while admirable, needs to change. In her view, Mr. Harris does not focus enough on the basic skills the students will need to pass their state-mandated high school exit exam. This is the stressful reality. How teachers do their job is directly related to the performance expectations that have become part and parcel of high-stakes standardized testing and accountability systems that are pervasive in K–12 education in the United States and perhaps to a lesser extent in Canada.

Numerous articles can be found in the educational literature that describe the history and current impact of high-stakes standardized testing on educational practice (Darling-Hammond 1985; Goertz 2003). The widespread adoption of accountability systems that rely on standardized tests to drive educational reform gained momentum in the 1980s and 1990s and has become accepted practice today. The assumptions behind the high-stakes testing movement are that testing will increase student performance outcomes, positively influence educational policy reform efforts, motivate student achievement, and increase teacher effectiveness (Stecher 2002). However, the research does not unambiguously support the validity of these assumptions.

A wide range of outcomes have resulted from the current accountability movement, with many representing dire consequences for students and teachers alike. Behaviours that have been documented, either in research or in the media, include such things as the narrowing of the curriculum to focus exclusively on the subjects covered on a state-adopted assessment instrument; increased class time spent on test-related activities to improve students' test-wiseness; increased incidences of academic dishonesty including direct coaching, divulging of test items, and other forms of cheating; student apathy and disengagement; teacher attrition; and encouragement of widespread testing exemption practices for low-performing students (Darling-Hammond 1985; Jones 1997; Hoffman 2001; Stecher 2002; Neill 2003; Goldberg 2004).

Nevertheless, the sheer practice of administering standardized assessments *in general* should not be portrayed as the destructive agent behind these undesirable changes. A holistic condemnation of the accountability movement denies the genuine benefits of having valid and reliable data on student performance. Test results are useful to determine whether students are meeting curricular standards. Furthermore, true progress in educational reform efforts can be accomplished only through rigorous evaluation of the efficacy of curricular change. With this said, there are clear practices in the current iteration of high-stakes standardized testing that continue to cause alarm. This chapter addresses how the use of basic-skills, factual-knowledge-oriented, state-mandated tests results in the systematic neglect of higher-order thinking skills and dispositions in the assessment process and, consequently, in classroom-based curricular design and delivery. The chapter highlights a rarely mentioned but worrisome concern: that critical thinking (CT) as an educational outcome, particularly the assessment of CT dispositions, may be an unintended casualty associated with high-stakes state-mandated testing programs.

Critical Thinking as an Educational Outcome

The expression "critical thinking" can be traced back to the work of John Dewey and Max Black in philosophy. It is also sometimes associated with the work of W.G. Perry and other developmentalists in cognitive psychology, where it has associations with reflective judgment, intelligence, logical thinking, and problem-solving. To some people the term is coextensive with informal logic, while others see it as an alternative way of talking about the scientific method.

There is broad consensus among critical thinking theoreticians that a central goal of education is to prepare persons who willingly and skillfully engage in CT. In short, the educational system should produce graduates who are willing and able to use their cognitive powers of analysis, interpretation, inference, evaluation, explanation, and self-monitoring meta-cognition to make purposeful judgments about what to believe or what to do (Paul 1984; Ennis 1985; Facione 1990; Carter-Wells 1992; Winn 2004). *Goals 2000: Educate America Act* called for all students to leave grades 4, 8, and 12 "having demonstrated competency over challenging subject matter" and every school in America to "ensure that all students learn to use their minds well, so that they may be prepared for responsible citizenship, further learning, and productive employment in our Nation's modern economy" (Education 1990). A national survey of employers, policy-makers, and educators found consensus that the dispositional dimension, as well as the skills dimension, of critical thinking should be considered an essential outcome of a college education (Jones 1995).

In 1990, under the sponsorship of the American Philosophical Association, a cross-disciplinary panel completed a two-year Delphi Project that yielded a robust conceptualization of critical thinking understood as an outcome of college-level education (Facione 1990). Before the Delphi Project, no clear consensus definition of critical thinking existed (Kurfiss 1988). Broadly conceived by the Delphi panelists, critical thinking was characterized as the process of purposeful, self-regulatory judgment. Throughout this cognitive, non-linear, recursive process a person gathers and evaluates evidence in order to form a judgment about what to believe or what to do in any given context. In so doing, a person engaged in critical thinking uses his or her cognitive skills to form a judgment and to monitor and improve the quality of that judgment (Facione 1990). This robust definition of critical thinking provided the conceptual framework to address the *Goals 2000: Educate America Act* mandate and was the focus of a replication study of the definition and valuation of critical thinking that resulted in a consensus among educators, employers, and policy-makers alike (Jones 1994). The Delphi Report's consensus expression of critical thinking was vital to advancing the national conversation beyond semantic disputations and into the more important realm of measurement.

The disposition toward critical thinking

Contemporary critical thinking scholars acknowledge that any discussion of critical thinking must include both thinking skills and thinking attitudes, or dispositions. The phrase *critical thinking disposition* refers to a person's internal motivation to think critically when faced with problems to solve, ideas to evaluate, or decisions to make (Facione 1997; Giancarlo 2004). These attitudes, values, and inclinations are dimensions of one's personality and motivational style which relate to how likely a person is to approach decision-making contexts or problem-solving situations by using their reasoning skills. The honing of one's critical thinking skills, as well as developing the disposition to use one's skills, is vital for success both in school and throughout a person's life. It is not sufficient for educators to nurture students' cognitive skills if, when faced with a decision on what to do or what to believe, the students fail to exercise what they have learned. When making decisions, students must apply sound reasoning over other strategies such as passive and unquestioning acceptance of the popular or consensus opinion. Valuing the disposition toward critical thinking as an educational outcome is a declaration of the centrality of this characterological dimension of the critical thinking process. It is only though the combined effort to teach thinking skills while nurturing the desire to be a confident and capable thinker that we will produce future generations of leaders who will be capable of solving the significant global challenges of the modern world (e.g., global warming, poverty, AIDS/HIV, etc.).

The dispositional portrait of the ideal critical thinker was described by the Delphi experts as follows:

> The ideal critical thinker is habitually inquisitive, well-informed, honest in facing personal biases, prudent in making judgments, willing to reconsider, clear about issues, orderly in complex matters, diligent in seeking relevant information, reasonable in the selection of criteria, focused in inquiry, and persistent in seeking results which are as precise as the subject and the circumstances of inquiry permit. (Facione 1990, 2)

Until only recently, the traditional assessment of a student's critical thinking has focused nearly exclusively on CT skills. It was not until the publication of the *California Critical Thinking Disposition Inventory* (CCTDI) in 1992 that researchers and educators had an instrument by which to assess a person's disposition toward critical thinking (Facione 1992; 2006). The CCTDI captures the Delphi description of the ideal critical thinker in terms of seven non-orthogonal subscales: truth-seeking, open-mindedness, analyticity, systematicity, CT self-confidence, inquisitiveness, and cognitive maturity. The introduction of the CCTDI led to investigations demonstrating a connection between critical thinking skills and dispositions, and the value of CT disposition for the prediction of educational success (Colucciello 1997; Walsh 1999; Giancarlo and Facione 2001; Kakai 2000; Zoller 2000; Giancarlo 2004; Nokes 2005; Lampart 2006).

The Impact of High-Stakes Testing on Educating for Critical Thinking Dispositions

Critical thinking is widely recognized as a liberating force in education and a powerful resource in one's personal and civic life. Many educators and researchers would concur that critical thinking instruction is vital in the K–12 curriculum (Lipman 1987; Kuhn 1990). Educators and scholars recommend that critical thinking instruction in the K–12 curricula develop CT skills and foster the disposition to use those skills as preparation for both college and later life. Reconciliation of the aforementioned educational goal with the goals of high-stakes standardized testing is the challenge to be faced (Chudowsky 2003). Tests that required only limited and lower-level thinking activities, such as memorization and recall of basic facts and skills, are not sufficient to meet the goal of educating students to become thinking members of society.

High-stakes testing and accountability programs have a direct impact on curriculum and instruction at the elementary and secondary levels (DiMartino 2007). Abrams and Madaus (2003) outline seven principles to describe consistent ways in which high-stakes testing affects teaching and learning. Most relevant to this discussion are principles 4 and 5. Principle 4 states, "In every setting where high-stakes tests operate, the exam content eventually defines the curriculum" (33). Highly related to this phenomenon is the practice captured in Principle 5: "Teachers pay attention to the form of the questions of high-stakes tests (short-answer, essay, multiple-choice, and so on) and adjust their instruction accordingly" (33). Through these principles the authors draw attention to influences such as the symbolic and perceptual importance of high-stakes testing, and the power high-stakes testing practices have to compromise the validity of test scores because of the potential to over-emphasize test preparation behaviours. The power to corrupt educational practice stems from the fact that the more likely a test result will be used for major educational decisions the more likely a teacher will "teach to the test." Research is readily available to suggest that teachers alter the emphasis placed on the core content areas being taught in the classroom to become nearly synonymous with the content included on state tests (Stecher 2002; Goldberg 2004).

It is clear that high-stakes testing affects K–12 curriculum. This impact is not limited, however, to the content being addressed. The thinking skills required by the assessment instruments also influence the instructional strategies teachers employ in their classrooms (DiMartino 2007). When state-mandated tests demand limited and lower-level thinking activities, such as memorization and recall of basic facts and skills, this conjures up the epistemological view of learning that is consistent with the tenets underlying direct instruction teaching: learning is best accomplished when subject-matter skills and knowledge are broken into their component parts and taught to students in a carefully planned, sequenced, and structured manner that is teacher centred (Palincsar 1998). For the acquisition of knowledge structures such as facts, rules, and action sequences, direct instruction is the preferred teaching method (Borich 2004). This is in contrast to the instructional techniques that serve to teach students broad concepts and abstractions, and to nurture critical thinking skills and dispositions. Indirect instructional strategies that emphasize inquiry, discovery, and engaging students in the construction of meaning, such as problem-based learning, are viewed as optimal when the cognitive activities associated with higher-order thinking are the educational aim (Palincsar 1998; Borich 2004). Results from national surveys of teachers provide undeniable evidence of a disconcerting shift toward direct instructional techniques that emphasize basic skills. This emphasis is now common practice, a move away from more innovative teaching approaches such as team-teaching, creative, and divergent thinking projects, long-term integrative units, and collaborative problem-solving (Costigan 2002; Pedulla 2003a; Pedulla 2003b; Taylor 2003).

The centrality of testing programs as a powerful force to be reckoned with for new and experienced teachers alike, and the ramifications of the pressure to teach in prescribed, restricted ways have been identified as potential threats to teacher retention. This issue was raised by Costigan (2002), who has written about the effects of the "Culture of High-Stakes Testing" on new teachers. Based on his work with beginning teachers in New York City, he describes how new teachers cope with the realization that mandated testing quickly becomes a primary focus in everyday classroom practice. Teachers in Costigan's study are quoted as saying that the pressure they experience from their principals to teach in a prescribed, direct-instruction fashion has made them frustrated and emotionally distraught to the point where they are questioning their vocational decision. The frustration and stress these teachers convey stem from the pressure to focus their teaching on only those activities that will help their students pass the tests. For these teachers it meant they could not implement creative activities that they felt would motivate the students and engage them in meaningful learning (Costigan 2002).

In this era of high-stakes testing, one might wonder what exactly new teachers are being taught when it comes to best practices for instruction. In teacher education methods courses—geared toward the teaching of the content areas—there is increased attention being paid to instructional practices that encourage thinking and the active engagement of students in their own learning. Topics such as student-centred instruction, collaborative problem-solving, problem-based or project-based learning, and constructivist pedagogy are commonplace. Instructional practices such as these have been shown to enhance students' critical thinking, including engaging students in critical thinking, modeling critical thinking behaviour, and creating a climate of inquiry in the classroom (Facione 1998; 2008). Furthermore, these instructional strategies represent what is known about how to maximize student motivation, engagement, and, ultimately, deeper understanding (Costa 1989; Johnson 2008). As was outlined above, ample research evidence suggests that there is a close connection between critical thinking and educational success (Baron 1987; Giancarlo 1994; Facione 1995; Williams 2006; McCall 2007). In a well-designed study by Williams et al., the scores based on critical thinking skills explained a significant variance in dental hygienist students' success on board scores, over and above all other measured variables.

Assessing Critical Thinking Dispositions among K–12 Learners

The majority of studies examining CT dispositions in relation to the academic experience have concentrated on post-secondary learners. To date, little is known about the critical thinking dispositions of elementary and secondary learners. This gap in the literature existed until a dispositional assessment tool suitable for use among adolescent and younger learners was developed. In 2000, the *California Measure of Mental Motivation* (CM3) was introduced as a valid measure of the disposition toward critical thinking among adolescent students (Giancarlo 2004). Since the initial publication of the validation work underlying the CM3 (hence known as the CM3 Level II for secondary students), three additional levels of the instrument have been developed: Level Ia for grades Kindergarten through 2nd grade (primary), Level Ib for Grades 3–5 (upper elementary), and Level III for post-secondary students and adults (Giancarlo 2006). Students who complete the CM3 Level Ia are asked to circle directly on the survey booklet the face that shows whether the sentence is true about them or false about them. CM3 Levels Ib, II, and III utilize separate answer sheets or can be administered in an online environment.

The CM3 is designed to measure the degree to which an individual is cognitively engaged and mentally motivated toward intellectual activities that involve reasoning. The dispositional domains measured by the CM3 are not linked with any particular curricular area. All forms (Levels Ia, Ib, II, and III) of the CM3 target four main dispositional aspects of critical thinking: learning orientation, mental focus, cognitive integrity, and creative problem-solving. These four domains of mental motivation can be identified in the writings of many researchers who have investigated how students differ in their problem-solving and decision-making (Ames 1984; Fisher 1990; Graham 1991). Table 1 presents the four scales of the CM3, and Table 2 provides a sample item from each CM3 form as well as the response format for each level of the instrument.

Scale Name	Scale Description
Learning Orientation	High scores in *learning orientation* indicate a motivation or desire to increase one's knowledge and skill base. These individuals value learning for learning's sake and express an eagerness to engage in the learning process. These individuals express an interest for engaging in challenging activities, and endorse information seeking as personal strategy when problem solving. Low scores indicate a muted desire to learn about new or challenging topics. These individuals express a lack of willingness to explore or research an issue and may even purposefully avoid opportunities to learn and understand. These individuals will attempt to answer questions with the information they have at hand rather than seeking out new information.
Mental Focus	High scores in *mental focus* indicate self-reported diligence, focus, systematicity, task-orientation, organization, and clear-headedness. While engaging in a mental activity this person tends to be focused in their attention, persistent, and comfortable with the problem solving process. Low scores indicate a compromised ability to regulate attention and a tendency toward disorganization and procrastination. These individuals may also express frustration with their ability to approach solving problems.

Cognitive Integrity	High scores in *Cognitive Integrity* indicate motivation to use one's thinking skills in a fair-minded fashion. These individuals are positively disposed toward seeking the truth and being open-minded, and are comfortable with complexity; they enjoy thinking about and interacting with others with potentially varying viewpoints in the search for truth or the best decision. Low scores indicate the expression of a viewpoint that is best characterized as cognitive resistance. These individuals are hasty, indecisive, uncomfortable with complexity and change, and are likely to be anxious and close-minded.
Creative Problem Solving	High scores on *Creative Problem Solving* indicate a tendency to approach problem solving with innovative or original ideas and solutions. These individuals pride themselves on their creative nature, and this creativity is likely to manifest itself by a desire to engage in challenging activities such as puzzles, games of strategy, and understanding the underlying function of objects. For these individuals, there is a stronger sense of personal satisfaction from engaging in complex or challenging activities than from participating in activities perceived to be easy. Low scores reflect the absence of feelings of personal imaginativeness or originality. This manifests itself by the tendency for these individuals to avoid challenging activities. They will choose easier activities over challenging ones.

Table 1: Four scales of the California Measure of Mental Motivation (CM3)[1]

CM3 Instrument	Target Grade Levels	Sample Question Prompt	Response Format
Level Ia (25 items)	K–2	Sometimes I stop listening even when I know I should be paying attention.	TRUE FALSE

Level Ib (25 items)	3–5	I like learning things that are hard for me when I first try them.	AGREE DISAGREE
Level II (72 items)	6–12	No matter what the subject, I am eager to know more about it.	Answered on a scale of 1–4 (Strongly Disagree–Strongly Agree)
Level III (72 items)	Post-secondary	I like trying to figure out how something works.	Answered on a scale of 1–4 (Strongly Disagree–Strongly Agree)

Table 2: Sample items and response formats from the CM3 family of instruments[2]

Reliability and validity studies have been conducted with the CM3 Level II instrument. Among secondary students, the scales of the CM3, as measures of the disposition toward critical thinking, have been shown to have strong positive correlations with academic motivation goals, academic self-efficacy, and self-regulation (Urdan 2001; Giancarlo 2004). Findings also demonstrate significant negative correlations between the CM3 and measures of self-handicapping and fear of failure. In relation to indicators of academic achievement and critical thinking skills, Giancarlo, Blohm, and Urdan (2004) report that the scales of the CM3 were positively correlated with all five content area tests of the Stanford 9 Content Area Test (1996). Other validity studies with the CM3 have been conducted and the publisher (http://www.insightassessment.com/pdf_files/CM3-Validity-Reliability.pdf)—as part of the instrument research and development process—has revealed positive correlations with the *Naglieri Nonverbal Abilities Test* (Naglieri 1988) and *The Test of Everyday Reasoning* (Facione 2000). In summary, the assessment literature on critical thinking dispositions at the K–12 level and the relationship to critical thinking skills and academic achievement indicators can be expected to grow at a rapid pace now that the CM3 is available to educators and researchers alike.

Authentic Assessments: Are They a Solution?

There is a growing acknowledgment in the educational assessment "best practices" literature that the evaluation of authentic student work products is the preferred method for measuring student learning outcomes (Allen 2006). There is reason to be hopeful that the trend in high-stakes testing is expanding to include not only the basic, core-content proficiencies but assessment tools that are more authentic and curriculum based. Authentic assessments, particularly when they are tied to real-world problems, require students to demonstrate not only content knowledge, but also the applied skills that they have acquired through instruction (DiMartino 2007). Students must recognize the appropriate skills to be applied to the problem context and be inclined to engage in these cognitive endeavours, whether it is the disposition to exercise creative problem-solving in the anticipation of consequences, the envisioning of alternatives, or the open-minded consideration of competing viewpoints and diverse perspectives on the topic at hand. In the classroom, this can include assessments based on live performances, such as speeches, debates, presentations, talk-aloud processes during problem-solving, and dramatic performances. Lest one think that the assessment of authentic student performances precludes the use of a paper-and-pencil or large group administration modality, the concept of authentic assessment can be applied to standardized testing because it encompasses the evaluation of outcomes or products of student work, such as essays, poems, short stories, and works of art (Taylor 2005).

Several states are exploring more innovative testing programs that permit students to respond to open-ended and free-response test item formats. For example, reporting on a study of 257 Grade 10 English, math, and science teachers in the state of Massachusetts, Vogler (2002) found that teachers were making observable changes in their instruction to give greater emphasis to creative and critical thinking, inquiry-based learning, and problem-solving activities. Teachers in this study attributed these instructional changes to the desire to help students perform well on the Massachusetts Comprehensive Assessment System (MCAS), a performance-based assessment tool that has been used in the state of Massachusetts since 1998 (Vogler 2002).

Other investigations into the effects of performance-based assessments on teaching practice have shown promising results that instructional emphasis on higher-order thinking and problem-solving have remained intact and in fact increased (Koretz 1996; Vogler 2002). The benefits of an instructional focus on higher-order thinking are not restricted to improved cognitive skills. Tiwari, Lai, So, and Yuen (2006) have demonstrated that problem-based learning strategies in the classroom can lead to gains in critical thinking dispositions.

A recent entrant into the large-scale assessment arena is the *Collegiate Learning Assessment* (CLA) (2007), available from the Council for Aid to Education for use at the post-secondary level. Used to ascertain "added value" in terms of student learning gains at the level of the institution rather than the level of the individual student, the CLA uses an open-ended question format that requires respondents to provide narrative responses that are then scored with a focus on the student's ability to make and critique an argument in the context of a performance task. The value of the CLA as a measure of critical thinking at the college level is untested and will, no doubt, be the focus of numerous research investigations. It remains to be seen what impact tools emphasizing performance-based testing formats will have on the widely accepted standardized testing strategies that characterize the contemporary K–12 educational environment. Any assessment plan for measuring learning outcomes can take the approach of measuring only a representative sample. Developers of the CLA suggest this approach, providing only institutional indicators as opposed to individual student results. This approach to assessment should be watched for its impact on the maintenance of classroom instruction that is grounded in inquiry and inclusive of both critical thinking skills and dispositions.

Conclusion

Care must be taken so as not to let accountability systems lead to the egregious neglect of breadth of content coverage and inquiry-based pedagogical techniques and assessment strategies. Many standardized tests continue to rely on question formats that tap factual content knowledge, or in other words, questions that demand thinking at the lowest levels—Knowledge and Comprehension—of Bloom's taxonomy (1956). Furthermore, it is inadequate to assess critical thinking skills alone and disregard the dispositions dimension of critical thinking despite the demonstrated relationship between dispositions and conventional indicators of student academic achievement. It is imperative to require students to demonstrate not only higher-order thinking and problem-solving skills but also critical thinking dispositions. State-mandated standardized testing programs must also be held accountable for effectively assessing not only basic knowledge and content standards, but also those curriculum standards that assure students are both willing and able to engage in high-order thinking.

The power wielded by the architects of accountability systems and mandated high-stakes testing programs must be directed toward positively affecting and maintaining our dedication to critical thinking as a central student learning outcome. We are committed at this time to the administration of standardized tests, and to the high-stakes decisions that are often linked to test results. At the highest levels there is faith in testing as the piston that can provide the driving force for reform of the American educational system. "Buy in" on the part of the general public and the educational community is commanding, and therefore testing compels pedagogical and curricular changes in the classroom. When there is faith in the goals and a presumptive validity of the testing program, teachers modify their practice in order to boost scores on the tests. If the state-mandated tests require critical/creative high-order thinking, student-centred teaching methods that promote critical thinking skills and dispositions and active learning will be implemented. The end result is high-quality teaching and the achievement of higher-level learning outcomes.

Negative trends related to high-stakes testing are changing the educational landscape of today's classrooms. These effects must be reversed if students are to receive a complete education that will prepare them for the complexities of the world we live in. If real improvement of schools is the goal, then we must recognize that the path to success is through teaching for deeper learning and understanding, not through teaching to a domain-restricted test. Only then will the goals of the accountability movement be actualized.

Notes

1. Reprinted, with permission, from the test manual for the *California Measure of Mental Motivation*. C.A. Giancarlo, *California Measure of Mental Motivation (CM3): An inventory of critical thinking dispositions. User Manual Supporting Levels IA, IB, II, and III Grades K–2, 3–5, 6–12, and Adults* (Millbrae, CA: The California Academic Press, 2006).
2. Reprinted, with permission, from the test manual for the *California Measure of Mental Motivation*, ibid.

References

Abrams, L., and G. Madaus. 2003. The lessons of high-stakes testing. *Educational Leadership* 61(3): 31–5.

Allen, M. 2006. *Assessing general education programs.* San Francisco: Jossey-Bass.

Ames, C. 1984. Competitive, cooperative, and individualistic goal structures: A motivational analysis. In *Research on motivation in education*, ed. R.A. Ames, 177–207. New York: Academic Press.

Baron, J. 1987. Evaluating thinking skills in the classroom. In *Teaching thinking skills: Theory and practice*, ed. J.B. Baron and R.J. Sternberg, 221–47. New York: W.H. Freeman.

Bloom, B., and D. Krathwohl. 1956. *Taxonomy of educational objectives: The classification of educational goals, by a committee of college and university examiners.* New York: Longman & Green.

Borich, G. 2004. *Effective teaching methods.* Upper Saddle River, NJ: Prentice Hall.

Carter-Wells, J. 1992. *Defining, teaching, and assessing critical thinking in a multicultural context.* Washington, DC: Association of American Colleges.

Chudowsky, N., and J. Pellegrino. 2003. Large-scale assessments that support learning: What will it take? *Theory Into Practice* 42(1): 75–83.

Colucciello, M. 1997. Critical thinking skills and dispositions of baccalaureate nursing students—A conceptual model for evaluation. *Journal of Professional Nursing* 13(4): 236–45.

Costa, A., and L. Lowery. 1989. *Techniques for teaching thinking.* Pacific Grove, CA: Critical Thinking Books and Software.

Costigan, A. 2002. Teaching the culture of high stakes testing: Listening to new teachers. *Action in Teacher Education* 23(4): 35–42.

Darling-Hammond, L., and A. Wise. 1985. Beyond standardization: State standards and school improvement. *The Elementary School Journal* 85(3): 315–6.

Duch, B., S. Groh, and D. Allen. 2001. *The problem of problem-based learning: A practical "how to" for teaching undergraduate courses in any discipline.* Sterling, VA: Stylus Publishing.

Ennis, R. 1985. The logical basis for measuring CT skills. *Educational Leadership* 43: 5.

Facione, P. 2000. *The test of everyday reasoning.* Millbrae, CA: Academic Press.

———. 1990. Critical thinking: A statement of expert consensus for purposes of educational assessment and instruction. *The Delphi Report: Research findings and recommendations prepared for the committee on pre-college philosophy.* Washington, DC: American Philosophical Association.

Facione, P., N. Facione, and C. Giancarlo. 2006 [1992]. *Test manual: The California critical thinking disposition inventory.* Millbrae, CA: Academic Press.

———. 1997. The motivation to think in working and learning. In *Preparing competent college graduates: Setting new and higher expectations for student learning,* ed. A. Jones, 67–79. San Francisco: Jossey-Bass.

Facione, P., N. Facione, S. Blohm, and C. Giancarlo. 2008 [1998]. *Test manual: The California critical thinking skills test, Revised edition.* Millbrae, CA: Academic Press.

Facione, P., C. Giancarlo, N. Facione, and J. Gainen. 1995. The disposition toward critical thinking. *Journal of General Education* 44(1): 1–25.

Fisher, R. 1990. *Teaching children to think.* Oxford: Basil Blackwell.

Giancarlo, C. 2006. *California Measure of Mental Motivation (CM3): An inventory of critical thinking dispositions. User Manual Supporting Levels IA, IB, II, and III Grades K–2, 3–5, 6–12, and Adults.* Millbrae, CA: Academic Press.

Giancarlo, C., S. Blohm, and T. Urdan. 2004. Assessing secondary students' disposition toward critical thinking: Development of the California measure of mental motivation. *Educational and Psychological Measurement* 64(2): 347–64.

Giancarlo, C., and N. Facione. 1994. *A study of the critical thinking disposition and skill of Spanish and English speaking students at Camelback High School.* Millbrae, CA: Phoenix Union High School District.

Giancarlo, C., and P. Facione. 2001. A look across four years at the disposition toward critical thinking among undergraduate students. *Journal of General Education* 50(1): 29–55.

Goertz, M., and M. Duffy. 2003. Mapping the landscape of high-stakes testing and accountability programs. *Theory into Practice* 42(1): 4–11.

Goldberg, M. 2004. The high-stakes testing mess. *The Educational Digest* 69(8): 8–15.

Graham, S., and S. Golan. 1991. Motivational influences on cognition: Task involvement, ego involvement and depth of information processing. *Journal of Educational Psychology* 83: 187–94.

Hoffman, J., L. Assaf, and S. Paris. 2001. High-stakes testing in reading: Today in Texas, tomorrow? *The Reading Teacher* 54(5): 482–92.

Johnson, L.S. 2008. Relationship of instructional methods to student engagement in two public schools. *American Secondary Education* 36(2): 69.

Jones, E., S. Corrallo, P. Facione, and G. Ratcliff. 1994. *Developing consensus for critical thinking.* Washington, DC: American Association of Higher Education.

Jones, E., S. Hoffman, L. Moore, G. Ratcliff, S. Tibbetts, and B. Click. 1995. *National assessment of college student learning: Identifying the college graduate's essential skills in writing, speech and listening, and critical thinking.* Washington, DC: National Center for Educational Statistics.

Jones, K., and B. Whitford. 1997. Kentucky's conflicting reform principles: High-stakes school accountability and student performance assessment. *Phi Delta Kappan* 79(4): 276–81.

Kakai, H. 2000. The use of cross-cultural studies and experiences as a way of fostering critical thinking dispositions among college students. *Journal of General Education* 49(2): 110–31.

Koretz, D., S. Barron, K. Mitchell, and B. Stecher. 1996. *The perceived effects of the Kentucky Instructional Results Information System (KIRIS)*. Santa Monica, CA: RAND.

Kuhn, D. 1990. Education for thinking: What can psychology contribute? In *Promoting cognitive growth over the lifespan*, ed. M. Schwebel, C.A. Mahlcr, and N.S. Fagley, 35–45 Hillsdale, NJ: Lawrence Erlbaum.

Kurfiss, J. 1988. Critical thinking: Theory, research, practice and possibilities. In *ASHE–ERIC Higher Education Report*. Washington, DC: Association for the Study of Higher Education.

Lampart, N. 2006. Critical thinking dispositions as an outcome of art education. *Studies in Art Education* 47(3): 215–28.

Lipman, M. 1987. Some thoughts on the foundations of reflective education. In *Teaching thinking skills: Theory and practice*, ed. J.B. Baron and R.J. Sternberg, 151–61. New York: W.H. Freeman.

McCall, K., E. MacLaughlin, D. Fike, and B. Ruiz. 2007. Preadmission predictors of PharmD graduates' performance on the NAPLEX. *American Journal of Pharma-critical Education* 71(1): 5.

Naglieri, J. 1988. *Naglieri nonverbal ability test: Individual administration kit.* San Antonio: Harcourt Assessment.

Neill, M. 2003. The dangers of testing. *Educational Leadership* 60(5): 43–6.

Nokes, K., D. Nickitas, and R. Keida. 2005. Does service-learning increase cultural competency, critical thinking and civic engagement? *Journal of Nursing Education* 44(2): 65–70.

Palincsar, A. 1998. Social constructivist perspectives on teaching and learning. *Annual Review of Psychology* 49: 345–75.

Paul, R. 1984. Critical thinking: Foundation to education for a free society. *Educational Leadership* 42(15): 4–14.

Pedulla, J. 2003. State-mandated testing: What do teachers think? *Educational Leadership* 61(3): 42–9.

Pedulla, J., L. Abrams, G. Madaus, M. Russell, M. Ramos, and J. Miao. 2003. Perceived effects of state-mandated testing programs on teaching and learning: Findings from a national survey of teachers. In *National board on educational testing and public policy*. Boston: Boston College.

Standford University. 1996. Stanford Achievement Test Series, Ninth Edition. Complete Battery. Online. Available at http://harcourtassessment.

com/haiweb/cultures/en-us/productdetail.htm?pid=E132C. Last retrieved October 12, 2007.

Stecher, B. 2002. Consequences of large-scale, high-stakes testing on school and classroom practice. In *Making sense of test-based accountability in education*, ed. L.S. Hamilton, B.M. Stecher, and S.P. Klein, 79–100. Santa Monica, CA: RAND.

Taylor, C., and S. Nolen. 2005. *Classroom assessment: Supporting teaching and learning in real classrooms.* Upper Saddle River, NJ: Pearson Education.

Taylor, G., L. Shepard, F. Kinner, and J. Rosenthal. 2003. *A survey of teachers' perspectives on high-stakes testing in Colorado: What gets taught, what gets lost.* Los Angeles: Center for Research on Evaluation, Standards, and Student Testing.

The Collegiate Learning Assessment. 2007. Online. Available at http://www.cae.org/content/pro_collegiate.htm#. Last retrieved October 10, 2007.

Tiwari, A., P. Lai, M. So, and K. Yuen. 2006. A comparison of the effects of problem-based learning and lecturing on the development of students' critical thinking. *Medical Education* 40(6): 547–54.

United States Department of Education. 1990. *National goals for education.* Washington, DC: U.S. Government Printing Office.

Urdan, T., and C. Giancarlo. 2001. A comparison of motivational and critical thinking orientations across ethnic groups. In *Research on sociocultural influences on motivation and learning*, ed. D.M. McInerney and S. Van Etten. Greenwich: Information Age.

Vogler, K. 2002. The impact of high-stakes, state-mandated student performance assessment on teachers' instructional practices. *Education* 123(1): 39–55.

Walsh, C., and R. Hardy. 1999. Dispositional differences in critical thinking related to gender and academic major. *Journal of Nursing Education* 38(4): 149–55.

Williams, K., C. Schmidt, T. Tilliss, K. Wilkins, and D. Glasnapp. 2006. Predictive validity of critical thinking skills and disposition for the national board dental hygiene examination: A preliminary investigation. *Journal of Dental Education* 70(5): 536–44.

Winn, I. 2004. The high cost of uncritical thinking. *Phi Delta Kappan* 85(7): 496.

Zoller, U., D. Ben-Chaim, and S. Ron. 2000. The disposition toward critical thinking of high school and university science students: An inter-intra Israeli–Italian study. *International Journal of Science Education* 22(6): 571–82.

Chapter Two

What's Wrong with the California Critical Thinking Skills Test?
CT Testing and Accountability

Leo Groarke

*I*t is not difficult to understand why critical thinking ("CT") has been proposed as a goal of education. How could one deny that students should be taught to be proficient, judicious, and open- and fair-minded thinkers? The skills that this requires—most notably, the ability to evaluate the evidence for conflicting points of view—might plausibly be identified as *the* core ingredient in a good education. A commitment to CT seems particularly important to democracy, because democracies rely on their citizens' ability to reach reasonable conclusions in the exercise of their democratic rights and influence.

Though the value of critical thinking thus seems unassailable, it is not obvious how critical thinking can and should be taught. Within universities (and, increasingly, at other levels of education), disciplines such as informal logic, rhetoric, pragma-dialectics, cognitive psychology, communication studies, and education theory have developed a variety of competing approaches to "stand-alone" and/or "subject-specific" critical thinking courses and curricula. The result has been hundreds of critical thinking texts, thousands of syllabi, and a growing cache of supplemental material which includes software, websites, bibliographies, lesson plans, data bases, and extensive collections of examples.

This is a positive development, but it raises many questions. Assuming that there are more and less successful ways to teach critical thinking (and it would be peculiar to imagine otherwise), what are the key components of successful texts and courses? Which of the many competing approaches to critical thinking is to be preferred? Should different approaches be used in different circumstances? What evidence justifies the assumption that the skills (or dispositions) we try to teach in any critical thinking course are successfully learned? How do we know that they are transferred to other contexts? Can we *prove* that attempts to teach critical thinking create more engaged, reflective citizens? These "critical questions" have special force in a discipline which claims that it is dedicated to reflective criticism. This is a goal which implies that those of us who teach and study critical thinking have an obligation to critically evaluate the extent to which our courses—and the curricula, texts, and theories on which they are founded—really do turn students into better thinkers.

In practice, evaluations of attempts to teach critical thinking tend to be informal: those who teach and study critical thinking form opinions on the basis of their observations and experience. One should not minimize the experience underpinning these informal impressions, but conclusions founded on them are inherently problematic. Among other things, such conclusions are frequently contradictory: teachers committed to formal logic conclude that it aids their students; teachers who reject formal logic conclude that it is a pointless exercise; and so on. It is hard to see how contradictory conclusions of this sort can substitute for a systematic and critical approach to the assessment of critical thinking—especially as they do not, in any careful way, distinguish among the different factors that may contribute to the improvement of students' ability to think critically (e.g., CT courses, other kinds of courses, and increased maturity).

Standardized critical thinking tests are sometimes suggested as a way to navigate these problems. According to this view, they provide a more consistent and objective way of measuring the results of critical thinking courses. In the context of attempts to defend critical thinking as an educational goal, they may seem particularly important. Van Gelder has even claimed that they cast doubt on the assumption that critical thinking courses improve students' thinking. On the basis of a review of studies using such tests, he wrote that "currently it is difficult to make a convincing case that CT/IL [Critical Thinking/Informal Logic] courses make an appreciable difference to CT or informal reasoning skills" (van Gelder 2000). In discussing the studies he reviews, van Gelder goes even further, suggesting that "an important question, which is left unresolved by these studies, is whether CT courses harm their students. It appears possible that typical CT courses actually reduce CT performance" (ibid.).

Despite his general skepticism, van Gelder does not reject all approaches to critical thinking. In defending particular approaches, one might cite studies by van Gelder et al. (2004), Hatcher (2003), and Hitchcock (2003), who have demonstrated that their courses in critical thinking improve their students' performance on standardized critical thinking tests. If it can be shown that this improvement is not plausibly attributed to other causes (e.g., increased maturity, general education), one might take this as proof that these courses successfully improve students' critical thinking skills. By studying changes in performance that occur in other kinds of critical thinking courses, one might try to assess the relative value of different courses—an intriguing idea that Hatcher develops in his chapter.

In this way, standardized critical thinking tests appear to provide us with a way to systematically study and evaluate attempts to teach critical thinking. This approach might seem to provide a ready answer to demands for educational accountability—demands that we prove that our teaching methods successfully attain our education goals. But I shall argue that this approach to the evaluation of CT raises as many questions as it answers.

The problem with standardized CT tests can be put simply: an appeal to standardized tests can settle questions about the effectiveness of critical thinking courses only if such tests are dependable instruments which measure critical thinking abilities in a valid and unproblematic way. This assumption, frequently made by those who use such tests, is problematic. In such a context, it is easily argued that standardized tests do not answer the question "Do critical thinking courses actually improve critical thinking?" so much as they replace it with the corollary "Do critical thinking tests actually measure critical thinking?"

The difficulties inherent in the second question reflect and exacerbate the many difficulties inherent in the first. It is difficult, for example, to be sure that attempts to teach critical thinking are successful because critical thinking (and higher-order thinking generally) is a complex activity that should, if the attempt to teach it is successful, be applicable to a broad array of different contexts (indeed, to all of life). The complexity and breadth that this complexity implies are, however, even more of a problem for testing than for teaching. How can one be sure that proficiency in such a complex and broadly applicable skills set can be measured by a standardized test which must be administered in artificial circumstances governed by so many practical constraints—the limited time available for testing, ease of marking, and so on?

These problems need further study. If they are considerable and serious, then standardized testing may not be the best way to evaluate critical thinking teaching. If critical thinking is, for example, too complex to be measured by standardized tests, then the informal assessments of critical thinking—assessments based on complex human judgments carried out over an extended period of time—may, for all their problems, be a more reasonable way to judge the efficacy of attempts to teach critical thinking (see, for example, Case 1997).

The California Critical Thinking Skills Test

Within this broader context, my goal is to assess one specific test: the *California Critical Thinking Skills Test* (the "CCTST"). Currently available from the California company Insight Assessment, the CCTST is a popular test which is available in three forms (Form A, Form B, and Form 2000) and seven languages. It is the test used by van Gelder (2000, 2004), Hatcher (2003), and Hitchcock (2003) in their studies of critical thinking courses, and it has been used by educational institutions to monitor their students' critical thinking skills.

Each of the CCTST forms consists of 34 multiple-choice questions designed to "target those core critical thinking skills regarded to be essential elements of a college education" (Facione et al. 2002, 1). Form 2000, which I discuss, retains 22 items from the original Form A, but adds 12 new items which "require one to apply reasoning skills to contexts more appropriate to the expectations of the new century" (ibid.). Despite its popularity (and even though it must be granted that the CCTST is an historically important attempt to formulate a test that measures critical thinking skills), I contend that the CCTST is a poor instrument for testing critical thinking skills.

In defending this conclusion I argue that

- ❖ answers in the CCTST are mistaken or unreflective;
- ❖ one can reasonably defend conflicting answers to many CCTST questions;

- ❖ the instances of reasoning the CCTST uses as a basis for its questions are vague and artificial;
- ❖ the CCTST does not recognize many essential components of critical thinking;
- ❖ the CCTST is biased in favour of an outmoded conception of critical thinking; and
- ❖ there is little reason for believing that the unproblematic questions the CCTST does contain provide even a rough measure of CT skills.

If these contentions are correct, then the CCTST cannot be used to answer the important questions I have already raised about critical thinking as a subject. At best, it is irrelevant to these questions. At worst, its continued use serves only to confuse possible answers to them.

Issues of independence

Those who create and distribute standardized tests have an ethical obligation to ensure that their instruments accurately measure what they claim to measure (all the more so when tests are used as high-stakes tests). Because test makers and test distributors have a vested interest in positive evaluations, it is difficult for them to act as neutral judges of their own tests.[1] Such an obligation can best be met through independent scrutiny and assessment. Openness to impartial test evaluation is not a criterion for a valid test, but it is a condition that needs to be satisfied before users of a test can be confident of its validity.

This is a condition which the distributors of the CCTST do not meet because they have refused to make its answers available for scrutiny.[2] Not all refusals of this sort are unreasonable. Distributors might reasonably protect their financial investment by placing limits on such reviews (by restricting access to established researchers, requiring non-disclosure agreements, etc.) but Insight Assessment has refused to make the CCTST answers available for scrutiny even under these restricted terms. Whatever motivates this refusal, it might easily be interpreted as an attempt to prevent a critical evaluation of the test. Given the nature of the CCTST, this lack of transparency cannot prevent its evaluation,[3] but it still fails to embrace an openness to critical assessment which is one important precondition for an acceptable critical thinking test.[4]

These issues are exacerbated by the way in which the creators and distributors of the CCTST have attempted to confirm its validity. They have attempted to investigate (construct) validity by studying the CCTST performance of students who complete critical thinking courses. On the basis of their finding that such students register statistically significant gains in CCTST scores, they conclude that "the CCTST proved successful as a valid and reliable measure of CT skills" (Facione et al. 2002, 20; see also Facione 1990b).

Instead of resolving questions about the CCTST (and the questions about critical thinking courses that motivate its use), such conclusions constitute a classic begging of the question: the evidence that the CCTST is valid assuming the validity of critical thinking courses, the proof that critical thinking courses are valid assuming the validity of the CCTST. This is a circle which would have to be broken (or at least explained) before one could reasonably claim that the CCTST studies provide independent evidence for the conclusion that the CCTST is valid. Without further argument, the correlation between improved CCTST performance and the successful completion of critical thinking courses may be just as plausibly attributed to similar biases that they may share. This is a hypothesis which is not easily dismissed given that the CCTST and the courses in question have been created by individuals who share a particular approach to critical thinking (one that places, for example, great emphasis on the aspects of critical thinking that correspond to introductory formal logic).

Problem questions, problem answers

Though these issues of independence are cause for concern, and though they raise serious questions about the evidence given for the validity of the CCTST, they do not themselves show that the CCTST is unreliable. In arguing that the CCTST is indeed unreliable, I want to begin with a catalogue of problems inherent in the test questions. In elaborating these problems, I will argue that the questions and answers the CCTST contains are often unreflective, sometimes mistaken (usually because they are imprecise), and founded on attempts to mimic ordinary reasoning, attempts that are artificial and ambiguous when they are presented outside the context of a more detailed description of the circumstances in which they are supposed to arise. In all the cases that follow, I argue that a critical thinker may reasonably favour a response to a question that is neither available on the CCTST nor favoured in its expected answers.

Question 1

The first question in the CCTST expects a critical thinker to conclude that the Sparklers will probably beat the Mustangs (but may lose) in a soccer match, on the basis of the knowledge that the Sparklers beat the Wildflowers and the Wildflowers beat the Mustangs (test answer B).

For a variety of reasons, this is a prediction a critical thinker should reject. First, one should recognize that the results of games are difficult to predict, especially in circumstances in which the Sparklers may have beaten the Wildflowers 3–2 in a penalty kick shootout, while the Wildflowers beat the Mustangs 1–0 on a single penalty kick. In a circumstance such as this, the teams are too closely matched to allow one to predict the outcome of their game. And all the more so given that teams in the "recreational" league in question have (according to the scenario described in the CCTST) been explicitly designed "to be evenly matched." As anyone familiar with such leagues is bound to know, the matches they sponsor are by their nature characterized by inconsistent play and dramatic changes in individual teams, as different players show up (or not), depending on other family obligations.

Faced with the scenario the CCTST proposes, a critical thinker in a real-life situation should not draw a conclusion; instead he or she should refuse to predict the outcome of the upcoming game. Critical thinking in such a circumstance requires that one recognize that the situation is too uncertain to allow any reasonable prediction about who will certainly or even probably win the game.

Question 5

The CCTST asks us to recognize that "Ezernians tell lies" "means the same thing" as "If anyone is Ezernian, then that person is a liar." This equivalence treats "Ezernians tell lies" as a universal statement equivalent to "All Ezernians tell lies." This equivalence is sometimes assumed in formal logic, but it misrepresents ordinary language in which statements of the form "Xs are Ys" function as general rather than universal claims. In ordinary language, this means that "Ezernians tell lies" claims a general truth which, unlike a universal statement, is compatible with exceptions. One might compare "The French are fond of red wine and cheese," which is not mistaken if a few French persons do not hold these preferences (or "Lions eat meat," which is not disproved if a vegetarian raises a lion on soy-based alternatives). In the CCTST, a generalization that is recognized as admitting of exceptions is included in question 7.

Question 8

We are asked to draw the conclusion that "Whatever else, Nero was certainly insane" on the basis of four premises:

1. Nero was emperor of Rome in the first century AD.
2. Every Roman emperor drank wine and did so using exclusively pewter pitchers and goblets.
3. Whoever uses pewter, even once, has lead poisoning.
4. Lead poisoning always manifests itself through insanity.

This is a peculiar inference on a test which purports to measure critical thinking skills because a critical thinker faced with premises such as these should not be drawing a conclusion, but should instead be asking how the premises can be justified. How could one ever know that *every* Roman emperor drank wine using *exclusively* pewter pitchers, that using pewter *only once* produces lead poisoning, and that such poisoning *always* manifests itself through insanity?

Even if we ignore the epistemological issues the above question raises, the CCTST inference cannot be justified. It is apparently founded on the notion that the conclusion of a deductive inference is always certain. This is a common misconception: deductive inferences produce conclusions which are only *as* certain as their premises (which in this case are notably *un*certain).[5] In the case in question, someone who accepts the proposed premises must certainly (on pain of contradiction) accept that Nero was insane, but he or she needs not accept that it is *certain* that Nero was insane. If the premises are marginally acceptable but not certain (as they appear to be) then the conclusion is acceptable but uncertain.

Question 12

We are asked to draw a conclusion on the basis of data gleaned from research on preschools and the extent to which they help prepare students for kindergarten. The intended conclusion is founded on the way that students who attended preschool and those who did not attend preschool perform on a standardized test of kindergarten readiness. Those students who attended preschool scored 50–60 points, whereas those who did not attend preschool scored an average of 32 points. The CCTST concludes that "attending preschool is correlated with kindergarten readiness" (test answer E) but one could reasonably argue that more testing is needed before a plausible hypothesis can be formed (test answer B). In this regard it is significant that the students who did not attend preschool "were all from low-income households" and that the students who attended may, for all we know, be from high-income households (a distinct possibility if the preschools were located in affluent neighbourhoods). In such circumstances, it may be life in a high-income household, not preschool attendance, which is correlated with kindergarten readiness. To find out, one would have to investigate how students in preschools in low-income areas perform on the test in question.

Question 17

"Little Christopher" presses his nose against the window, wishes for the sun to come up, watches it rise, and concludes that he can make the sun come up whenever he wishes. The CCTST asks one to explain this as poor reasoning because it is an instance of the fallacy *post hoc ergo propter hoc* (test answer A). This is the answer one expects from a logic student (or professor), but it is a mistake to think that it must, therefore, be the "best" way to explain what is wrong with the reasoning. If one wants to explain to little Christopher's friend, Jamie, why the reasoning is wrong, one will do better to point out that the world goes around the sun with or without Christopher's wishing it (test answer B). One can even imagine contexts in which one could plausibly argue that Christopher's reasoning is good because he is "only a child" (test answer C): one might argue that, despite his erroneous conclusion, it is significant that someone as young as Christopher has recognized that causal conclusions should, in some crucial way, be founded on an observed correlation between a cause and an effect.

Question 19

We are told that there are "two popular arguments in favour of the death penalty." The problems with one of the arguments are explained and the test-taker is asked to evaluate the reasoning. But one might easily object that this is difficult to do without knowing more about one's goals in arguing. If one's goal is the argument that is the most philosophically defensible (the traditional goal of logic), one might lean in one direction. If one's goal is to convince an audience (the traditional goal of rhetoric) then one might lean in another direction. If one imagines oneself at a philosophy conference where one is trying to establish the morality of the death penalty, one might reasonably object to question 19's focus on popular arguments in favour of the death penalty (test answer A). In such a context, one might argue that the popularity of an argument is irrelevant.

One might evaluate the argument in a different way if it is propounded by a politician in the context of an upcoming referendum on the death penalty—a circumstance where popular opinion (even if misguided) is an appropriate focus of attention. In these new circumstances, one might argue that the reasoning is poor because only one of two popular arguments has been addressed (test answer B). In yet another context—say, a conversation with a group of social scientists (who typically reject the deterrence argument)—it might not matter that a popular argument based on deterrence is mentioned but not addressed. In this context, one might argue that the argument is a good argument (test answer C).

Question 23

We are provided with a list of height relations (L is shorter than X, Y than L, M than L, M than Y) and asked what information "*must*" [the test's emphasis] be added to require that Y is shorter than J. Of the answers given the only possibility is C ("J is taller than L") but J could be shorter than L and still taller than Y—if, to take one example, L is 5', X is 6', Y is 4', M is 3' and J is 4.5'. Thus, it is not true that the information "J is taller than L" *must* be added to imply that Y is shorter than J. There are many possibilities one could add (for example, "Z is taller than Y and shorter than J"). In this particular case, it appears that the CCTST question is misstated. It should ask: "Which of the following would imply that Y is shorter than J?" This question would require the intended answer. Though precision is one of the hallmarks of critical thinking, the CCTST mistakenly treats it as equivalent to the question "What information *must* be added to make this true?"

Question 24

A paragraph of reasoning begins with the sentence "A standard deck of 52 playing cards contains exactly four kings, four queens, and four jacks" and ends with the sentence "So, from what we know now, we can conclude that among the 52 playing cards in a standard deck, there are precisely four each of jacks, queens, and kings." According to the CCTST, the reasoning is "poor" because "It proves nothing, as in 'The sky is blue because it's blue'" (test answer A).

But the claim that reasoning in the paragraph has the form "The sky is blue because it's blue" is contentious. The latter is an inference of the form "A, therefore A." The reasoning in Question 24 has the form "A, B, C, D, E, therefore A." These are importantly different inferences. In one, the conclusion repeats the premise; in the other, the conclusion is deduced from a list which contains it. It is difficult to think of plausible inferences of the form $A \vdash A$ (I don't doubt that there are some), but it is not difficult to think of examples of the form $A, B, C, D, E \vdash A$.

The latter, for example, is the form of inference I use when checking a grocery list to deduce what should be put in the shopping cart. In other situations, such an inference might be appropriate when teaching deductive reasoning or when dealing with children, or in other cases where one needs, in painstaking ways, to make things clear; or when the passage in question is one part of a long argument in which it is particularly important to recognize that there are four of each face card in a standard deck of cards (i.e., a circumstance in which it makes good sense to repeatedly reinforce an audience's commitment to this proposition).

It is true that the argument in question is circular, but it cannot be dismissed on these grounds. The same can be said of all good deductive arguments—which might be approved, not rejected, because they are (as test answer B explains) inferences in which "the reasoning is an accurate restatement of the facts."

Question 33

In a situation in which an assistant fails to send an important package, we are asked to judge a friend's argument that there are (setting aside union issues) sufficient reasons for firing him: "He has lied. He is disorganized and loses important things. He did not even check with you about sending the package late once he found it." One could argue that the reasoning is "good, because the assistant has performed in exactly these substandard ways" (test answer D). It is plausible to suppose that someone should be fired if he has acted in these ways.

However, one can imagine contexts in which it is more plausible to conclude that the friend's reasoning is "poor, because the friend does not know the circumstances of work in your office" (test answer A). Imagine a situation where the assistant who has misbehaved has a long record of superior performance and his unhelpful behaviour can be attributed to difficult circumstances that require some compassion (e.g., his father has died, his teenager is in trouble with drugs, etc.).

Someone who reflects on the vicissitudes of human conflict may reasonably argue that one can never understand a situation of this sort until one has heard "both sides of the story." But this suggests that the right answer to Question 33 is B: that the friend's reasoning is poor because he or she has not given the assistant a chance to explain himself.

Faced with Question 33, how can the critical thinker choose between answers A and D and possibly B? On the one hand, one might reasonably suppose that all the essential information has been given in the test question, and that one should not imagine further complicating circumstances (a supposition that favours answer D). On the other hand, one might reasonably hypothesize that the CCTST is designed to test one's care in reasoning, and that in this instance it is testing one's ability to recognize that complicating circumstances have not been explicitly ruled out.

Question 34

The same kinds of problems are evident in Question 34, which refers again to the misbehaving assistant. In this case, we are asked to imagine that our daughter elaborates the argument that "If you fire your assistant you will get in trouble with the union; but if you do not, you will get in trouble with your boss! No matter what, you will get in trouble eventually." This is reasonably judged to be a good dilemma argument "because right now there seem to be no other options" (test answer C). It is, however, possible to make a case for rejecting one of the conditionals in the dilemma, i.e., the claim that "if you fire your assistant you will get in trouble with the union." This is not explicitly stated in the CCTST's original description of the situation. One might say on these grounds that the reasoning is poor "because you cannot be sure what the union will do" (test answer B).

Without more information, it is difficult to choose between answers B and C. On the one hand, this is the kind of contract violation that is likely to precipitate a union grievance. On the other hand, violations of a union contract may not result in grievances (because the individual affected does not wish to pursue a grievance, because the union leadership decides not to pursue it, and so on). There is no way to tell what should be expected in this particular case.

Why such problematic questions?
Putting aside the problems with specific questions, the CCTST might be criticized for its commitment to artificial examples of reasoning that are, at best, distantly related to the kinds of reasoning or critical thinking required in real-life contexts. Within the CCTST, this artificiality is reflected in premises that are fanciful ("*Whenever* it is snowing, streets and sidewalks are wet and slippery," "*All* college students graduate sooner or later," etc.); in arguments presented out of context; and in inferences that are embedded in scenarios which are described in a manner that does not provide the details necessary to properly assess them.

In such contexts, the CCTST asks us to judge arguments and explanations without knowing to whom they are addressed, what circumstances prompted them, and the argumentative details of the situation in which they are advanced. In these and many other cases (consider Questions 3, 6, and 16), one may wonder whether the examples that form the basis of CCTST questions can reasonably be used to test one's ability to think critically in the "complex and many layered" situations that demand real-life reasoning. Why should we believe that an ability to answer the CCTST's artificial questions shows that someone can think critically about politics, his or her favourite television show, advertising on the Internet, a business proposition, ethics, and so on? What compelling evidence shows that this is so?

Anyone familiar with the development of critical thinking and its related disciplines will recognize that the artificiality that tends to characterize the examples in the CCTST reflects the artificiality that characterized early attempts to teach logic in a manner suited for general students (notably, in early editions of Copi: see, for example, Copi 1961). In both cases, the attempt to teach reasoning skills is characterized by constructed rather than actual examples of reasoning; focuses on answers that only reflect aspects of thinking explained in terms of the limited resources available in propositional and syllogistic logic; and emphasizes many of the simplest kinds of inference making to the exclusion of many more complex aspects of ordinary reasoning (e.g., questions of premise acceptability and more complex kinds of inference).

In the wake of developments in informal (and even formal) logic, critical thinking, and related disciplines, this approach to critical thinking reflects an outmoded conception of critical thinking which has been roundly criticized (for an overview of some of the standard criticisms, see the articles by Johnson and Blair in Johnson 1996). There is therefore little reason to believe that test questions reflecting the CCTST's limited conception of reasoning can validly measure critical thinking abilities as they are understood when critical thinking is proposed as a goal of education—a goal that implies the ability to think critically in the midst of the complexities and nuances that characterize reasoning in real-life contexts.[6]

What's Missing From the CCTST?

The issues raised by the artificial examples in the CCTST suggest that it fails to test one's ability to deal with many of the complexities that characterize critical thinking in real-life situations. It is reasonable, then, to ask whether key critical thinking competencies are missing from the CCTST. In attempting to answer this question, something must be said about the definitions of critical thinking, because it is one's definition of critical thinking that determines what competencies and complexities critical thinking must encompass.

The CCTST is based on the definition of critical thinking proposed in the American Philosophical Association's 1990 "Delphi" report (*Critical Thinking: A Statement of Expert Consensus for Purposes of Educational Assessment and Instruction*). It identifies six core critical thinking skills: interpretation, analysis, evaluation, inference, explanation, and self-regulation; and defines critical thinking as the "purposeful, self-regulatory judgment which results in interpretation, analysis, evaluation and inference, as well as explanation of the evidential, conceptual, methodological, criteriological or contextual considerations upon which that judgment is based" (Facione 1990a, 2). The Delphi Report associates each of the six core skills identified in this definition with a specific set of sub-skills.[7]

A detailed discussion of the Delphi definition—or the general issues raised by any attempt to define critical thinking—lies beyond the scope of this chapter.[8] In place of such a discussion, it will suffice to note that the different definitions of critical thinking that have been proposed recognize it as an ability (or set of abilities, or set of abilities and dispositions) applicable to a broad array of real-life contexts. When those of us who champion critical thinking say that we want students to be critical thinkers, we mean that we want them to be individuals who critically evaluate the claims, beliefs, arguments, attempts at persuasion, etc., that surround them in the many different facets of their lives: when they argue in class; when they watch television; when they read magazines, newspapers, and books; when they participate in formal and informal conversations; when they graduate and pursue professional careers; and so on.

This aspect of critical thinking raises an obvious question about the CCTST: Does its interpretation of the Delphi definition[9] encompass the essential skills and competencies that characterize critical thinking in a broad array of real-life contexts? In answering this question, one might usefully compare the understanding of ordinary reasoning implicit in the CCTST and that evident in current research coming out of disciplines usually associated with critical thinking (which are often referred to as the interdisciplinary amalgam of disciplines and sub-disciplines called "argumentation theory"). In the last twenty years such argumentation theories have made great progress in the attempt to establish and extend a more sophisticated understanding of informal argument, discussion, dialogue, and debate. It is significant that they are, in marked contrast with the CCTST, characterized by both a much clearer focus on real, rather than concocted, examples of critical thinking, and a much more sensitive account of the nuances and complexities of real-life reasoning.

Though space does not allow a detailed account of the understanding of critical thinking that has emerged in argumentation theory (for an overview, see Johnson 1996; Groarke 2002; van Eemeren 2002), I will note that its scope encompasses, among others, the following elements:

❖ the principles of argumentative communication that inform critical inquiry;

❖ the different expectations that govern dialectical exchange in different kinds of circumstances (see, e.g., Van Eemeren 2002);

❖ techniques of persuasion, bias, and the relationship between argument, audience, and ethos (see, e.g., Tindale 1999, 2004);

❖ an in-depth understanding of fallacies and argument schemes which play a central role in ordinary reasoning (see, e.g., Walton 1992, 1998; Hansen and Pinto 1995);

❖ the dialectical obligations that attend arguments in real-life contexts (see Johnson 2000, and in this volume); and

❖ the nature of visual argument and persuasion that surround us on television, in advertising, and on the Internet (see Groarke 1996; Blair 2003).

These aspects of reasoning, which have been shown to play a crucial role in reasoning in real-life contexts, are conspicuously absent from the CCTST, which has no questions that would allow us to measure a thinker's ability to evaluate real-life problems appropriately or to make sound decisions about what to believe or do. Even if there were no problems with the questions and answers assumed in the CCTST, the failure to recognize and test for such abilities would make it difficult to accept that this particular test can function as a reliable measure of critical thinking skills.

Some Concluding Comments

The ruminations in this chapter leave little room for confidence in the CCTST's ability to reliably measure critical thinking skills. The test is problematic in many ways. Most notably, it contains many contentious answers, relies on artificial examples which are removed from the real-life contexts where critical thinking must take place, fails to recognize key aspects of ordinary reasoning that play a role in critical thinking, and focuses on rudimentary reasoning skills which represent a very limited conception of critical thinking. For these reasons, it is difficult to defend the use of the CCTST as a way to test critical thinking abilities and, more broadly, to teach these skills.

It would be premature to conclude that reliable tests of critical thinking are impossible. The problems with the CCTST highlight the many nuances and complexities of ordinary reasoning that make the design of a good test difficult. That said, other tests (like the Ennis-Weir) and other approaches to testing (like Fisher and Scriven's multiple rating items) must be judged on their own merits. More significantly, perhaps, we should not prejudge attempts to create better tests because it is possible that they will provide valuable instruments that will allow us to study and understand attempts to teach critical thinking. More study and discussion will have to determine the extent to which testing can adequately measure the complex and difficult aspects of critical thinking (e.g., what the Delphi Report calls "self-regulation"). Such work will be worthwhile even if it reaches negative conclusions because it will still clarify the nature of critical thinking teaching and assessment.

In the meantime, it should be said that the value of standardized critical thinking tests is easily exaggerated. My attempt to answer the questions about critical thinking stated at the beginning of this chapter has not shown that standardized tests provide a better measure of critical thinking abilities (and the efficacy of critical thinking courses) than the informal assessments that have characterized the field. We need to remain open-minded, but we should also be wary of the kind of standardized testing Giancarlo-Gittens warns about in Chapter One of this book—tests often used in high-stakes situations that have major ramifications for students and teachers, and for the development of critical thinking as a field.

Notes

1. As Paul and Elder (2003) recognize, vested interests of this sort are one of the major obstacles to critical thinking, and manifest themselves in a natural tendency to "think of the world in terms of how *it* can serve *us*" (214).

2. I personally discussed this issue with Insight Assessment (the test distributors) on two occasions, asking them for the official answers. I purchased the test packet and explained that I would only use the answers to assess the test, but they would not release the official answer key.

3. Many of my criticisms (for example, that the CCTST is founded on ques-
    tions which are vague, founded on mistaken assumptions, and susceptible
    to different interpretations) hold no matter what answers one proposes.
    That said, most of the questions on the CCTST have obviously intended
    answers that will be evident to anyone who knows the field. In order to
    deal with a few cases about which I was unsure I consulted with research-
    ers who worked on the original test.
4. One might question whether, as a matter of standard practice, the critical
    thinking community should use any test which is not made available for
    independent assessment.
5. The intended answer illustrates a fallacy of misplaced modality which
    often characterizes assessments of deductive arguments. It assumes that
    the conclusion of a deductive argument is certain—that such an argu-
    ment, with premises P and conclusion C, has the form $P \vdash C$. However,
    a deductive argument has the form $(P \vdash C)$ and establishes only that the
    conclusion is *as* certain as the premises (Groarke 1999).
6. The more one is sensitive to the different aspects of real-life reasoning
    (context, audience, premise acceptability, etc.), the more the questions on
    the CCTST must strike one as puzzling, peculiar, and open to different
    interpretations. Especially in view of its time constraints, one will score
    better on the CCTST if one ignores the nuances of good reasoning (as
    formal logicians sometimes do) and answers questions without the reflec-
    tion they invite.
7. Interpretation, for example, is defined as the ability "to comprehend and
    express the meaning or significance of a wide variety of experiences, situ-
    ations, data, events, judgments, conventions, beliefs, rules, procedures or
    criteria" and said to include as sub-skills "categorization," "decoding sig-
    nificance," and "clarifying meaning" (Facione 1990a, 6–7).
8. For an overview of these issues, see Fisher and Scriven (1997); see also
    the discussion in the Introduction and Chapter Three by Ralph Johnson
    in this book.
9. The CCTST interpretation is only one of many possibilities—and one
    that might be criticized in many ways. One aspect of the Delphi defini-
    tion, for example, is its commitment to "self-regulation." Putting aside
    the question of whether it is a disposition rather than a skill, self-regula-
    tion encompasses a willingness to critically examine and re-examine one's
    beliefs. There is no doubt that regulation of this sort is a cornerstone of
    critical thinking, but it is difficult to see how it can be tested in a test like
    the CCTST. In circumstances in which we wish to establish the extent
    to which someone is committed to an open-minded examination of their
    beliefs, we need to observe their willingness to engage criticisms of these
    beliefs, their response to countervailing evidence, and so on. These are

skills and dispositions that are not tested by the CCTST, which function as a more general test of reasoning skills. The difference between reasoning skills and self-regulation is evident in individuals who have sophisticated reasoning skills but are dogmatic about their beliefs.

References

American Philosophical Association. 1990. *Critical thinking: A statement of expert consensus for the purposes of educational assessment and instruction.* ("The Delphi Report"). ERIC Doc. No. ED 315-423.

Blair, J. 2003. The rhetoric of visual arguments. In *Defining visual rhetorics*, ed. C. Hill and M. Helmers, 41–62. Mahwah, NJ: Lawrence Erlbaum Associates.

Case, R. 1997. Principles of authentic assessment. In *The Canadian anthology of social studies: Issues and strategies for teachers*, ed. R. Case and P. Clark, 389–400. Vancouver: Pacific Educational Press.

Copi, I. 1961. *Introduction to logic.* New York: Macmillan.

Dumke, G. 1980. *Chancellor's executive order 338.* Long Beach, CA: California State University.

Ennis, R., and E. Weir. 1985. *The Ennis-Weir critical thinking essay test.* Pacific Grove, CA: Midwest Publications.

Facione, P., N. Facione, S. Blohm, and C. Giancarlo. 2002. *The California critical thinking skills test.* Millbrae, CA: Academic Press/Insight Assessment.

Facione, P. 1990a. *Critical thinking: A statement of expert consensus for purposes of educational assessment and instruction. Executive summary "The Delphi Report."* Millbrae, CA: Academic Press.

———. 1990b. *The California critical thinking skills test: College level technical report #1—Experimental validation and content validity.* Millbrae, CA: Academic Press. ERIC Doc No. ED 327-549.

Fisher, A., and M. Scriven. 1997. *Critical thinking: Its definition and assessment.* Norwich, UK: Centre For Research In Critical Thinking, University of East Anglia.

Groarke, L. 2002. Informal logic. *Stanford Encyclopedia of Philosophy.* Online. Available at http://plato.stanford.edu/entries/logic-informal.

———. 1999. Deductivism within pragma-dialectics. *Argumentation* 13: 1–16.

———. 1996. Logic, art and argument. *Informal Logic* 18(2 and 3): 116–31.

Hansen, H., and R. Pinto. 1995. *Fallacies: Classical and contemporary readings.* University Park: Pennsylvania State University Press.

Hatcher, D. 2003. On assessing and comparing critical thinking programs: A response to Hitchcock. Paper presented at *Informal Logic @ 25*, University of Windsor, May 14–17. Online. Available at http://www.humanities. mcmaster.ca/~hitchckd/response.htm.

Hitchcock, D. 2003. The effectiveness of computer-assisted instruction in critical thinking. In *Informal Logic at 25: Proceedings of the Windsor Conference*, ed. J. Blair, D. Farr, H. Hansen, R. Johnson, and C. Tindale. CD-ROM. Windsor, ON: Ontario Society for the Study of Argument.

Johnson, R. 2000. *Manifest rationality: A pragmatic theory of argument.* Mahwah, NJ: Lawrence Erlbaum Associates.

———. 1996. *The rise of informal logic: Essays on argumentation, critical thinking, reasoning and politics.* Studies in Critical Thinking and Informal Logic No. 2. Newport News, VA: Vale Press.

Paul, R., and L. Elder. 2001. *Critical thinking: Tools for taking charge of your learning and your life.* Upper Saddle River, NJ: Prentice-Hall.

Tindale, C. 2004. *Rhetorical argumentation.* Thousand Oaks, CA: Sage Publications.

———. 1999. *Acts of arguing: A rhetorical model of argument.* Albany: SUNY Press.

van Eemeren, F., ed. 2002. *Advances in pragma-dialectics.* Amsterdam and Newport News, VA: Vale Press.

van Gelder, T. 2000. The efficacy of undergraduate critical thinking courses: A survey in progress. Online. Available at http://www.philosophy.unimelb.edu.au/reason/efficacy.html.

van Gelder, T., M. Bissett, and G. Cumming. 2004. Cultivating expertise in informal reasoning. Special issue on informal reasoning. *Canadian Journal of Experimental Psychology.*

Walton, D. 1998. *Appeal to popular opinion.* University Park: Pennsylvania State University Press.

———. 1992. *Slippery slope arguments.* Oxford: Clarendon Press.

Chapter Three

The Implications of the Dialectical Tier for Critical Thinking

Ralph H. Johnson

Introduction

'Most theorists agree that a thinker who thinks critically must be able to deal with arguments, that is, he or she must be able to construct, interpret, evaluate, and criticize arguments. A critical thinker should also have the ability to process arguments: to take criticisms of his or her views, and to engage critically with the arguments of others.

I have recently proposed that an important aspect of argument has been under-represented in theories of argument. In *Manifest Rationality* (2000), I argued that one's theoretical apparatus for understanding argument is incomplete unless it contains the concept of the "dialectical tier" a layer of argument in which the arguer discharges his or her dialectical obligations by anticipating and responding to objections, criticisms, and so on.

If my view is correct, then critical thinkers must possess, as part of their argumentative skills, what I call *dialectical* skills. They must be familiar with the standard objections to their positions and respond to them, facing off against alternatives. This implies an extension of our understanding of critical thinking skills. Although critical thinking theorists traditionally have concurred that skills in argument are a necessary part of critical thinking, they have not taken the dialectical components of these skills into account.

The proposal to include what I call dialectical skills in the skill set of the critical thinker has important implications for many issues, including the following:

1.   how we evaluate and/or criticize arguments;
2.   how we teach our students about argument; and
3.   how we test for critical thinking.

In this chapter, I attempt to flesh out these implications. The next section begins with some comments on the problems that arise when one tries to define critical thinking. This is central in a discussion of assessment issues as they relate to critical thinking. The attempt to construct a valid test for critical thinking remains compromised by the sheer diversity of conceptions of critical thinking and the assorted underlying theories. I discuss this problem at greater length in Johnson (1996), and I want to review the current situation in light of that discussion to see whether (a) there has been any improvement in the situation (I do not think there has been), and (b) the standoff between different conceptions necessarily compromises our ability to test for the argumentative skills that we associate with critical thinking (I do not think it does). This is followed by a discussion of the dialectical tier and its implications for understanding the argumentative skills of the critical thinker. In the last section of the chapter I discuss the implications for all of the issues listed above, especially the testing of critical thinking.

The Nature of Critical Thinking:
The Definition Problem

In Johnson (1992) I discussed, in detail, the problem of defining critical thinking. Briefly, the problem is that there are many definitions of critical thinking, all of which propose to explicate the same idea, yet they are not in any obvious sense the same definition. There are important differences that separate the Ennis (1987) and the McPeck (1981) definitions, these two definitions from the Paul (1982) definitions, and so on. For example, McPeck's definition is closely wed to his claim that critical thinking is discipline specific. Paul, a generalist, takes a different view.

In the concluding section of my 1992 paper, I proposed a moratorium on the attempt to formulate definitions. I classified the prevailing definitions as stipulative and proposed a set of criteria for such definitions.[1] Such a change does not materially affect the point I made: that any definition should be broadly reflective of current practice and should not be idiosyncratic. I made four other suggestions.

1. The definition should be imbedded in a theory of critical thinking.
2. The definition should make plain why critical thinking is "critical" thinking, that is, the force of the term "critical" should be evident. It should make clear how this type of thinking differs from just plain old thinking, or good thinking.
3. The definition should yield assessment tools. (Different modes of assessment would follow from different definitions.)
4. The definition should not assume an *a priori* relationship between critical thinking and problem-solving, creative thinking, or any other cognitive operation.

My proposal and suggestions appear to have had no effect. New freestanding attempts to define critical thinking continue to appear with little awareness of, or sensitivity to, the dialectics of the situation as I have outlined them.

Some textbook definitions

It seems to me that almost everyone who works in the critical thinking area feels the need, indeed the right, to offer his or her own definition of critical thinking. This trend is certainly evident in the work of textbook authors, some of whose efforts (but only some) appear to be informed by the scholarly literature. Consider two fairly recent definitions from critical thinking texts. Parker and Moore (1992) state, "Critical thinking is simply the careful, deliberate determination of whether we should accept, reject, or suspend judgment about a claim—and of the degree of confidence with which we accept or reject it" (4). Their focus, which is on probating claims, seems too limited. It ignores arguments, inferences, and explanations.

Romain (1997) defines critical thinking this way: "Critical thinking, as I define and teach it, consists of those activities of the mind that are indispensable to making decisions we can live with" (1). The focus of this definition is practical decision-making that affects our lives. Although this is certainly sometimes the focus of critical thinking, there are also instances where there is no such decision in the offing, such as when we think about whether to accept certain theories or arguments. I think a third party would be surprised to learn that both of these texts were attempting a definition of the same term.

A definition from educational policy

Then there is the famous "definition" of critical thinking imbedded in Executive Order #338, which mandated critical thinking as a requirement for graduation from nineteen California State University campuses and many California community colleges and high schools:

> Instruction in critical thinking is designed to achieve an understanding of the relationship of language to logic, which should lead to the ability to analyze, criticize and advocate ideas, to reason inductively and deductively and to reach factual or judgmental conclusions based on sound inferences drawn from unambiguous statements of knowledge or belief. The minimal competence to be expected at the successful conclusion of instruction in critical thinking should be the ability to distinguish fact from judgment, belief from knowledge, and skills in elementary deductive and inductive processes, including an understanding of the formal and informal fallacies of language and thought. (Dumke 1980, 1)

To satisfy this particular definition, critical thinkers would have to accept the inductive–deductive distinction, be able to distinguish between the two, and apply the proper criteria in given instances. They would also have to embrace fallacy analysis as a central component of critical thinking. Much of this is highly contentious: there are many critical thinking theorists who reject the distinction between inductive and deductive reasoning as either exhaustive or as incapable of clear articulation. Applying that distinction to individual examples is a highly problematic exercise. Moreover, many critical thinking theorists (Scriven [1976], for example) eschew fallacy analysis.

One might contrast the definition in Executive Order #338 with the conception of critical thinking proposed by Halpern (1996), who ties critical thinking to the ability to assess probability. Among the key skills she identifies are recognizing regression to the mean and understanding and avoiding conjunction errors. If Halpern's view were correct, it could easily be demonstrated that many of the people who are critical thinkers (on her account) do not satisfy the definition imbedded in Executive Order #338.

Definitions by critical thinking theorists

Theorists have proposed several new definitions of critical thinking. I discuss only two: that of Scriven and Fisher (1997), and that of Hatcher and Spencer (2000).

Scriven and Fisher (1997) define critical thinking as "the skilled and active interpretation and evaluation of observations and communication, information and argumentation" (21). In this account, the focus of critical thinking is very broad: observation, communication, information, and argumentation. This way of specifying the focus of critical thinking is not altogether sensible. Communication is a broad category and would certainly include argumentation, so a separate mention of the latter seems unnecessary. The term "active" also seems redundant; being skilled implies being active. The Scriven and Fisher (1997) definition raises the question of how evaluation relates to criticism, that is, to the "critical" in critical thinking. Finally, might not one interpret and evaluate in a skilled way, without being critical? Think of the not uncommon situation in which someone shows evidence of skill but fails to see any of the weaknesses in his or her own position or any of the real strengths in alternatives.[2]

Hatcher and Spencer (2000) define critical thinking as "thinking that attempts to arrive at a conclusion through honestly evaluating the position and its alternatives with respect to the available evidence and arguments" (20). I believe this definition is close to what critical thinking theorists want. Thus understood, critical thinking has three major components: (1) the clarification and understanding of the issue in question; (2) the evaluation of the position through the application of accepted standards of evaluation to the various alternatives; and (3) the articulation of the evaluation.

I like this definition's emphasis on standards, and particularly the fact that it includes as part of the process of critical thinking the articulation of the thinking! I also like the authors' rules for critical discussion, which they use as a way of supplementing and breathing life into their definition. Still there are some problems.

First, the definition seems too narrow in that it appears to be limited to positions and arguments. Although I regard positions and arguments as natural focal points, there are other items about which to think critically (e.g., news reports, hypotheses, truth-claims, and even advertising). If Scriven and Fisher (1997) are correct, then even these focal points are too narrow.

Second, the authors appear to build morality and moral character into the very definition of critical thinking, and so Paul's (1982) view is problematic. Missimer (1990), for example, has argued that critical thinking must be defined in terms of the skills alone. Debates about the role of character in reasoning are profound and long lived, extending as far back as Plato.

Third, the Hatcher and Spencer (2000) definition faces the challenge I call "The Identity Question." What in this definition captures the idea of "critical"? How is *critical* thinking different from just plain old thinking?

The problem with definitions

The question of what critical thinking is and how it is to be understood or defined remains both unsettled and unsettling. It is unsettled because

1. it remains the case that there are a great many definitions of critical thinking—almost as many as there are textbook writers and theorists;
2. it is not at all clear that all of them are attempts at defining the same thing;
3. it is not at all clear that those who propose them are aware of this variety; and
4. it is clear (from 3) that many who offer definitions of "critical thinking" do so without discharging their dialectical obligations.

The definitional question is unsettling because one can quite readily imagine how this diversity of definition might be viewed by those skeptical of the critical thinking initiative. They want to see evidence that teaching students to think critically works and is not just the latest fad in higher education. This requires assessments of critical thinking abilities which can prove whether attempts to teach these abilities work. But I can imagine the skeptic saying "You people don't seem to know what you're doing. No two of your many definitions seem to agree." Thus, there would be one test for those who accept McPeck's definition, another for those who accept Ennis's definition, still another for those who favour Halpern's approach. A person might pass one test but fail one or all of the others. It seems that the term "critical thinking" is too woolly, too flabby, too ill-defined to support decent educational objectives, especially if one proposes to test for them.

This is a reasonable objection that needs to be taken seriously. A failure to overcome the diversity of definitions may yet prove to be the Achilles heel of the critical thinking initiative.

Why this divergence?

I cannot help but wonder why this diversity of definitions character-izes critical thinking as a field. Perhaps it is because the term "critical thinking" is so rich in meaning (like the term "philosophy") that it is inevitable that there will be a wide variety of ways of understanding it.[3] Another possible explanation resides in the ambiguity of the word "critical." This fact was first brought home to me in a personal ex-change with Margaret Lee, who observed that "critical" is a word with an interesting story, and that its synonyms—faultfinding, captious, caviling, carping, and censorious—suggest the first and most popular understanding of the word. As she pointed out, the *Oxford English Dic-tionary* traces its changing nuances from its first known use, which is notably attributed to Shakespeare's *Othello*: Iago says "For I am noth-ing if not critical," meaning given to judging in an especially adverse or unfavourable ways to its use by Sir Thomas Browne in the seven-teenth century to mean "involving or exercising careful judgement or observation on the basis of which right decisions might be made," to Jefferson's use of the word to designate "a turning point of decisive importance in relation to an issue."

The common meaning of "critical" is the first one noted by Lee—the one that none of us takes to be the intended referent. Most take critical thinking to be something good but in ordinary parlance the term "critical" has a negative connotation.

Suppose that the definers intend to offer a definition of the "good" kind of critical thinking. In that case, it appears that there are the two quite different senses, both of which Lee has identified. First, there is critical$_j$ (Jefferson), in the sense of a critical moment, a crucial point: the patient is in critical condition; deliberations have reached a critical stage, i.e., a significant stage. In this sense of "critical," critical

thinking would be important thinking—the kind that is perhaps necessary for one's survival or well-being. I think some definitions attempt
to capture this sense of the term. I take Halpern's definition to be a
case in point.

But there is a second, different sense of the term—critical$_b$
(Browne), which means being skilled in reasoned judgment, being able
to see both the strengths and weaknesses of the object of one's scrutiny. I call this "the dialectical" sense of critical thinking.

How are these two senses related? Critical$_j$ seems to have the
broader scope: it can be argued that not all instances of critical$_b$ will be
critical$_j$ but not the reverse. Halpern sees critical thinking as providing
skills that are crucial in this society, but they are not skills which are
equivalent to the ability to see strengths and weaknesses in an argument. On the other hand, Paul (1982) and Lipman (1988) seem to be
defining critical$_b$. This is in keeping with my own belief that critical$_b$ is
the important sense of "critical"—the one that best fits with the phrase
"thinking critically." I conclude that this is the sense on which definitions of critical thinking should be focused.[4]

One further thought may help explain the diversity of definitions. For some theorists (Richard Paul may be one example, Ennis
another) the term "critical thinking" becomes in effect synonymous
with "good thinking." In such definitions, the scope of critical thinking broadens to include problem-solving, creative thinking, etc. I agree
that critical thinking is "a good thing," but not that all good thinking is
critical thinking. For example, problem-solving is an important kind
of thinking that has similarities to critical thinking, but it should not be
identified with it.[5] Creative thinking is good thinking, but it is not the
same as critical thinking, even though it is widely believed and likely
true that there is a relationship between them (one explored in this
volume by Hoogland, Sobocan, and Hare).[6]

In addition to the factors I have mentioned, other considerations may help to explain the plethora of ways in which "critical
thinking" has been defined. Different definitions may, for example,
reflect deep philosophical differences, mainly of an epistemological
sort. Whatever the reason for so many different definitions, an already
astonishing diversity is only increasing. Instead of pursuing further the
reasons for this definitional divergence, I will turn next to the dialectical aspects of critical thinking. Whatever the causes of the multitude

of definitions, the important point is that most definitions, and the approaches they typify, are insufficiently attentive to the dialectical/critical dimension of the task.

The Dialectical Tier and Its Implications for Critical Thinking

In trying to understand critical thinking, it may be helpful to distinguish between critical thinking, an activity that occurs in a specific setting, and the critical thinker, the person who regularly carries out such activity. In my view, this distinction contains an important clue to the skills versus disposition debate, but I shall not press that matter here. In what follows, I focus principally on critical think*ing*. In doing so, I discuss the dialectical aspects of the issues to which I have already referred.

The role of argument in critical thinking

Because most accounts of critical thinking include argument analysis and construction as crucial components, it follows that the theory of argument has implications for critical thinking in terms of both theory and practice. If, for example, one thinks that the syllogism is a crucial type of argument, then one will want to build that into the idea of what is required for critical thinking. One will want to familiarize students with this mode of argument. I would not take this view, and very few theorists still regard mastery of the syllogism as necessary for critical thinking. Judged from this point of view, such a test would be inadequate because the concept of critical thinking imbedded in that test is inadequate.

The point is that as we conceive of critical thinking, so we teach critical thinking, and so test for it. In my work I have been arguing that traditional ways of conceiving argument fall short because they do not include the dialectical dimension of critical thinking. This suggests that there are related problems with the way we teach and test for critical thinking. In addressing these issues, I will begin by outlining a better way of conceiving argument, involving the dialectical tier, then move on to discuss the teaching and testing of the dialectical dimensions of critical thinking.

The dialectical tier

When most of those who discuss a concept of critical thinking present their views, it seems clear to me that they have embraced the traditional conception of argument. It construes an argument as reasons presented in support of a conclusion, or as "premises" leading to a conclusion. In my view, that is just the first level of argument (what I call its "illative" core). Given the contexts in which critical thinking occurs—namely, contexts characterized by conflicts between different positions—arguers must, in addition to providing reasons for their conclusion, also deal with objections and possible objections. They must respond in some fashion to at least some of the alternative positions that characterize the point in issue. That is what happens in what I call "the dialectical tier"—the second level of an argument.

When I introduced the notion of the dialectical tier in *Manifest Rationality* (2000), I wanted to point to a limitation in the way in which logicians and argumentation theorists conceived of argument. My view was that they tended to see argument only vertically, in terms of the relationship of reasons to the conclusion, while ignoring the horizontal (or dialectical) dimension. Arguers—particularly in the context of critical thinking—have a responsibility not just to provide evidence for their conclusions but also to situate their arguments against the field, for example, by showing how they would handle the standard objections. I conceived of this engagement as taking place in the dialectical tier of argument.

Many have pointed out difficulties in the way that I presented my ideas.[7] I will not review those objections and criticisms here, or my responses to them. Suffice to say that I would now formulate my views differently. Nonetheless, most theorists have accepted that there is something like a dialectical tier of argument (see, e.g., Groarke in this volume) and I want to focus on the implications that this has for the concerns about testing that motivated this book.

Most texts on critical thinking and most tests of critical thinking presuppose a traditional account of argument and ignore, or certainly minimize, the skills associated with what I have called the dialectical dimension. One can find tests that assess a person's inferential capacity and also his or her capacity to handle premise/conclusions structures. But not much has been done to take into account the dialectical dimension of critical thinking. For example, the Ennis-Weir test, which I discuss below, appears to be an adequate test of the subject's ability to judge the illative core of an argument, but it does not do a very good job of testing the subject's ability to assess the dialectical dimension. Let me continue by discussing this dimension in greater detail.

Dialectical properties of a critical thinker
I think it is clear from this discussion that my proposed view of argument has important implications for the conception of a critical thinker. In addition to inferential skills (the ability to tell when a set of reasons are good reasons), it suggests that a critical thinker must have certain dialectical habits and skills. One I have already mentioned is the ability to deal with objections and alternative positions. This is an important skill, but it seems to me that the dialectical properties of a critical thinker go further and include the following skills and traits (or dispositions).

1. *The critical thinker is someone who overcomes resistance to criticism.* In a way this is included in the common idea that critical thinkers are not dogmatic. Far from resisting criticism, which is a naturally human standpoint, critical thinkers are interested in criticisms of their views; indeed, they seek them out.[8]

2. *The critical thinker knows what would count against his or her position as well as for it; that is, a critical thinker can pass "The Flew Challenge."* By this I mean the kind of challenge Anthony Flew (1955) posited in a famous paper about the meaningfulness of religious language. In this context, his version of this challenge was presented to his opponents (who were defending a belief in God) in the following question: "The question I want to pose to my fellow symposiasts is this: what would have to occur, or to have occurred, to constitute for you a disproof of the love of, or the existence of, God?"

Part of what it means to be a critical, as opposed to a dogmatic, thinker is having some sense of what would cause you to give up your position.[9] For the dogmatist, the answer (usually not stated) is "nothing." I take it that this cannot be an acceptable answer from a critical thinker, who might reason as follows: "The crucial issue/question/proposition for me is X. If that should turn out to be false, then I would be forced, or at least inclined, to give up my position."

The Flew Challenge seems to be a reasonable one that might be incorporated in conceptions of and tests for critical thinking. Since a critical thinker holds his or her position mindful of its weaknesses no less than its strengths, it follows that he or she should be able to indicate what sort of contrary evidence would cause him or her to abandon that position. Being unable to do so could be taken as evidence that the individual is not thinking critically.

3. *A critical thinker changes his or her mind when it is appropriate to do so, for example, as a result of being confronted with a strong objection or alternative position.* A dogmatist sees no need to change. We all know the default position here: "*You* display *your* critical mentality by coming around to *my* position, by being persuaded by the superior rational force of my position." But if I never display such conversions or changes or revisions as a result of engaging in argumentation, what would that mean? What defines a critical thinker is not just the willingness to change his or her mind but having done so—*and done so on more than one occasion. And done so for something like the right reasons!*[11]

4. *A critical thinker is defined as much by what he or she does* not *say or do as by what he or she does say or do.* Because a critical thinker thinks about his or her views in relationship to alternatives and is aware of possible objections and limitations, he or she will often *not* say certain things. A critical thinker knows full well the value of the pause for reflection; taking the time out to think it over, sort it out, rather than rushing to judgment.

If these are important properties of the critical thinker, how do we educate for them? And more importantly, how do we test for them? How, for example, do we test people for what people *do not* think, for having avoided a hasty judgment, or for having carefully considered and then rejected a certain line of thought?[11]

Implications of the Dialectical Tier for Arguments

How do we evaluate / criticize arguments?

One implication of the dialectical tier is the need to develop a doctrine of dialectical adequacy: what are the arguer's dialectical obligations, and what is required for the arguer to meet them? As a start in that direction, I proposed (2003) the "AAA" doctrine: the arguer's handling of dialectical material must be accurate, acceptable, and appropriate.

To illustrate, let us suppose that the arguer is anticipating an objection to his or her position: "Now someone is bound to object that O*. Here is my response." In such a context, I propose that three questions be asked.

Q1: Is the objection (O*) accurately stated? One way in which people go wrong in arguments is by mischaracter-izing and distorting the views of those who oppose them, thus committing the straw man fallacy.[12] To know whether this is the case, and the answer to Q1, one must be familiar with the argumentation and discussion of the issue.

Q2: Is the response to the objection acceptable? That is, has the arguer managed to defuse the objection? To answer this question one must know what is required to defuse the objection, and what other responses there might be.

Q3: Is the response appropriate in the circumstances? Are there more pressing and salient objections that the arguer ought to have addressed? To know the answer to these questions, one needs to be familiar with the relevant argu-mentative space. If, for example, the arguer failed to antici-pate and respond to a particularly salient objection, then he or she has a less than critical response.

How do we teach students about constructing arguments?

Textbooks do pretty well in this area, typically advising students to anticipate and respond to objections (see, e.g., Johnson and Blair 2006; Groarke and Tindale 2004). Sometimes, however, authors ignore or forget this component when presenting the evaluative part of their crit-ical thinking theory. There may be no better illustration of this than Solomon's (1989) *Introducing Philosophy* text. When Solomon provides directions to students about how to construct an argument, he makes a special point of telling them that they should anticipate objections. But, later, when he is giving standard formal deductive logic instruc-tion about what counts as a good argument (true premises and valid form), his theory makes no provision for considering how well the arguer does in the previously assigned task of anticipating objections. In this way his theory of evaluation fails to reflect his theory of analysis.

How do we test for critical thinking?

It seems clear to me (though others, like Scriven, probably disagree) that you cannot test for critical thinking without accessing the thinking of the subject. This is why I contend that objective tests (using multiple-choice items) are problematic. In view of this, I believe that of the available tests, the Ennis-Weir Test comes closest to being a valid test of critical thinking. Even the Ennis-Weir has important limitations when one considers whether a subject can handle arguments in a critical fashion, in the dialectical ways I have been discussing.

The Ennis-Weir test asks the subject being tested to write an argumentative response to an argumentative letter, "The Moorburg Letter." The letter is editorial in nature, where the arguer is asserting the conclusion that "Overnight parking on all streets in Moorburg should be eliminated" (Ennis-Weir Critical Thinking Essay Test). It asks for a response to each paragraph and then for a final paragraph in which an overall evaluation is made. The directions stress the importance of giving reasons in defence of one's response to the arguer's reasons for wanting a ban on overnight parking in Moorburg. These reasons are (basically) as follows:

1. It is illegal for anyone to have a garage in the city streets.
2. Three main streets in Moorburg are very narrow and so there is no room for heavy traffic.
3. Traffic on some streets is very bad when factory workers try to make their 6:00 am shift.
4. Overnight parking is generally undesirable.
5. Any "intelligent citizen" would regard the near elimination of accidents as highly desirable.
6. During a four-hour experiment on one of the busiest streets whereby parking was banned from 2:00 am to 6:00 am, there were no accidents.
7. Conditions are not safe if there is even the slightest possible chance for an accident; those who oppose banning or overnight parking don't know what "safe" really means and the conditions are not safe as they are now.

8.   The police and the national Traffic Safety Council has recommended traffic be banned on busy streets.

One will be inclined to regard such a test as a valid test of critical thinking to the degree that one believes that (a) the ability to appraise argumentative discourse is a crucial critical thinking skill; and (b) this test actually assesses the ability of the subject to appraise arguments. I am inclined to accept (a). The great strength of this test is that it does focus on what I and many others regard as the central critical thinking skill—argumentation. A second signal feature is that this test requires subjects to set forth their thinking, not just the results of their thinking.

I am less certain about (b). The guide for the test evinces that, for the most part, what is being tested are skills in detecting flaws in arguments at the level of the illative core. There is not much in this test that tests the subject's *dialectical* skills. The closest the Moorburg Letter comes to this dimension occurs in paragraph 7 where the arguer makes a dialectical move by taking into consideration the "suggestions made by my opponents." The arguer mentions the suggestion (I would call it an objection) that "conditions are safe enough now" and then responds to that suggestion.[13] According to the account I have outlined above, the dialectical adequacy of this response needs to be evaluated by asking the following questions:

Q1: Have the objections in question been accurately stated? To know the answer one would have to be familiar with the context of the argument in which the issue in question occurs.

Q2: Is the response to the objections adequate? In their guide to the test, the authors have addressed this question. They point out a number of ways in which the defect in paragraph 7 can be put.[14] I would put the defect somewhat differently: I would say that the arguer's response to this objection is inadequate and that the arguer has failed to achieve dialectical adequacy.

Q3: Are there other more pressing and salient objections that the arguer ought to have dealt with? To know the answer, one would need to be familiar with the dialectical situation: what objections have been made by other authors, which is most serious, etc?

Unless students are practised in asking and answering such questions (something which would require changes in how argumentation is taught), they will not be able to answer them in the context of the test, even if it makes such opportunities available.

Something similar might be said of the one other place where the Ennis-Weir test provides for the dialectical dimension. In this case, the test requires the subject to make a summary judgment in paragraph 9, taking into account the strengths and weaknesses of each paragraph of the letter (each contains a reason for the conclusion). A subject could well mention weaknesses in the dialectical dimension. This represents another step in the direction of testing dialectical skills, though it is not a step which is likely to be taken if students have not been taught the importance of dialectical considerations.

One other limitation of the Ennis-Weir test should be mentioned when it comes to testing dialectical skills. In taking the test, a critical thinker is to assess an argument, taking into account both its strengths and its weaknesses. In the Moorburg letter, Raywift presents reasons for his position. Some are good reasons, some are not. The test subject will be graded according to how well he or she evaluates these reasons (the illative core). However, Raywift's argument is weak from a dialectical point of view. It does not discuss, for example, any potential weaknesses in his own proposal: What are the effects, consequences, costs of adopting this proposal? What are the likely problems? What is/are the alternative position(s)? There is no explicit provision for testing these skills, which are part of dialectical assessment, though there could be.

So long as one does not build an assessment of such considerations into test construction and marking, the test will remain a good test of reasoning as it applies to the illative core of argument, but not a test that does a good job testing skills in the dialectical dimension.

Conclusion

If the initiative to incorporate critical thinking into education at all levels is to be evaluated and held accountable, as it surely should, we need to be able to show that students who take critical thinking courses do learn to think critically. Our ability to do this on a widespread scale is compromised by two important limitations I have discussed in this chapter: the sheer diversity of conceptions of critical thinking, and the absence of a reliable test of critical thinking (where a reliable test is understood as one which tests the analysis of both the illative core and the dialectical tier of argument).

In addressing the second issue, I have argued that one important dimension of critical thinking—the dialectical—seems not to have been taken into account in tests of critical thinking, particularly the Ennis-Weir test, which is one of the more effective tests of critical thinking on the market. The Ennis-Weir test represents an important advance in testing critical thinking. It requires subjects to produce their thinking; and that is, in my view, the proper way to make a judgment on whether that thinking qualifies as "critical." Ennis-Weir does a reasonably good job of testing the thinking skills of the subject, but the dialectical element of critical thinking is not as thoroughly tested. So although the Ennis-Weir test tests the *thinking* dimension of critical thinking, I have argued that it does not go far enough in testing the *critical* dimension. What possible revisions might be made to rectify these limitations remains for me an interesting question.

Notes

1. I think now that my classification was not the most apt. These proposed definitions of "critical thinking" might rather be called "theoretical" (following Hansen 2002), or perhaps better "programmatic" (following Scheffler 1968). I thank Fred Ellett, Jr. for calling this to my attention.
2. See, for example, Koehler (2003, http://www.commondreams.org/ views03/0228-06.htm, last accessed November 1, 2007). Koehler exposes all of the fallacies in the Bush administration's position, but can see none of the strengths.
3. Some would push this point further by arguing that philosophy and critical thinking are virtually identical. There is no denying that philosophy has been a principal sponsor of critical thinking, yet I would not equate the two. While some theorists (Richard Paul) do urge that critical thinking be constituted as a discipline, most view it as a skill, or a complex of skills (plus information, plus character traits).
4. It is tempting to think that this sense of "critical thinking" is necessary for survival, but I am afraid this is more a case of wishful thinking. In any

event, there is a great deal of evidence to the contrary.

5. See my chapter "Reasoning, critical thinking and the network problem" in Johnson (1996), 246–7.

6. I do not believe that the relation between the two is analytic, i.e., that critical thinking is necessarily creative thinking, or vice-versa. I suspect that there are any number of counterexamples: individuals who have been highly creative thinkers but were not particularly critical. Beethoven was highly creative but also resistant to criticism. Einstein, for all his brilliance, was unable to see any merits in quantum theory. He was certainly creative but not critical (in this respect).

7. See Hansen (2002), Tindale (2002), Groarke (2002), and Hitchcock (2002) and my response (2004).

8. This is a trait that I think Scriven embodies admirably.

9. Notice, by the way, that Flew neglects to appreciate the bilaterality of this situation (Johnstone, Jr. 1978). Flew seems to think it is only those who disagree with him who must pass the test. But Flew should also take the test, answer the question on the other side of the debate. Flew seems unaware of this dialectical (and perhaps epistemic) responsibility.

10. One might illustrate this point by pointing to episodes in the history of philosophy, which could include Russell's abandonment of his theory of judgment in light of Wittgenstein's 1914 criticisms; Wittgenstein's abandonment of the *Tractatus* theory in light of objections from Ramsey and Sraffa; and Ayer's gradual acceptance that the verifiability criterion could not be properly stated (Church's 1949 objection).

11. Part of the issue here involves the difference between testing for critical think*ing* and testing for when someone is a critical think*er*. The former is easier than the latter.

12. The strawman fallacy is a, perhaps the pre-eminent, *dialectical* fallacy.

13. Note that only one objection is taken into account and that it is by no means obvious that this is the strongest objection that could be made to the argument. In fact, I think there are much stronger objections: such as that the arguer has failed to take into account significant consequences of his proposal that would suggest to many that the negatives outweigh the positives.

14. Ennis states the defect is a "recognition of winning an argument by definition, that a word has been made useless for empirical assertion, and/or claim that an incorrect definition has been asserted" (Ennis-Weir Critical Thinking Essay Test).

References

Ennis, R. 1987. A taxonomy of critical thinking dispositions and abilities. In *Teaching thinking skills: Theory and practice*, ed. J.B. Baron and R.J. Sternberg, 2–26. New York: Freeman.

Flew, A. 1955. Theology and falsification. In *New essays in philosophical theology*, ed. A. Flew and A. MacIntyre. London: SCM Press.

Groarke, L. 2002. Johnson on the metaphysics of argument. *Argumentation* 16: 277–86.

Groarke, L., and C. Tindale. 2004. *Good reasoning matters*, 3d ed. Oxford: Oxford University Press.

Halpern, D. 1996. *Thinking critically about critical thinking*. Mahwah, NJ: Lawrence Erlbaum.

Hansen, H. 2002. An exploration of Johnson's sense of "argument." *Argumentation* 16: 263–76.

Hatcher, D., and L. Spencer. 2000. *Reasoning and writing: From critical thinking to composition*. Boston: American Press.

Hitchcock, D. 2002. The practice of argumentative discussion. *Argumentation* 16: 287–98.

Johnson, R. 2004. Still more on arguers and their dialectical obligations. In *Argumentation and its applications: Proceedings of the Fourth OSAA Conference*, University of Windsor, May. CD-ROM.

———. 2003. The dialectical tier revisited. In *Anyone who has a view: Theoretical contributions to the study of argumentation*, ed. F. Van Eemeren, J. Blair, C. Willard, and A. Henkemans, 41–54. Dorrecht: Kluwer Academic Publishers.

———. 2002. The dialectical tier reconsidered. Keynote address, International Society for the Study of Argumentation, Amsterdam, June 26.

———. 2000. *Manifest rationality: A pragmatic theory of argument*. Mahwah, NJ: Lawrence Erlbaum.

———. 1996. *The rise of informal logic*. Newport News, VA: Vale Press.

———. 1992. The problem of defining critical thinking. In *The generalizability of critical thinking*, ed. S. Norris, 38–53. New York: Teachers College Press.

Johnstone, Jr., H. 1978. *Validity and rhetoric in philosophical argument: An outlook in transition*. University Park, PA: Dialogue Press of Man & World.

Johnson, R., and J. Blair. 2006. Reprint. *Logical self-defense*. New York: Idea Press, 1994.

Koehler, D. 2003. *Fallacies and war: Misleading a nervous America to the wrong conclusion*. Online. Available at http://www.commondreams.org/archive/2008/02/28/7363/.

Lipman, M. 1988. Critical thinking: What can it be? *Analytic Teaching* 8: 5–12.

McPeck, J. 1981. *Critical thinking and education.* New York: St. Martin's Press.

Missimer, C. 1990. Perhaps by skill alone. *Informal Logic* 12(3): 145–53.

Parker, B., and B. Moore. 1992. *Critical thinking.* 3d ed. Mountain View, CA: Mayfield.

Paul, R. 1982. Teaching critical thinking in the strong sense: A focus on self deception, world views and a dialectical mode form analysis. *Informal Logic Newsletter* 4(2): 2–27.

Romain, D. 1997. *Thinking things through: Critical thinking for decisions you can live with.* Mountain View, CA: Mayfield.

Scheffler, I. 1968. Definitions in education. In *The language of education,* ed. I. Scheffler, 11–35. Springfield, IL: Thomas.

Scriven, M. 1976. *Reasoning.* New York: McGraw Hill.

Scriven, M., and A. Fisher. 1997. *Critical thinking: Its definition and assessment.* Point Reyes, CA: Edgepress.

Siegel, H. 1988. *Educating reason: Rationality, critical thinking and education.* New York: Routledge.

Solomon, R. 1989. *Introducing philosophy.* New York: Harcourt Brace College Publishers.

Tindale, C. 2002. A concept divided: Ralph Johnson's definition of argument. *Argumentation* 16: 299–309.

Chapter Four

Investigating and Assessing Multiple-Choice Critical Thinking Tests

Robert H. Ennis

Stephen Norris and I have long urged (e.g., Norris and Ennis 1989) the following basic steps in the investigation and assessment of a critical thinking test.

1. Make sure that the test is based on a defensible conception of critical thinking that is acceptable to you—and that the test does a reasonable job of covering that conception.
2. Examine the arguments, including your own, regarding the test's validity for students at the level of your students, in a situation like theirs.
3. Take the test yourself and score it with the key or guide to scoring. Assure yourself that the set of answers or the guide is appropriate for the situation.

Although the first and third of these steps are listed separately (to focus on conveniently identifiable actions), they are actually part of the second step, that is, examining the arguments in support of claims about the test's situational validity, the topic of this chapter.

In pursuit of this topic, I shall suggest a structure for appraising a claim regarding the situational validity of a critical thinking test, and apply the structure to a real case: my recent attempt to revise the manual for the Cornell critical thinking tests (Ennis, Millman, and

Tomko 2005). The suggested structure applies a broad inference-to-best-explanation approach to particular features involved in test validation, and assumes some, but not all, recent stances and insights of leading psychometricians, including Samuel Messick (1989a, 1989b) and members of the Joint Committee on Standards for Educational and Psychological Testing of the American Educational Research Association, the American Psychological Association, and the National Council on Educational Measurement (1999).

Three Contemporary Stances

Validity: A unitary concept
One stance adopted by Messick and the Joint Committee is that validity is a unitary concept; that is, there are not different types of validity, such as criterion validity, predictive validity, content validity, and discriminant validity, but only validity. This stance is not universally accepted, but I shall assume it here, without arguing the point.

Test validity versus validity of inferences from, or interpretations of, test scores
One significant difference between my approach and that of Messick and the Joint Committee concerns the bearer of validity—what it is that can be valid. They hold that inferences from, or interpretations of, test scores, and not tests themselves, are the bearers of validity. This view was endorsed and called the "consensual understanding" by David Frisbie in his 2005 Presidential Address to the National Council on Measurement in Education (Frisbie 2005). I urge something less radical, namely, that a test in a situation (or set of circumstances) is the bearer of (situational) validity. In my paper "Situational Test Validity" (in process), I urge that we define situational test validity as follows: A test is a valid test of X in a situation to the extent that it is an adequate measure of X in the situation. It is significant that this definition is situation specific and does not provide "test validity" with a meaning outside of a situation or type of situation.

In this definition, "the situation" can refer to a particular situation in which the specified test has been given or is to be given (for example, the testing of the fifty-two psychology and humanities students in Tom Solon's (2001) study; or it can refer to a type of situation (such as the testing of lower-division college students under standard conditions). Although both are of interest, the former is of primary interest to a test user. Even if a test is substantially valid in standard situations, what matters most to a user is whether the test was or will be at least substantially valid in the user's situation. In contrast, people preparing a test manual will be interested in the myriad of situations under which a test might be or has been used, but cannot take account of all of them. For this reason, they are likely to focus on standard situations, or the types of non-standard situations that are most likely to be encountered by test users.

The different kinds of situations imply an ambiguity in the definition of test validity, but it is not a destructive one as long as the person interested in the situational validity of a test is clear about the difference. In my investigation of the situational validity of the Cornell tests, I focused on standard-situation validity, though I was very interested in the particular-situation validity of the tests in the various studies in which they were used.

Non-quantitative appraisal of validity arguments
A third stance adopted by Messick and the Joint Committee, which I infer from what they say about arguments about validity, and with which I agree, is that the strength of a validity argument is not to be stated in numbers (such as 0.82), but in more vague normative terms. The terms they use are "consonant with," "less well supported," "scientifically sound...argument," and "support." Such words do not invite the attachment of numbers and are not replaceable by them.

In his essay "Validity," in Robert Linn's highly regarded third edition of *Educational Measurement* (1989), Messick equates validity with the consonance of evidence for an inference and lesser support for alternative lines of evidence: "To validate an interpretative inference is to ascertain the degree to which multiple lines of evidence are consonant with the inference, while establishing that alternative lines of evidence are less well supported" (Messick 1989a, 13). The Joint Committee has stated that test validation is the process of developing a "scientifically sound" validity argument to support an interpretation: "Validation can be viewed as developing a scientifically sound validity argument to support the interpretation of test scores and their relevance to the proposed use" (Joint Committee 1999, 9).

To the terms "consonant with," "lesser support," and "scientifically sound," I would add other words that can be used to express a judgment about degree of support. These words include "fully," "substantially," "moderately," "basically," "apparently," "seemingly," "probably," "likely," "for the most part," "by and large," "reasonably well," "sufficiently for the purpose," "somewhat," "possibly," "weakly," "hardly," and "minimally." These words are not replaceable by numbers, but are used to express less precise normative judgments.

The most frequent question I receive about the Cornell critical thinking tests (Ennis and Millman 2005a, 2005b) and The Ennis-Weir Critical Thinking Essay Test (Ennis and Weir 1985) is "What are the reliability and validity of this test?" This usually means that the questioner thinks that there is a number that can be given for the reliability and the validity of the tests. Reliability indices can be numbers, which are generally correlations (I shall have more to say about this later in this chapter), but if one agrees with the Joint Committee and Samuel Messick, as I do, the degree of situational validity cannot be captured in a number.

Numbers can be attached to correlations with other critical thinking tests and to correlations with other criteria (such as first-year grades in graduate school). Such numbers have been given names like "criterion validity" and "predictive validity." These names, in accord with the unitary conception of *validity* assumed earlier, are better expressed as "-related evidence of validity." The first example would then read: "criterion-related evidence of validity." This would make it clear that the numbers sometimes given for validity are evidence for validity, not validity itself.

Best-Explanation Reasoning

Given that the appraisal of situational validity ultimately calls for the construction of an argument, I find it helpful to work from the assumption that such an argument is a best-explanation argument. In this context, the best-explanation argument is an argument in which, very briefly, the hypothesis that a test is valid to a substantial degree in a given situation (or type of situation) is supported by (a) the ability of the hypothesis to best explain, or best contribute to explaining, the observations about the test; and (b) the inability of alternative hypotheses to explain them (roughly what Messick suggested in the quote above).

In more detail, in accord with the broad approach that I have developed,[1] a hypothesis of situational validity is supported roughly to the extent to which, given reasonable assumptions,

1. it can explain (account for) evidence—or help to do so;
2. there is no evidence that is inconsistent with the hypothesis;
3. evidence is inconsistent with alternative explanations of the data;
4. the hypothesis is plausible—it fits with what else we know;
5. realistic and earnest attempts have been made to find counter-evidence and alternative hypotheses;
6. the hypothesis implies new evidence (especially helpful if the new evidence is surprising); and
7. the evidence is well established.

Criteria 4, 5, and 6 overlap at least to some extent with some others, but it is helpful to make them explicit. These three, together with the other criteria, have been topics of discussion and debate for many years, but here I assume them.

Types of Evidence

The best-explanation structure of validation arguments provides broad criteria for making validation judgments. Messick (1989b, 6) has suggested specific types of information that are relevant to these broad criteria. Inspired by his suggestions,[2] with some supplementation by me, I propose the following ten (somewhat overlapping) types of evidence that are likely to be relevant when making a judgment about situational validity in regard to a critical thinking test:

1. the rationale upon which the tests are built;
2. the degree to which the tests cover the items in the rationale;
3. reasonable judgments about the acceptability of the keyed answers;
4. internal statistical analyses: item analyses, internal consistency indices (the latter being called "reliability" in psychometric language), and factor analyses;

5.   consistency of test results over time for individuals, including test-retest consistency and inter-rater consistency, which are also called "reliability" in psychometric language;

6.   appropriate consistency across groups or settings (generalizability);

7.   correlations and other relationships between the test and other variables;

8.   correlations between the test and other tests of and criteria for critical thinking;

9.   results of experimental studies in which teaching critical thinking was attempted, and in which the test was used as an indicator of success; and

10.   the extent to which test results fit into our general knowledge, including the contribution the tests have made to our knowledge of the relationship between critical thinking ability and other things.

This list is not intended to include all possible types, but I think it is fairly comprehensive. Each of these types is relevant to one or more of the seven criteria for best-explanation arguments I outlined earlier.

On the basis of my experience revising the Cornell manual, I can testify that a large amount of information must be gathered and interpreted when one makes a validity judgment in accord with the proposed ten types of evidence and the seven criteria for best-explanation arguments. The task is difficult if one is to produce anything approaching a reasonable judgment about validity. This is one of the reasons that validity is often slighted in descriptions of tests. It is much easier and less expensive to present an internal consistency index (by applying a Kuder-Richardson or Cronbach alpha formula to the results of a single administration of a test), which is a number, such as 0.85, and which is misleadingly called "reliability." More about this later.

An Example: Making a Validity Judgment About the Cornell Critical Thinking Tests

To illustrate the process of making a validity appraisal along the lines just suggested, to exhibit some distinctions and problems, and to show that the process is not an easy one, I shall describe my recent experience with revising the manual (Ennis, Millman, and Tomko 2005).

Level Z is the Cornell critical thinking test aimed at gifted and advanced high school students, college students, graduate students, and adults. Level X is aimed at students at middle or secondary levels of education, including 4th or 5th graders under special conditions of administration (Ennis and Millman 2005a, 2005b). My hypothesis is that the two tests I appraised are, to a substantial degree, situationally valid in standard situations, but I shall not here indicate the extent to which I believe the hypothesis to be established. My primary purpose is to present and comment on a process, not to defend a judgment about the Cornell tests.

Anyone trying to develop a picture of the validity of a particular test faces the problem of securing data. Large testing organizations have resources to conduct independent studies, but the cost impinges on their income, so they try to use information from the administration of their tests by other people. In reviewing the Cornell tests, our first problem was to secure data from the use of the tests. We were fortunate that a large number of studies have been done with Cornell Level X and Level Z. For earlier versions—as well as the most recent version—of the manual, we reviewed the *Dissertation Abstracts International* and the *Social Science Citation Index* from 1970 to 2000 to find sources of data. Most sources we located had some usable data. These, combined with several studies we did ourselves and several sent to us voluntarily, resulted in a total of sixty-nine usable studies for Level X and forty-two for Level Z.[3]

I shall refer to some of these studies as I discuss the problems and processes involved in evaluating critical thinking tests in accord with the ten types of evidence in the list above. The first three types in the list come under the heading "content-related evidence of validity."

Evidence types 1–3: A clearly defensible conception of critical thinking and its incorporation in the test

In generating or appraising a test, it is important to have a clear and defensible conception of critical thinking on which the test is based, partly because this will clarify one's hypothesis about the test's situational validity. The presentation of the conception provides the opportunity to decide whether it is close enough to what the test user has in mind, and whether critical thinking so conceptualized is worthwhile (required by the commendatory tone of "critical thinking").

Approaches to critical thinking do vary. Some approaches emphasize the degree to which the argument, presentation, or statement under consideration is persuasive, not whether it is justified. The Cornell-Illinois conception,[4] on which the Cornell critical thinking tests are based, is concerned with justification. We might begin with the following brief definition: Critical thinking is reasonable reflective thinking focused on deciding what to believe or do. This definition is too general to provide much guidance in the construction and evaluation of a critical thinking test, but the following more detailed definition can serve as a bridge from the brief definition to an even more detailed specification of abilities and dispositions: Critical thinking is focused, skilled, active, reasonable thinking, incorporating the identification, clarification, and due consideration of the situation, relevant background information, reasons, evidence, and alternatives in deciding what to believe or do.[5]

Based on the brief and the bridging definitions is an elaborate and detailed set of critical thinking abilities and dispositions of critical thinkers. This set can be the basis for a detailed table of specifications for a critical thinking test. The most readily accessible version of this detailed set is the outline of goals for a critical thinking curriculum and its assessment on my academic website (http://faculty.ed.uiuc.edu/rhennis). For a similar presentation in print form, see Ennis (2001); for exemplification and interpretation, see Ennis (1962, 1987, 1991, 1996).

But a clear and defensible conception of critical thinking is not enough. The conception must also be well incorporated in the test. This calls for an examination to determine whether the conception is adequately covered (although complete coverage is unlikely for any test of critical thinking) and whether the keyed answers to test questions are justified. In making this judgment, a prospective user should examine the extent of coverage and take the test, checking the adequacy of the prospective user's answers as well as the answers in the key. The keyed answers for the Cornell tests are defended at the end of the manual, but a prospective user should still take the time to check them.

The Cornell tests do not fully cover the Cornell-Illinois detailed conception, as can be seen in Table 1, which lists most of the main topics included in the detailed conception. One must decide whether the coverage is adequate for one's purposes.

Aspect of Critical Thinking	Items of Level X (for K–12)	Items of Level Z (for UG, Grad, Adult)
Induction	3–25, 48, 50	17, 26–42
Deduction	52–65, 67–76	1–10, 39–52
Value Judging	Not tested	Not tested
Observation	27–50	22–25
Credibility of Sources	27–50	22–25
Assumptions	67–76	43–52
Meaning	Not directly tested	11–21, 43–46
Dispositions	Not directly tested	Not directly tested

Table 1: A rough assignment of test items to aspects of critical thinking[6]

The multiple-choice format has some significant desirable features: multiple-choice tests can be graded easily and cheaply, and can assure coverage of specific aspects of critical thinking. But this also means that some significant aspects of critical thinking mentioned in Table 1 are not tested—value judging and dispositions for both tests and meaning abilities for Level X. It is difficult to have value-judging items because this would probably require the assessment of a test taker's value judgments, which would be unfair. The multiple-choice testing of dispositions would appear to be useful only for situations in which students do not reveal their names to people who matter to them (savvy students are not likely to admit that they are not open minded, for example, even if they are not open minded). And it is difficult to phrase questions designed to test meaning abilities in a way likely to be understood by less sophisticated students.

The creative aspects of critical thinking also tend to be neglected in multiple-choice tests. These include formulating hypotheses, doing the creative parts of planning experiments, formulating definitions, and formulating appropriate questions. These aspects require more open-ended kinds of assessment.

Other limits on multiple-choice testing can be found in attempts to test for skill at best-explanation induction and the judging of credibility. When we draw inductive and credibility conclusions, judge them, and even decide the bearing of evidence upon them, we rely on a vast array of auxiliary assumptions about the way things happen. As in real life, the need for all of these background-belief assumptions exists in a test situation when we ask students to make a commitment to some view that students might not share.

A second problem arises because a less sophisticated person is sometimes justified in calling true something that a more sophisticated person would justifiably call only probably true. In the same circumstances, a very sophisticated person might justifiably judge that there is insufficient evidence for either position (problems Groarke raises in his chapter in this volume with respect to certain multiple-choice questions on the *California Critical Thinking Skills Test*). These problems can be reduced in best-explanation induction test items by asking for merely the direction of evidential support, if it has a direction, rather than whether the conclusion is true, probably true, etc. With credibility test items, one can ask which of two statements is more credible, if either is, instead of asking whether a statement is credible. This again avoids the requirement that one make an absolute judgment.

The first problem with best-explanation induction and the judging of credibility is somewhat more difficult to handle, because different people bring different auxiliary assumptions to bear on decisions of this sort. Though not always a solution, the most reasonable approach calls for auxiliary assumptions on which most people will agree. For example, we believe *most* people would agree on the following auxiliary assumption of Item 1 of Level X: "If a hut is not lived in or used, a layer of dust will probably develop." But we are not certain that *all* test takers would agree on even this auxiliary assumption, and do not want to penalize them for holding a different belief about the way the world works. Accordingly, we have provisionally adopted a stance that deems as indicative of mastery any induction or credibility section score with a greater than 85 percent agreement with the answer key.

These content problems must be faced in making a situational-validity judgment.

Evidence types 4 and 5: Internal consistency and consistency over time ("reliability")

Some internal consistency is desirable because a test should hang together in some reasonable way if it is to be named by a single noun or noun phrase, such as "critical thinking." Standard measures of internal consistency are the extent to which students who do well on the total test do well on a particular item (item discrimination), and (roughly) the average correlation of each item with every other item. The latter is what we get with the Kuder-Richardson and Cronbach alpha formulas, which are the indices most frequently used and reported under the label "reliability."

Calling these indices "reliability indices" is unfortunate (Ennis 2000) because they indicate only internal consistency, not what is ordinarily meant by "reliability" (a combination of consistency and accuracy). According to the psychometric concept of *reliability* (which is only consistency, whether internal or not), a bathroom scale that consistently reads 15 pounds low is totally reliable, as is a compass that consistently reads 180 degrees off (that is, reads just the opposite of what it should read). This is a serious problem because, when information is called "reliability," many test users think they are being given test-validity information.

Internal-consistency psychometric reliability is especially attractive to test makers. The numbers run higher than validity-related numbers and they are inexpensive to secure. One has only to run a computer program on the item scores obtained in one administration of a test to get an internal-consistency index. Consequently, test makers can get inexpensive and misleading indicators that are indicators only of internal consistency, but advertise them as "reliability" indices. Inevitably there is pressure on test makers to increase the internal-consistency indices.

One way for test makers to increase internal consistency is simply to lengthen the test by adding more, similar items. Another way is to discard any items that do not correlate well with the total score, that is, those with low item discrimination (also a misleading label, unless the test is uni-dimensional). This increases the correlations items have with each other and thus internal consistency, but also increases the uni-dimensionality of the test.

But critical thinking is not uni-dimensional, as can be seen by looking at the wide variety of aspects associated with it (as Johnson argues in his chapter in this volume). For example, in Cornell Level Z, deduction, meaning, fallacies, observation, credibility of sources, hypothesis testing, planning experiments, definition, and assumption identification are all assessed.[7]

Empirical support for the multi-dimensionality of critical thinking appears in the Level Z manual (Ennis, Millman, and Tomko 2005; from Mines 1980). Part-score "reliabilities" for Level Z ran almost as high as the total-score "reliability." That is, 0.76, 0.66, 0.60, 0.55, 0.72, 0.65, and 0.65 are about as high as 0.76, the "reliability" for the total score (N=40 graduate students at the University of Iowa). Adjusting these part-score "reliabilities" (using the Spearman-Brown formula) for the lengthening of each part to 52 items (the actual number of items in the total test), these part-score "reliabilities" become 0.94, 0.90, 0.95, 0.83, 0.97, 0.96, and 0.94, which are considerably higher than the 0.76 for the full test. This strongly suggests multi-dimensionality and justifies not expecting internal-consistency ("reliability") indices of over 0.80 on comprehensive critical thinking tests. A very high internal-consistency index (e.g., 0.92, or 0.95) would be undesirable. Admittedly, this reasoning involved stretching the Spearman-Brown formula beyond its original intent, but the results are still rather striking.

A second and more defensible kind of internal consistency for multi-dimensional critical thinking tests is "split-half" consistency. In this case, a test is split in half (typically into odd items and even items, sometimes into equal-length sets of items judged comparable), the two halves are correlated with each other, and the correlation is adjusted upward (by the Spearman-Brown formula) to compensate for each half's being shorter than the full test. Split-half consistency is more defensible than some of the other measures of consistency because sums of composites are correlated with sums of fairly comparable composites (assuming a roughly equal number of items from each part of the test), instead of each item being correlated with every other item. Computing such measures is more troubling than the Kuder-Richardson and Cronbach alpha internal-consistency estimates, however, and it is still misleading to call split-half internal consistency "reliability," because it provides a measure of consistency, not situational validity.

Another type of consistency is test-retest consistency. It is not vulnerable to the complaint that it unduly penalizes a test for multi-dimensionality. But it, too, is wrongly called "reliability." It is (only) a measure of consistency from one administration of a test to the next, and does not show that the test is assessing what it claims to be in the situation. Test-retest consistency is investigated less often. Many things can happen from one administration of a text to the next and this may interfere with a consistency measure. Even without this complication, test-retest consistency is generally avoided because the required two administrations (reasonably separated in time) of the same test to the same population are generally much more trouble than one administration.

Inter-rater consistency is important for tests, typically essay tests, that must be graded according to some rubric or criterion. Again, consistency is not validity though it is more likely to tend in that direction if the graders are familiar with the goals and their meaning, and if they are competent. Inter-rater consistency, however, does not apply to multiple-choice critical thinking tests, the topic of this chapter.

For both Cornell tests combined, we have twenty-six examples of Kuder-Richardson internal consistencies, as contrasted with fourteen examples of the split-half type of internal consistency, and two examples of test-retest consistency. Variation among groups and settings is expectable, but simple arithmetic means give a good indication of central tendencies.[7] For Level X the simple mean for Kuder-Richardsons is 0.79, and for split halves it is 0.83; for Level Z, it is 0.67 for Kuder-Richardsons and 0.67 for split halves. For identifiable graduate students on Level Z, the split-half internal consistencies averaged 0.78, and the only Level Z Kuder-Richardson I found is 0.76. This suggests that Level Z is more internally consistent for more sophisticated students than it is for less sophisticated students. The test-retest consistencies were obtained for Level Z only, and averaged 0.79. Results like these are quite acceptable, if the multi-dimensionality thesis is acceptable. These "reliabilities" are not as high as those in good uni-dimensional tests, such as the verbal, quantitative, and analytic parts of the former Graduate Record Examination (GRE) general test, which are listed at 0.92, 0.92, and 0.88 respectively (GRE Board 1995–6, 30).

The simple mean of the item discrimination indices is 0.24 (N=6) for Level X and 0.22 (N=5) for Level Z. These are reasonable, especially for multi-dimensional tests. Item discrimination is a type of internal consistency that is not called "reliability," and not one that yields anything like the high numbers of Kuder-Richardsons.

The Kuder-Richardsons and other internal-consistency results are roughly explainable by the tests' being multi-dimensional and the Level Zs' being aimed at more sophisticated students. As such, they are quite adequate, though not as high as the ones in uni-dimensional tests, for example, the verbal and quantitative parts of the GRE, which run approximately 0.92. But note that the GRE program did not combine three components—verbal, quantitative, and analytic—to compute internal-consistency estimates. Combining them would produce a multi-dimensional test and lower the internal-consistency index.

It is sometimes held that psychometric reliability is a necessary condition for validity. This is generally true for test-retest and split-half consistency. A test with inconsistent retest results raises the question "Which is right: the test or the retest?" And a test with inconsistent, supposedly comparable halves would seem odd. But for intercorrelation internal-consistency indices, the claim that consistency is a necessary condition for validity is an exaggeration because of the multi-dimensionality possibility, although at least some internal consistency is generally desirable for a test named by a noun.

In sum, when judging consistency one must carefully consider the type of consistency measure used and interpret it accordingly. It is important to compare critical thinking tests using the same type of consistency, and, if comparing internal consistencies, to consider whether the tests attempt to assess only one or a few similar aspects of critical thinking, or attempt to assess a more comprehensive conception of critical thinking. In all considerations of consistency, it is important to be wary of treating consistency (psychometric reliability) as validity.

Evidence types 6 and 7: Relations with other factors, and appropriate generalization

One can generalize from the twenty studies that checked for gender differences using either Cornell Level X or Level Z. There seems, in general, to be no difference in critical thinking ability between mature males and females, assuming that these tests were valid in the situation of their use, although there was some evidence for the superiority of females among younger students. Using Level X, there was occasionally a leaning toward a conclusion that girls were better critical thinkers, but with Level Z, there was no indication of superiority of one gender over the other. The slight difference between the tests could result from the fact that Level Z is given to older students. It is possible that girls are a bit more advanced in critical thinking in grades four to twelve, as they are in many mental activities, and that boys catch up in college and above.

The results for gender seem consistent across groups. The values of the gender variable are clearly identifiable, and we have reason to expect that males and females who are tested together represent the same level of critical thinking ability within their gender groups (that is, that the males were roughly in the same male percentile range as the female percentile range of the females to whom they are compared). The results are explainable by these factors, by the combination of a set of what I believe to be reasonable beliefs about male/female critical thinking levels, and by the hypothesis that the tests were valid in the situation of their use.

In contrast, one would expect less consistency in relationships between test results and grades given by an instructor, because there is considerable variation in the types of prowess rewarded by grades in institutions in the United States. With both Level X and Level Z we found relationship to grade point averages to vary considerably. The greatest disparity was for Level Z, its correlations ranging from −0.02 to +0.60. The 0.60 value was obtained at Cornell University. This is in keeping with my experience there, which leads me to believe that critical thinking is commonly taught and rewarded at Cornell. It is different, however, from experiences in other situations. But even with the obtained variation, the central tendency in the studies surveyed is a moderate relationship with grades.

The lesson here is that complete generalizability is not always to be expected. What should be expected depends on the situation, including the factors related to critical thinking ability, and whether generalizability, or lack of it, can reasonably be explained. Generalizability is more expectable for gender than for grades. For grades, less generalizability is expectable.

Other areas of seemingly moderate consistency were also evident. They included improvement in critical thinking across grade levels; negative correlations with dogmatism; low positive correlations with socio-economic status, independence, and first-year grades in graduate school (the latter being about the same as those obtained with the Graduate Record Examination and the Miller Analogies Test; see Linn 1982); and moderate correlations with IQAA (IQ and Academic Admissions tests) and grades, though there were wide variations for grades, as I pointed out earlier. All of these findings are explainable by the hypothesis that the Cornell tests are situationally valid, together with other plausible assumptions, for example, the assumption that critical thinkers are not dogmatic.

Evidence type 8: Other critical thinking tests

The correlations between the Cornell tests and other critical thinking tests, especially the Watson Glaser test, are high to moderate, and are explainable by the situational validity hypothesis, taken in conjunction with the assumption that the tests assess some things in common but also differ somewhat.[9] It is unfortunate that there are not more data for correlations with other critical thinking tests, but they are difficult to obtain, partly because students and teachers resist testing that is done solely for the sake of research. Because it is desirable that an argument for the situational validity of a critical thinking test include correlations with other critical thinking tests, the situational-validity hypothesis receives less support or challenge here than it should. Ideally, for the hypothesis, there would be more correlational studies with other critical thinking tests, producing fairly high to high correlations, depending on the nature of the tests.

Evidence type 9: Experimental studies of teaching

Suppose that, in a teaching experiment, the experimental group improved significantly more than the control group. If critical thinking had been taught—and taught well—to the experimental group only and the experiment had otherwise been run well, then the hypothesis that the test was a situationally valid test of critical thinking is supported. This is because, together, the hypothesis and the two conditional clauses above roughly explain the results. The hypothesis gets further support if the two conditional clauses are established, and the explanation of the results is not plausibly completed other than by the situational-validity hypothesis.

A third type of support can come from a situation in which critical thinking is not taught (even if the investigator thought it was, or might have been), the experiment is otherwise run well, and the experimental group does no better on the test than the control group. The situational-validity hypothesis would help explain the lack of difference between the experimental and control groups. So, in this type of case, negative results would also support the hypothesis.

The above reasoning is schematic, but it shows how best-explanation reasoning can guide our thinking about the relevance of experimental results. There are other possible combinations of the factors involved, but these three exhibit a general strategy when there is a control group. When there is no control group, but only a test-retest situation, support provided by positive and negative results is generally weaker because there is more opportunity for other possible explanations of the results.

The application of the above type of schematic thinking is difficult because each case is unique—with many details in doubt, even for the investigator. Nevertheless, experimental evidence is relevant, even though claims about its relevance must usually be qualified by words like "probably," "possibly," and "it seems that...".

From the twenty-seven experimental reports using Cornell Level X that we found, it seems that all but one provided support for the hypothesis. Some of the experiments seemed bound to fail because of the nature of the experimental variables (some of which I think were mistakenly called "critical thinking"), and they did fail to yield a significant difference. Others seemed likely to succeed because a reasonable conception of critical thinking was used, critical thinking principles were made explicit, and probably sufficient time was devoted to the task. In all but one case these experiments did succeed. These results lead me to say that the situational-validity hypothesis for Level X is substantially supported.

In the Level Z experiments with college students, the desirable conditions for learning critical thinking seemed to be present and statistically significant results were obtained in all four experiments we found—with respectable Cohen's d's of 1.1, 1.5, and 0.6 (Cohen 1992) in those experiments that produced this statistic (Solon 2001,

2003). The situational-validity hypothesis for Level Z, together with additional assumptions, explains these consistently favourable results. But more data are needed.

Evidence type 10: Contributions to knowledge

Tom Solon (2007), the investigator in some above-reported experiments using Level Z, asserts that his experimental class in which he infused critical thinking in psychology instruction did as well in psychology as the one in which the infusion did not occur. In the other two studies I found that investigated the matter, subject-matter comprehension did not suffer. This is not difficult to understand because the involvement occasioned by critically thinking about the subject matter could easily compensate for the reduced time spent on standard subject-matter instruction. In this context this result satisfies the sixth best-explanation criterion, "the hypothesis [helps imply] new evidence, especially if the new evidence is surprising," and constitutes the tenth evidence type, "contributions the tests have made to knowledge."

Other contributions to the sixth best-explanation criterion and the contribution-to-knowledge type of evidence are the findings about gender, grades, socio-economic status, independence, dogmatism, IQAA, and general improvement in critical thinking across grade levels. These findings are explained by the situational-validity hypothesis and a set of plausible assumptions. As in the case of experiments, more data would, of course, be helpful.

Summary and Comment

In this chapter I propose a program for investigating and assessing multiple-choice critical thinking tests. The program assumes a focus on the test and the testing situation rather than on inferences from, and interpretations of, test scores. In concurrence with psychometric lore, I have assumed that numbers are not a good way to try to indicate the extent of validity, and have assumed a unitary conception of validity.

It is helpful to view test-validity claims as inference-to-best-explanation hypotheses which can be assessed on the basis of seven criteria. A hypothesis of situational validity is supported roughly to the extent to which, given reasonable assumptions, (1) it can explain (account for) evidence—or help to do so; (2) there is no evidence that is inconsistent with the hypothesis; (3) evidence is inconsistent with alternative explanations of the data; (4) the hypothesis is plausible—it fits with what else we know; (5) realistic and earnest attempts have been made to find counter-evidence and alternative hypotheses; (6) the hypothesis implies new evidence (especially helpful if the new evidence is surprising); and (7) the evidence is well established.

Ten categories of information inspired by a list by Messick (1989b) particularize the best-explanation approach for this context:

1. the rationale upon which the tests are built;
2. the degree to which the tests cover the items in the rationale;
3. reasonable judgments about the acceptability of the keyed answers;
4. internal statistical analyses—item analyses, internal consistency indices (called "reliability" in psychometrics), and factor analyses;
5. consistency of test results over time, including test-retest consistency and inter-rater consistency (also called "reliability" in psychometrics);
6. appropriate consistency across groups or settings (generalizability);
7. correlations and other relationships between the test and other variables;
8. correlations between the test and other tests of and criteria for critical thinking;
9. results of experimental studies in which teaching critical thinking (or something else) was attempted, and in which the test was used as an indicator of success; and
10. the extent to which test results fit into our general knowledge, including the contribution the tests have made to our knowledge of the relationship between critical thinking ability and other things.

By looking at these categories in the case of the Cornell critical thinking tests, I have tried to illustrate the complexities involved in making a reasonable validity decision about critical thinking tests, the difficulty of obtaining firm and clear results in critical thinking research, and the need for attending to many features of the situations in which the data were (or might be) obtained. The resulting challenge may, in part, explain test makers' heavy reliance on psychometric reliability, which is fairly easily determined and a misleading name for consistency. In examining consistency, it is important to be aware of the kind of consistency that is claimed for any test. Different types of psychometric-reliability consistency vary in their import, partly because tests vary in their degree of uni-dimensionality and partly because different factors can be checked for consistency.

The desirability of the generalizability of relationships depends on the factor which is in question. For instance, considerably less consistency in relation to subject-matter grades than in relation to gender is to be expected for critical thinking.

As a by-product of this investigation and assessment of the situational validity of the Cornell tests, some of the more interesting results of a review of the literature using the Cornell tests are (1) the genders are essentially equal in critical thinking ability, given mature students (though among less mature students, girls might have an edge); (2) there is a great deal of variation in the sorts of activities that people evaluate for their efficacy in promoting critical thinking; (3) critical thinking can be taught; (4) infusing critical thinking into subject-matter instruction does not appear to interfere with subject-matter learning; (5) critical thinking is a multi-dimensional concept; (6) critical thinking is negatively related to dogmatism; and (7) critical thinking is positively related to independence, socio-economic status, IQAA tests, subject-matter grades (though there is variation here, presumably attributable to institutional and classroom variation in what is valued and taught), and (using Level Z only) first-year grades in graduate school.

These results are subject to further investigation and depend on the situational validity of the tests used to produce them. This reflects the standard bootstrap situation in science: these results are part of the support for the situational-validity hypothesis, and the hypothesis is part of the support for the acceptability of the results.

Notes

1. Although somewhat similar in spirit to the best-explanation-inference approach advocated by Gilbert Harman (1973), my approach does not treat enumerative induction as a special case of best-explanation inference (Harman 1965, 1968; Ennis 1968), and adds some popular features.
2. Omitting his controversial value-implication and social-consequences criteria.

3. Both locating and reviewing these studies were difficult, and we are deeply indebted to the University of Illinois Library.

4. I call it the "Cornell-Illinois conception" because it was conceived and developed while I was at these two universities, where I had much help from colleagues, students, and administrators. John McPeck called the first readily available statement of this conception (Ennis 1962) "the prevailing view of the concept of critical thinking" (see Chapter 3 in McPeck 1981).

5. I am indebted to Michael Scriven for some content of this bridging definition.

6. Reproduced with permission from the Critical Thinking Company (www. CriticalThinking.com).

7. See the "Outline of goals..." on my academic website (http://faculty. ed.uiuc.edu/rhennis) for a more complete list.

8. For simplicity, I used ordinary averages rather than go through Fisher's z transformations because it makes so little difference in this situation.

9. In the past, I argued (Ennis 1958) that the then-current version of the Watson-Glaser test had significant problems. Most of those concerns still hold.

References

Cohen, J. 1992. A power primer. *Psychological Bulletin* 112(1): 155–9.

Ennis, R. In process. Situational test validity.

———. 2001. Goals for a critical thinking curriculum and its assessment. In *Developing minds*, 3d ed., ed. A. Costa, 44–6. Alexandria, VA: ASCD.

———. 2000. Test reliability: A practical exemplification of ordinary language philosophy. *Philosophy of education 1999*. Champaign, IL: Philosophy of Education Society.

———. 1996. *Critical thinking*. Upper Saddle River, NJ: Prentice-Hall.

———. 1991. Critical thinking: A streamlined conception. *Teaching Philosophy* 14(1): 5–25.

———. 1987. A taxonomy of critical thinking dispositions and abilities. In *Teaching thinking skills: Theory and practice*, ed. J. Baron and R. Sternberg, 9–26. New York: W.H. Freeman.

———. 1968. Enumerative induction and best explanation. *The Journal of Philosophy* 65(18): 523–9.

———. 1962. A concept of critical thinking. *Harvard Educational Review* 32: 81–111.

———. 1958. An appraisal of the *Watson-Glaser critical thinking appraisal*. *Journal of Educational Research* 52: 155–8.

Ennis, R., and J. Millman. 2005a. *Cornell critical thinking test, Level X.* Seaside, CA: The Critical Thinking Company.

———. 2005b. *Cornell critical thinking test, Level Z.* Seaside, CA: The Critical Thinking Company.

Ennis, R., J. Millman, and T. Tomko. 2005. *Cornell critical thinking tests Level X & Level Z manual,* 4ᵗʰ ed. Seaside, CA: The Critical Thinking Co.

Ennis, R., and E. Weir. 1985. *The Ennis-Weir critical thinking essay test.* Pacific Grove, CA: Midwest Publications.

Frisbie, D. 2005. Measurement 101: Some fundamentals revisited. *Educational Measurement: Issues and Practice* 24(3): 21–8.

Graduate Record Examination Board. 1995–96. *Guide to the graduate record examination programs.* Princeton, NJ: Educational Testing Service.

Harman, G. 1973. *Thought.* Princeton, NJ: Princeton University Press.

———. 1968. Enumerative induction and inference to best explanation. *The Journal of Philosophy* 65(18): 529–33.

———. 1965. The inference to the best explanation. *Philosophical Review* 74(1): 88–95.

Joint Committee on Standards for Educational and Psychological Testing of American Educational Research Association, American Psychological Association, and National Council on Educational Measurement. 1999. *Standards for educational and psychological tests.* Washington, DC: American Educational Research Association.

Linn, R. 1982. Ability testing: Individual differences, prediction and differential prediction. In *Ability testing: Uses, consequences, and controversies* (Part II: Documentation section), ed. A. Wigdor and W. Garner, 335–88. Washington DC: National Academy Press.

Linn, R., ed. 1989. *Educational measurement,* 3d ed. New York: Macmillan.

McPeck, J. 1981. *Critical thinking and education.* New York: St. Martin's Press.

Messick, S. 1989a. Validity. In *Educational Measurement,* 3d ed., ed. R. Linn, 13–103. New York: Macmillan.

———. 1989b. Meaning and values in test validation: The science and ethics of assessment. *Educational Researcher* 18(2): 5–11.

Mines, R. 1980. Levels of intellectual development and associated critical thinking skills in young adults. *Dissertation Abstracts International* 41: 1495A.

Norris, S., and R. Ennis. 1989. *Evaluating critical thinking.* Pacific Grove, CA: Midwest Publications.

Solon, T. 2007. Generic critical thinking infusion and course content learning in introductory psychology. *Journal of Instructional Psychology* 34(2): 95–109.

———. 2003. Teaching critical thinking: The more, the better. *The Commu-*

nity College Enterprise 9(2): 25–8.

———. 2001. Improving critical thinking in an introductory psychology course. *Michigan Community College Journal* 7(2): 73–80.

Chapter Five

Testing Critical Thinking in a Pluralistic Democracy

Frederick S. Ellett, Jr. and Allan Pitman

$\mathcal{M}$odern post-industrial societies face serious problems. In Canada, for example, the costs of providing health care have been rising so quickly that the viability of a public health system with free universal access is being undermined (see Gratzer 1999, Rachlis and Kushner 1994). There are also serious problems with public education. It is true that most citizens in democratic states recognize the importance of public education, and they know that a system of education accessible to all serves some of the deepest interests of the state. At the same time, however, many doubt the quality of their education systems. And according to more than a few, it is not clear that they achieve the democratic ideals of excellence (quality), equity, and accountability.

The situation is further complicated by considerable disagreement over the basic principles of a pluralistic democracy. The courts in North America have held that schools should teach the basic democratic values. One of the most central democratic values is respect. But what *is* respect? And, how is it to be shown? Respect toward *what*? According to Charles Larmore (1987), respect does not mean respect for the beliefs a person holds so much as his or her capacity to reason (theoretically) about key issues. In contrast, Kantian scholars like Thomas Hill (1992) and Allan Wood (1999) hold that respect is due all persons in view of their practical rationality. Another neo-Kantian, John Rawls (1993), holds that respect is due persons for their capacity for rational action and their sense of fair play. Broadening the notion of respect, the communitarian Charles Taylor (1994) argues that

99

a democratic society should show respect for cultural groups as well as individuals.

Other important controversies characterize contemporary discussions of democracy. Commentators, including Alasdair MacIntrye (1984) and John Kekes (2003), have argued against the egalitarian tendencies contained in much contemporary theory. An even deeper critique of traditionally accepted notions of democracy has been forwarded by feminists like Nel Noddings (2003) and Martha Nussbaum (2001), who argue that they place too much emphasis on reason (and all forms of rationality) and that they should instead emphasize human capacity for caring or compassion. As Annette Baier (1987) argues, a good society needs more than "just institutions."

We agree with those who hold that there are good reasons for a democratic society to have a good civic (or political) education as one of the primary goals of its public schools. This civic education should teach the socio-historical settings of modern democracy and discuss the institutions which may help (or hinder) the development of democratic values. It should help students understand and evaluate the different views of democracies, and foster the attitudes and emotions conducive to responsible citizenship. As much as possible, it should be democratic in both its ends and means (Gutmann 1987; Levinson 1999).

In a "pluralistic" democracy, individuals may choose different yet reasonable lives for themselves. One of democracy's cental strengths is its ability to allow its citizens to live their lives as they judge best. To paraphrase John Dewey (1938), it follows that one of the aims of democratic education should be a power of "self-control" (in the sense of "positive freedom" for Dewey, and "autonomy" for Kant). Students who emerge from schools should be ready and able to make the choices this aim implies. Citizens in a democracy also need an education that prepares them for the political decisions with which they are entrusted by their political system. In addition to the ability to deliberate, they need to be able to understand what their institutions are doing, and they need good, relevant information on which to base their decisions. This is why the institutions in a democratic society must strive to be open and transparent. And, within education, this means that the relevant information about these institutions (and their policies and programs) must be collected, analyzed, and debated.

Many hold that critical thinking is one of the key components in fostering civic education, positive autonomy, and the ability to understand and discuss democratic institutions. More broadly, this suggests that critical thinking is a crucial part of education for democracy. But what is it to be a critical thinker? In one of the earliest discussions of the topic, Max Black (1952) suggests that critical thinking is coextensive with formal logic and the scientific method, and that a critical thinker is a person who has mastered this set of narrow skills. In response, John Passmore (1967) argues that a student who has mastered the exercises in Black's book has not learned to *be critical* unless he or she can apply these skills to something else. Passmore concludes that a critical thinker must have various attitudes—what might be called "a critical spirit." In keeping with this, an educated person should be independent, critical, and capable of facing problems. Such a person is able to participate "in the great human traditions of *critico-creative thought*: science, history, literature, philosophy, and technology..." (1967, 200). For Passmore, philosophy includes ethics and social and political theory, so this characterization of critical thinking implies thinking in the broadest sense. He suggests a partnership of critical thinking and creativity to evaluate and develop new possibilities.

The remarks of Black and Passmore suggest that critical thinking includes the following components:

- ❖ the ability to reason according to the formal principles of logic (perhaps including probability theory);
- ❖ the ability to reason logically and to employ the scientific method;
- ❖ the capacity for theoretical reason (in all its forms);
- ❖ the capacity (and attitudes) for being a practically rational agent;
- ❖ the capacity (and attitudes) for being a rational and morally responsible agent; and
- ❖ the capacity (and attitudes) for being a caring and nurturing person.

This list is not exhaustive, nor are the options mutually exclusive. Although we agree with Passmore that productive critical thinking should be accompanied by creativity, we do not pursue this point because it would require that we get suitably clear about creativity.[1]

Supposing that this notion of critical thinking is clear enough for the purposes at hand, is it possible to construct a test to determine whether a person is a critical thinker? For argument's sake, let us take Passmore's fairly broad conception of critical thinking and focus on higher-order thinking skills, attitudes, and dispositions. In the rest of this chapter we will defend the thesis that it is possible to construct tests for determining whether a person is a critical thinker (in a given context). In doing so, we will argue for a broad concept of "test" that is not restricted to paper-and-pencil, multiple-choice settings. It is this broader notion of test (and the rubrics of assessment that can accompany it) which looks most promising in this context.

In discussing the validity of tests, like many other researchers, we will embrace a shift in the meaning of "test validation" away from the notion that judgments of validation must limit their concerns to statistical reasoning. According to the view we favour, these judgments involve more complexity—indeed, they are judgments of the sort that critical thinking emphasizes. We will also argue that judgments about test-based validity in educational contexts almost always involve moral and socio-political issues. Finally, we will argue that conclusions about the validity of a test crucially depend upon the purpose for which the test is used.

The last point suggests that different standards and procedures are appropriate in different testing circumstances. In the current testing climate, it is particularly significant that one set of standards and procedures may be appropriate when "high-stakes" tests are used to decide whether one should be admitted to a program (or should graduate from a program), and another set when "classroom" (or "curricular") tests are used in the course of teaching. In the debates over these two kinds of tests, we side with James Popham (2001; 2003), who argues that the quality of education is best served by tests which are directly relevant to classroom teaching.

Principles of Interpretation

We hope that all (with the possible exception of some postmodernists[2]) will agree that whenever teachers judge, interpret, test, or assess whether students have learned, their judgments (interpretations, tests, or assessments) should be defensible, that is, based on good reasons. This seems a matter of basic fairness: judgments must be based on both *defensible* and *commonly agreed upon and applied* criteria, not the arbitrary views and conclusions of individual teachers. In understanding and evaluating teachers' judgments, it seems appropriate and natural to say that teachers *interpret* their students' test results, their performances and actions, and so on. We therefore take the term "interpretation" to be the key term in these contexts.

The general task at hand now becomes the following: When a teacher attributes a specific property to a student, what counts as adequate evidence for the teacher's attribution? What are we to make of the notion "adequate evidence" (good reasons, warrants)? The related question is this: How is it determined whether someone has adequate evidence? Is there an algorithm? Is there a mechanical recipe? Or does one have to judge? The answer seems clear enough to us: one has to *judge!*

Consider a simple example. Suppose a student hands in a well-written assignment which answers the teacher's question about the historical influences of legal concepts in education law. Suppose the paper directly answers the question in a clear manner with detailed explanations and telling cases. How is the teacher to interpret the student's actions? What could *explain* such a good paper? It is always possible that the student retrieved it from the Internet! But if the teacher's question was specific, then this seems unlikely. In that case, the student may have had a friend write the paper for him or her. Alternatively, the student wrote the paper.

How does a sensible and fair teacher choose from among these three explanations? Among other things, he or she employs a *principle*: if the student has truly learned something, then such thought is *likely to be manifested* in the student's performance(s). The student's new learning (or thoughtfulness) can in this way help *explain* the performance(s). If the student has written the paper by himself or herself (or has mastered a particular know-how or a higher-order thinking skill), then he or she can be expected to do well in another situation which is similar to the first. If the student has the capacity in question, then one can expect that he or she will exhibit it in other related situations. Suppose the student has used the term "reliable witness" properly and consistently in the paper. What should be expected if the teacher then asks the student, "What does the term 'reliable witness' mean and how is it used? Can you give examples?" Here we employ another principle: if the student has truly learned something, and has demonstrated that learning, a teacher will be able to make *predictions* about the future performances of the student.

Whenever one is trying to reach an interpretation (albeit fallible) about events, one is entitled to bring to bear all relevant background knowledge. It is often said the interpreter must come to an interpretation with an *open mind*, but having an open mind does not mean that the interpreter disregards all that he or she has reason to believe. Indeed, it is this resource of vast background information that enables one to use the newly collected information to reach a plausible interpretation. This principle holds that we should always check to see whether the interpretation accords with previous background knowledge. In the example we have suggested, let us suppose both that the student had written a paper which was appropriate for a much older student and that the student had never before shown such capacities. In such a context, the teacher sensibly would, so far, regard the interpretation [the student wrote this paper] to be implausible because it conflicted with the teacher's background knowledge.

In summary, this case involving cheating illustrates that good thinking typically relies upon the principles of simplicity, explanatory power, predictiveness, and consistency. Since all human attributions are fallible, the teacher is not guaranteed to be correct when judging that the student did (or did not) cheat. But given suitable evidence, the judgment asserts (at least) that it is more likely that the student did cheat. We say that the teacher's judgment is *valid* (to a certain degree) when it coincides (to a certain degree) with the truth of the interpretation that the student did cheat.

Interpreting a student's actions as cheating is not just an "attribution" problem for the teacher. Almost always, the attribution of cheating will be the basis for a suitable sanction: the paper may not be accepted, but another attempt may be allowed; the student may get a zero for the assignment; the student might fail the course; or the student may be suspended or expelled. We believe there is a *moral-political* principle of fairness involved here: as the possible harm to the student increases, the teacher must take extra steps to increase the defensibility of the attribution of cheating.

Let us suppose that the teacher has reasonably concluded that the student did write the paper. Having judged the quality of the student's analysis and arguments, the teacher will perform actions based on that interpretation. For example, the teacher may grade the paper to determine 20 percent of the student's course grade. We hold that the kind of action the teacher takes will in part determine the degree of plausibility (defensibility) the interpretation of the paper must satisfy.

Tests

Writers like Grant Wiggins (1993) and Linda Darling-Hammond (1999) restrict the word "test" to tests which employ *standardized* methods made up of *multiple-choice* items with *uniquely* right answers. They use the term "authentic assessments" (or "performance-assessments") for those more informal procedures that use *open-response* (or *constructed-response*) questions to determine whether students have learned something which will be useful in their lives. In our view, however, this hard-and-fast distinction between a "test" and "an assessment" is needlessly contentious and quarrelsome. We think the less rigid distinctions in the following table are more useful.

Kind of Tool	*Kind of Item*	*Item Selection*	*Aggregation of Items*
A typical **standardized** test	tends to use *multiple-choice* items for which there are correct answers	tends to use items which have a high level of difficulty to differentiate students from each another (norm-referenced)	tends to regard all items as "indicators" of the same characteristic (and therefore to sum up to get a total score)
A typical **performance assessment** test	tends to use *open-response* items which allow for several good answers (as estimated by competent judges)	has no perceived idea of levels of difficulty; tries to find out what each student can do (which may have quality levels) (criterion-referenced)	tends to regard the test as a collection of items which are "indicators" of quite different characteristics

Table 1: Kinds of tests

Our broader account of tests, we think, is in keeping with the acknowledged and official position of The American Educational Research Association, The American Psychological Association, The American Psychoanalytic Association, and similar groups. They now recognize that the term "test" is properly applied to a surprisingly wide range of activities, methods, and procedures; it is no longer restricted to such things as standardized methods which employ multiple-choice items. Samuel Messick (1989), for example, has written that "the term test score is used generically here in its broadest sense to mean any observed consistency, not just on tests as ordinarily conceived but on any means of observing or documenting consistent behaviours or attributes" (13). Similarly, Lorrie Shepard (1993) has commented, "As stated by Cronbach (1971), 'one validates, not a test, but an interpretation of data arising from a specified procedure' (p. 447). Procedure may refer to a formal test or other data-gathering instrument and includes the conditions of examinee preparation, test administration, and so forth" (19).

In the example discussed above in which the teacher suspected that the student might have cheated, all of the (relevant) information gathered by the teacher (by direct questioning or by background knowledge and so on) is used to judge whether the student wrote the (good) paper. This is, on the broader account of tests, a *test situation* in which one is collecting various kinds of data to test whether the student can (and did) write the good history paper.

"Reliable" and (Comparatively) "Valid"

One of the key concepts in testing is "reliability." In educational (or psychological) contexts, a "reliable test" is a test which yields approximately the same results when it is given again in similar situations. Though it is intuitively peculiar, measuring a person's shoe size would be a *reliable* test of the person's intelligence because it would give very nearly the same results when repeated. As this example shows, one needs to be very careful not to confuse the educational (or psychological) use of "reliable" with the way the term might be used in law (in talk of a "reliable witness" for example) or with the way the term might be used in medical science (where a "reliable test" is an accurate indicator of a disease.)

Although a good test must have some moderate degree of reliability, the crucial question that must be asked about an educational test is whether and to what degree the test is *valid*. In our example about the student's cheating, to say that the teacher's judgment (that the student cheated) is valid is to say that the judgment coincides with its being true that the student cheated. In the traditional way of expressing this point, the "student's cheating" is called a *construct*. The teacher's attribution is *construct valid* (to a certain degree) when it coincides with the student's having the attribution (of being a cheater).

In many books one finds the following slogan: A test is a valid measure of something if the test really measures that something. This statement may be true in the abstract, but it does not explain what is involved in validating a test. Unfortunately, most texts spend very little time on the complex and multi-dimensional aspects of the "validation process." In general, the validation process involves collecting the various forms of evidence in order to defend the attribution of the construct (the property) to the student. It must also be kept in mind that the strength (or the quality) of the evidence is not the same as the validity of the attribution. For example, in their critical discussion of IQ tests, Block and Dworkin (1976) argue that there are strong reasons for holding that the IQ tests account for only 25 percent of the variance of intelligence and are, therefore, *invalid*.

In preparation for our look at critical thinking tests, let us draw out a plausible (and standard) account of the key term "validation." First, it should be clear that the *validation process* is wide ranging and multi-dimensional. Messick (1989) defines validity as "an integrated evaluative judgment of the degree to which empirical evidence and theoretical rationales support the adequacy and appropriateness of inferences and actions based on test scores or other modes of assessment....Broadly speaking, then, validity is an inductive summary of both the existing evidence and the potential consequences of score interpretation and use" (13). He adds that validity is "a matter of degree" and that validation is an evolving process as "new findings and projections of potential social consequences of testing become transformed by evidence of actual consequences and by changing social conditions" (13).

Shepard (1993) similarly emphasizes the multi-dimensional nature of test validation when she writes that "[e]very test use involves inferences or interpretation; therefore, all validation requires the combination of logical argument and empirical argument needed to support those inferences" (19). In the present context, it is worth noting that this conception of the test validation process implies that the skills emphasized in critical thinking (reasoning, argumentation, etc.) must play a key role in validating tests.

Adapting Messick (1989) and Lorrie Shepard's (1993) elaboration of his analysis, we would describe the process involved in test validation in terms of the role that different values—epistemic, scientific, moral, and political—play within it. Consider Table 2 below.

	Test Interpretation	Test-based Actions
Evidential basis	Construct validity	Construct validity + epistemic relevance/ utility + socio-political relevance/ utility
"Consequential" basis	Epistemic value and socio-political value presuppositions or implications.	Socio-political "consequences"

Table 2: Kinds of values and construct validation

Let us begin by looking at the column entitled "Test Interpretation." One plausible way to understand "test interpretation" is to see it as a process which is primarily concerned with the role of the test in the formation, development, and testing of hypotheses (or conjectures) in the social sciences. Given this interpretation, the values that matter would be scientific values in the domain of inquiry. This account is supported by some of Lorrie Shepard's (1993) remarks (see, for example, 424), but she also writes,

> Test uses are obviously derived from value positions that are amendable to political debate, as, for example, when meritocratic or egalitarian principles are the basis for allocating educational opportunities. It is less widely recog-

nized, however, that much scientific research is also value directed, to a greater or lesser degree. Values assumptions shape how research questions are framed, what data are gathered, and how results are interpreted. It is these perspectives, which influence scientific inquiry, that should be acknowledged in the validity framework. (60)[3]

Shepard seems to be suggesting that other kinds of values are involved in test validation as well. Educators have been interested in IQ tests because they are interested in a student's intelligence. In such a case, the educator's socio-political interest in intelligence informs the evaluation of test scores. Decisions about what research gets funded (and by whom) also reflect various socio-political interests.[4] If this is the kind of point Shepard is trying to acknowledge here, then it seems to be clearer to distinguish the kinds of values involved, which we have tried to do in Table 2.

Because it seems that socio-political values can enter the validation process before, during, and after the process, we have added quotation marks around the word "consequential." We have also emphasized (in the upper-right cell of the table) the distinction between epistemic values and socio-political values. The column we call "Test-based Actions" implies evaluations involving the relevant socio-political (moral) values, the purposes for which an educational test is being used in schools (selection, sorting, information feedback to students or parents, assessment, accountability, high-stakes certification, and so on) and the consequences of so using the test.

Within test validation, then, *construct validation*—the empirical or scientific process of defending one's attribution of a characteristic to someone on the basis of testing—plays a central role. Like Lorrie Shepard (1993), we would emphasize that construct validation is not separate from value considerations:

> [V]alue perspectives influence construct hypotheses and counter interpretations that must be entertained as part of the initial delineation of a nomological network....Our epistemic principles—the standards of predictive accuracy, internal coherence, and the like used to accept or reject hypotheses—represent value choices, and the concepts we

study are evaluative of human behavior. (427)

Kenneth Howe (1985), Samual Messick (1989), and Lorrie Shepard (1993) all accept the point that the "epistemic values" play a central role in construct validation. Epistemic values are used to decide (scientifically) whether to accept a particular interpretation (or theory)—on the basis of the epistemic values of simplicity, empirical adequacy, power, scope, fruitfulness, and consistency.[5] However one defines the terms "assessment" and "test" and whether one is considering relatively simple constructs (such as whether a student did indeed write the paper he or she submitted), or is considering complex constructs (such as "innate intelligence"), central to all these activities will be the (empirical) validation process in which the inquirer must use the epistemic values to judge which interpretation of the test results is comparatively plausible.

The other values in the process are the moral and socio-political values. There is a danger that the upper right cell in Table 2 will be taken to suggest that in the validation of a test-use, the socio-political values and principles are somehow *merely added onto* the process of construct validation, and *do not interact* with the process of construct validation. Consider Shepard's (1993) words:

> In my view, validity investigations cannot resolve questions that are purely value choices (e.g., should all high school students be given an academic curriculum versus being tracked into vocational and college programs?). However, to the extent that contending constituencies make competing claims about what a test measures, about the nature of its relations to subsequent performance in school or on the job, or about the effects of testing, these value-laden questions are integral to a validity evaluation. For example, the question as to whether students are helped or hurt as a result of a test-based remedial placement is amenable to scientific investigation. (428)

The key phrases here are "claims about what a test measures," "[claims] about the nature of its relations to subsequent performance in school or on the job," and "[claims] about the effects of testing." In our view,

Shepard (and Messick) mean these claims to be empirical claims. As Shepard puts it, such claims are "amenable to scientific investigation."

We do not deny that in any interesting case of test validation there will be such claims that are amenable to scientific investigation. There might be a claim that using the test in this situation probably results in the outcome G (which is morally good). Almost always there will be related claims that using the test in this situation likely results in the outcome B (which is morally bad). Such claims are amenable to scientific investigation. But is this all that is involved in test validation? How can the use of the test be evaluated here? It seems clear that a moral judgment is needed which will take into account the fact that using the test will probably result in good outcomes and bad outcomes. Because we reject the idea that some kind of cost-benefit calculus can resolve the questions raised by these good and bad outcomes, we hold that evaluation of the way a test is used in a specific situation must make a moral (qualitative) judgment. That judgment will place special emphasis on socio-political values and principles.

Perhaps Shepard and Messick desire a "test validator" who focuses only on those aspects of evaluation which are amenable to scientific inquiry. Perhaps most people who call themselves "test validators"—or "measurement professionals" (Shepard 1993, 407, 441–2)—prefer to restrict themselves to scientific inquiry. This is not a major problem so long as the general public and educators recognize that such "test validators" are performing only *some* of the crucial tasks of test validation. Perhaps there is a division of labour here. What must not be lost is that some suitably placed moral agent must make a moral judgment which weighs relevant positives and negatives in the course of a complete test validation. Indeed, we think the following can be justified: the person who performs the action based upon the test has the moral responsibility to justify the action by using the relevant epistemic values and the relevant socio-political values. The person performing a test-based action cannot "shift" his or her own moral responsibility.

We agree with Messick and Shepard (and others) that the more limited matters of construct validation are a major part of all validations of test-use actions. But, in education, where tests will almost always be used for some purpose (to punish for cheating, to sort, to promote, to award, and so on), the left-hand (column one) of our table is possibly misleading, because all test uses (all test-based actions) occur in column two. We think a better way to represent the key issues involved here is therefore given in Figure 1 below, where the socio-political values are represented as backgrounding, focusing, and shaping the validation of the test-based actions.

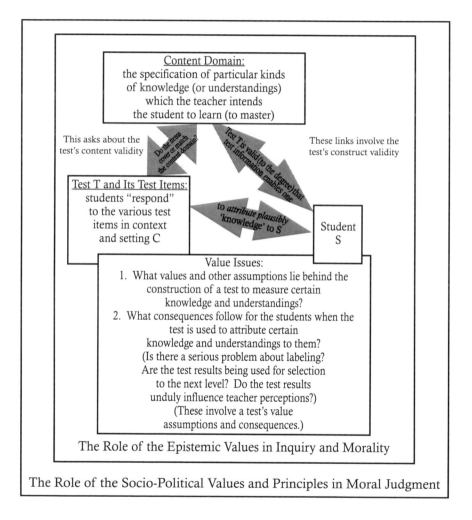

Figure 1: Issues in the validation of test-based action

Tests and Assessments: Rubrics for Critical Thinking

We are now in position to see how our general remarks on test validity are related to the recently developed tools called "rubrics." Rubrics guide the assessment of open-ended test questions. In the course of introducing rubrics, we will focus on the core, "interpretive" aspect involved in all test situations (i.e., construct validity). Almost all teachers will perform test-based actions that are open to full moral evaluation. In view of this, test-based actions are likely to interactively set restrictions on the adequacy of the interpretations.

We begin with an example of a test. The following testing exercise—"Cuthbert: Hero or Scoundrel?"—is suggested by Roland Case in a paper on assessment methods (Case 1997). The test is made up of a *constructed-response* item which requires that students construct a suitable answer. It is designed to test critical thinking skills in the context of the higher-order skills employed in the interpretation of a story. In a case such as this, the assessment process needs to aim for a consistent standard of assessment which is applied to all students. For obvious reasons, this is one of the difficulties that arises when one grades open-ended questions.

Cuthbert: Hero or Scoundrel?

After reading the story *It's So Nice To Have A Wolf Around the House* (Henry Allard 1977) decide whether the main character in the story, Cuthbert Q. Devine, is a hero or a scoundrel. Consider carefully the evidence for each interpretation and defend your own interpretation. (Case 1987, 410)

Consistent grading can be promoted by the use of rubrics. The following five-level *rubric* which we have adapted from Wiggins and McTighe's (1998) *Understanding By Design* can be applied to the case at hand. In this case, the rubric "reflects a continuum of performance— from naive understanding (at the bottom) to sophisticated understanding (at the top)" (74–6).

Critical Interpretation
Profound: a powerful and illuminating critical interpretation and analysis of the importance/meaning/significance; tells a rich and insightful story; provides a rich history or context; sees deeply and incisively any ironies in the different interpretations.
Revealing: a nuanced critical interpretation and analysis of the importance/ meaning/significance; tells an insightful story; provides a telling history or context; sees subtle differences, levels, and ironies in diverse interpretations.
Perceptive: a helpful critical interpretation or analysis of the importance/ meaning/significance; tells a clear and instructive story; provides a useful history or context; sees different levels of interpretation.
Interpreted: a plausible interpretation or limited critical analysis of the importance/meaning/significance; makes sense of a story; provides a history or context.
Literal: a simplistic or superficial reading; mechanical translation; a decoding with little or no interpretation; no sense of wider importance or significance; a restatement of what was taught or read.

Figure 2: Five-level rubric for critical interpretation. Adapted from Wiggins and McTighe (1998).

This rubric uses words (e.g., literal,...,profound) to *rank order* the quality of interpretation exhibited.[6] Using rubrics for higher-order skills requires that several things be considered. For an inquirer—a teacher—to *validly* use a rubric, it is necessary that the inquirer/teacher have a deep understanding of the subject matter being taught at this level. The deep mastery of the subject matter (for the relevant grade level) provides the background beliefs and the standards for judging whether the content of the critical interpretation is a profound (as com-pared to a literal) one. Another set of abilities which is often underem-phasized (or overlooked) comprise the ability to understand persons in general and the students at this level of learning. This ability provides the background beliefs and standards for judging how to interpret val-idly the student's actions and responses (see Figure 1 above). Again, remember that the teacher will perform actions based upon the assessments that result from the rubric.

We consider next a quantitative rubric developed from Young and Wilson (2000).

Category	Good	Better	Best
Core Content and Concepts	• demonstrates *limited* understanding of *some* of the required concepts • provides appropriate but *incomplete* explanations that incorporate *some* content ideas and relationships	• demonstrates *general* understanding of *most* of the required concepts • provides the appropriate and *complete* explanations that *consistently* incorporate some content ideas and relationships	• demonstrates *in-depth* understanding of *all* of the required concepts • provides the appropriate and *complete* explanations of content ideas and relationships, and incorporates the concepts in a *variety* of contexts
Reasoning and Applications	• selects and applies *some* of the appropriate procedures and operations • has *several minor* errors or omissions • constructs a *few minor* criticisms	• selects and applies *most* of the appropriate procedures and operations • has a *few minor* errors or omissions • constructs *several good* criticisms	• selects and applies *almost all* of the appropriate procedures and operations • has *rare* errors or omissions • constructs *central or key* criticisms

Communica-tion	• provides justifications that have *some* clarity and precision • uses *some* appropriate content terms and symbols	• provides justifications that are *generally* clear and precise • uses content terms and symbols that are usually appropriate	• provides justifications that are clear and precise • always uses a *range* of appropriate content terms and symbols
Problem Solving	• demonstrates limited understanding • chooses and carries out appropriate strategies • sometimes arrives at plausible solutions	• demonstrates a general understanding • consistently chooses and carries out appropriate strategies • usually plausible solutions	• demonstrates a thorough understanding • chooses and carries out *innovative* and appropriate strategies • always plausible solutions

Figure 3: Quantitative content rubric. Adapted from Young and Wilson (2000, 36), which was adapted from *The Ontario Curriculum: Grades 1–8 Mathematics* (1997).

To use this rubric validly, the teacher needs to have and be able to execute the *two abilities* we have already noted: an understanding of the subject and an understanding of the students. This so-called "quantitative rubric" is, moreover, really a kind of "qualitative rubric," because what counts as "few," "some," or "many" will depend upon the context. It should be clear that rubrics help teachers organize their judgments, especially when the standards are explicitly formulated. But rubrics cannot replace teacher judgment.

　　Because we are interested in the assessment of critical thinking, we have emphasized rubrics in the domain of higher-order cognitive skills. But it is arguable that critical thinking also requires dispositions and attitudes that fit the *affective* as well as the cognitive domain. It is, arguable, for example, that critical thinking requires respect for others, in part because it requires the ability to understand and appreciate others' views. The following figure shows how a rubric can be created for assessments of this sort.

Deep respect	The student shows a deep and steadfast respect for the views, thinking, and feelings of all students in the class.
A very good respect	The student shows, most of the time, a very good respect for the views, thinking, and feelings of all students in the class.
An adequate respect	The student shows, fairly often, an adequate respect for the views, thinking, and the feelings of all students in the class.
A very limited and inconsistent respect	The student shows, at best, a very limited and inconsistent respect for the views, thinking, and feelings of all students in the class.

Figure 4: Attitude (Respect) rubric

This rubric might be used to judge students who engage in dialogue, a key competency for democracy.

A teacher who is trying to foster critical thinking must try to understand their students' deeper values. Although it is generally held, as a matter or morals, that the teacher should not test for the values (or attitudes) of any individual student, the teacher can anonymously test the class to get a sense of what values (or attitudes) the class members have. The following figure offers an example of an assessment tool that could be used (see Popham 2003; Anderson and Bourke 2000).

Critical thinking and me: An affective inventory
Directions: Please indicate how true or untrue the statements in the following inventory are for you. Some of the statements are positive; some are negative. Decide if each statement is true for you. There are no right or wrong answers. Please answer honestly. Do not write your name on the inventory. Only make X marks. Your answers will be anonymous. An example is provided below.

Statement	**Response (one per statement)**		
	Very true for me	Not true for me	I'm not sure
I enjoy going to the movies.	☐	☒	☐

Statements	**Responses (one per statement)**		
	Very true for me	Not true for me	I'm not sure
1. Most of the time, I really like doing critical thinking.	☐	☐	☐
2. I really feel that I can learn to think critically.	☐	☐	☐
3. I don't really like to do the formal logic exercises.	☐	☐	☐
4. I really enjoy finding good reasons for my claims.	☐	☐	☐
5. Overall, I feel that, for me, critical thinking is valuable.	☐	☐	☐
6. When I have to analyze actual passages, I don't like it.	☐	☐	☐
7. I like to do the statistics problems.	☐	☐	☐
8. Overall, I really don't like doing critical thinking.	☐	☐	☐
9. I am afraid that I cannot learn to do critical thinking.	☐	☐	☐
10. Finding good reasons for my claims is not very enjoyable.	☐	☐	☐
11. I enjoy doing the formal logic exercises.	☐	☐	☐
12. I feel the statistics problems are boring.	☐	☐	☐
13. Mostly I feel that, for me, critical thinking is irrelevant.	☐	☐	☐
14. I enjoy analyzing actual passages.	☐	☐	☐

Figure 5: A Likert-like multi-dimensional inventory. Adapted from Popham (2003).

If student responses show that they do not like critical thinking, one might follow up with a question which asks them why they do not like it. This feedback can then be used in the planning of future classes.

Conclusion

We began this chapter by considering the need for education for democracy. Our arguments are built upon rather recent conceptual and epistemic renderings of "test" (or assessment) and "validity." Although we argued that testing for critical thinking is possible, we fully acknowledge that constructing tests that are valid is no simple task. The most crucial considerations are twofold: that increased stakes are cause for ensuring critical thinking on the part of teachers insofar as they can and must use critical thinking to validly defend their own scoring and assessment criteria (including epistemic values). Second, if teachers are going to assess and evaluate their students' higher-order thinking, they ought to begin using rubrics and testing instruments that measure the attitudes and dispositions that lead to the exercise of critical thinking: no doubt the most difficult task of all, but perhaps the most essential for students learning how to be good citizens in a pluralistic democracy.

Notes

1. Cornelia Hoogland and Jan Sobocan explore the relationship of critical thinking and creativity in Part Two of this book.
2. The term "postmodernist" has been applied to many different views. One group uses the term to refer to views which reject the correspondence theory of truth; such a group could adopt, say, one of the pragmatist conceptions. Radical postmodernists, however, reject the use of the term "true" in all ways. Such radical views are, in our judgment, deeply incoherent and self-defeating. Other radical postmodernists reject the view that reasons are universal and go on to refuse to accept any reasons at all. This latter view is also, in our judgment, deeply incoherent and self-defeating. Having acknowledged these incoherent, radical postmodernisms, we will say little more about them, but the reader should see Gross and Levitt (1994) and Koertge (2001).
3. Again, it must be kept in mind that the strength (or the quality) of the evidence is not the same as the validity of the attribution (see Block and Dworkin 1976).
4. One must not overreact to this kind of influence, per se, because medi-

cal science research and public health care research are also deeply (and should be) influenced by such socio-political (or moral-political) interests and values.

5. Kenneth Howe has argued that the judgments employing epistemic values typically *compare* one interpretation against another interpretation. Here Howe has drawn on the philosophic tradition which includes Elgin (1996), Lycan (1988), Kuhn (1977), and Quine (1960).

6. The acceptability of nominal (category) scales and ordinal (rank ordering) scales, along with the standard interval (e.g., temperature) and ratio (e.g., length) scales, was settled a long time ago (see Stevens 1960).

References

Anderson, L., and S. Bourke. 2000. *Assessing affective characteristics in the schools*, 2d ed. Mahwah, NJ: Lawrence Erlbaum.

Baier, A. 1987. The need for more than justice. *The Canadian Journal of Philosophy, Supplementary* 13: 41–56.

Black, M. 1952. *Critical thinking: An introduction to logic and scientific method.* New York: Prentice-Hall.

Block, N., and G. Dworkin. 1976. IQ, heritability, and inequality. In *The IQ controversy*, ed. N. Block and G. Dworkin, 410–73. New York: Pantheon.

Case, R. 1997. Assessment methods. In *The Canadian anthology of social studies: Issues and strategies for teachers*, ed. R. Case and P. Clark, 409–20. Vancouver: Pacific Educational Press.

Cronbach, L. 1971. Test validation. In *Educational measurement*, 2d ed., ed. R. Thorndike, 443–507. Washington, DC: American Council on Education.

Darling-Hammond, L. 1999. Performance-based assessment and educational equity. In *Contemporary issues in curriculum*, 2d ed., ed. A. Ornstein and L. Behar, 382–402. New York: Allyn and Bacon.

Dewey, J. 1938. *Experience and education.* New York: Collier-MacMillan.

Elgin, C. 1996. *Considered judgment.* Princeton, NJ: Princeton University Press.

Gratzer, D. 1999. *Code blue.* Toronto: ECW Press.

Gross, P., and N. Levitt. 1994. *Higher superstition: The academic left and its quarrels with science.* Baltimore: Johns Hopkins University Press.

Gutmann, A. 1987. *Democratic education.* Princeton, NJ: Princeton University Press.

Hill, T., Jr. 1992. *Dignity and practical rationality in Kant's moral theory.* Ithaca, NY: Cornell University Press.

Howe, K. 1985. Two dogmas of educational research. *Educational Researcher* 14(8): 10–18.

Kekes, J. 2003. *The illusions of egalitarianism.* Ithaca, NY: Cornell University Press.

Koertge, N., ed. 2001. *A house built on sand: Exposing postmodernist myths about science.* Oxford: Oxford University Press.

Kuhn, T. 1977. *The essential tension: Selected studies in scientific tradition and change.* Chicago: University of Chicago Press.

Larmore, C. 1987. *Patterns of moral complexity.* Cambridge: Cambridge University Press.

Levinson, M. 1999. *The demands of liberal education.* Oxford: Oxford University Press.

Linn, R., ed. 1989. *Educational measurement,* 3d ed. New York: Macmillan.

Lycan, W. 1988. *Judgment and justification.* Cambridge: Cambridge University Press.

MacIntyre, A. 1984. *After virtue: A study in moral theory,* 2d ed. Notre Dame, IN: University of Notre Dame Press.

Messick, S. 1989. Validity. In *Educational measurement,* 3d ed., ed. R. Linn, 13–103. New York: Macmillan.

Nodding, N. 2003. *Happiness and education.* Cambridge: Cambridge University Press.

Nussbaum, M. 2001. *Upheavals of thought.* Cambridge: Cambridge University Press.

Passmore, J. 1967. On teaching to be critical. In *The Concept of education,* ed. R. S. Peters, 192–211. London: Routledge & Kegan Paul.

Popham, W. 2003. *Test better, teach better.* Alexandria, VA: Association for Supervision and Curriculum Development.

———. 2001. *The truth about testing.* Alexandria, VA: Association for Supervision and Curriculum Development.

Quine, W. 1960. *Word and object.* Cambridge, MA: MIT Press.

Rachlis, M., and C. Kushner. 1994. *Strong medicine.* Toronto: HarperCollins.

Rawls, J. 1993. *Political liberalism.* New Haven, CT: Yale University Press.

Shepard, L. 1993. Evaluating test validity. In *Review of research in education.* Vol. 19, ed. L. Darling-Hammond, 405–50. Washington, DC: American Educational Research Association.

Stevens, S. 1960. On the theory of scales of measurement. In *Philosophy of Science,* ed. A. Danto and S. Morgenbessor, 141–9. New York: Meridian Books.

Taylor, C. 1994. The politics of recognition. In *Multiculturalism: Examining the politics of recognition,* ed. A. Gutmann, with C. Taylor, K. Appiah, J. Habermas, S. Rockefeller, M. Walzer, and S. Wolf, 25–73. Princeton, NJ:

Princeton University Press.

The Ontario Curriculum: Grades 1–8 Mathematics. 1997. Toronto: Ministry of Education and Training.

Wiggins, G. 1993. *Assessing student performance.* San Francisco, CA: Jossey-Bass Publishers.

Wiggins, G., and J. McTighe. 1998. *Understanding by design.* Alexandria, VA: Association for Supervision and Curriculum Development.

Wood, A. 1999. *Kant's ethical thought.* Cambridge: Cambridge University Press.

Young, S., and R. Wilson. 2000. *Assessment and learning: The ICE approach.* Toronto: Portage & Main Press.

PART TWO

Critical and Creative Thinking

Introduction

*O*ne of the least understood aspects of critical thinking is its relationship to creative thinking. On reflection, most would agree that critical thinking manifests itself—perhaps most completely— in creative thinking. But the nature of creative thinking is elusive and poorly understood. Though the critical thinking movement has spawned extensive literature on the nature, teaching, and assessment of critical thinking, this is a literature that, for the most part, ignores the relationship between creative and critical thinking.

To some extent, our failure to fully come to terms with creative thinking may be inevitable; creativity by nature is an elusive phenomenon that breaks free of the established standards of thinking and reasoning. Because creativity is most often conceived of as invention, then perhaps it is a cognitive activity that must necessarily reach beyond the structure of what has been studied and written about. The theoretical and pedagogical questions that this raises are particularly acute in the area of assessment, especially standardized assessment, because it seems impossible to develop answer keys to capture the range of answers under the umbrella "all answers imaginable." It is relatively easy to see whether students can detect standard logical or linguistic flaws in a piece of reasoning, but far more difficult to assess whether they are capable of developing new ways of looking at things, and to then score them according to that "newness" or on some scale of imagination. To do so seems counterintuitive.

More deeply, one might wonder whether the unimaginative exercise of the rote skills emphasized on most standardized tests encourages habits of thinking which are, by their nature, not free and creative. With this consideration to mull over, creative thinking seems untestable by, and in fact seems bound by, this and almost any other testing format (most notably, the ubiquitous multiple-choice question).

The chapters in Part Two of the book address this very issue: how the creative aspect of a critical thinking process might best be taught and assessed. In Chapter Six, William Hare argues that the importance of imagination has been overlooked in discussions of critical thinking, and promotes a view of teaching and critical thinking which is squarely founded on a belief in imagination and the openness and creativity it encompasses. Cornelia Hoogland looks at the "critical" in arts-based inquiry in Chapter Seven, examining the relationship between critical thinking and creative thinking in the Ontario Curriculum and illustrates her perspective with an account of her own creative work.

In the final chapter of this section, Jan Sobocan examines the format of the *The Ontario Secondary School Literacy Test* and discusses whether or not this particular instrument solicits any creative thinking skills that would be considered higher-order thinking as outlined in *The Ontario Curriculum* documents that supplement the test. More generally, she considers how tests might more validly assess the creative components of a critical thinking process.

Chapter Six

Imagination, Critical Thinking, and Teaching

William Hare

> *New ideas thrive in the imagination, which negates what is and ponders what might be.*
> —Israel Scheffler, *In Praise of the Cognitive Emotions*

Imagination and Critical Thinking

*I*n the wealth of material which has appeared on critical thinking, there is precious little attention paid to imagination. "Critical thinking" has become something of an educational slogan and everyone, it seems, subscribes to the view that teachers need to both have and foster critical ability. Imagination has had fewer champions.[1] Some philosophers of education, of course, have long claimed a link between criticism and imagination, notably John Passmore (1967), who took the view at the very outset of the modern debate on critical thinking that a critical person must possess initiative, independence, courage, and imagination (198). Not surprisingly, John Dewey (1985) also resists the tempting dichotomy between criticism and creativity, pointing out that criticism, especially self-criticism, is the road to the release of creative activity (30). Gilbert Ryle (1963) reminds us that "there are hosts of widely divergent sorts of behaviour" which can be appropriately described as imaginative, including the business of criticism itself (242–3).[2] On the whole, however, these suggestions have not been pur-

127

sued, and it has been assumed that imagination and criticism are in conflict.

No one who has followed recent educational theory can have failed to notice that critical thinking has effectively supplanted creativity as the preeminent aim of education. During the past thirty years, there has been a veritable deluge of articles and books on critical thinking, and a parallel decline in work on creativity which had so captured the headlines in the 1960s.[3] It may be that imagination has suffered by its association with creativity and the sense that critical thinking and creativity are unrelated, or even incompatible. This is quite mistaken; criticism and imagination are intimately connected. In thinking critically, we are not merely offering a stock response. Critical thinking can take us beyond our present beliefs and practices to new, unanticipated, and imaginative possibilities. We need imagination if we are to see how an idea might be supported or how it might be applied. Similarly, imaginative work draws on critical judgment; ideas that genuinely deserve to be considered creative, or imaginative, must be critically evaluated and deemed to meet an appropriate standard.[4]

Teachers who value imagination need to see critical ability and imagination as complementary, as Dewey (1985) clearly does when he describes one vital phase of reflective thought as involving "anticipation, supposition, conjecture, imagination" (198).[5] Robert Ennis (1987) attempts to catalogue the dispositions which distinguish the critical thinker, calling attention to the importance of *looking for alternatives*, a disposition which translates into a number of relevant abilities. That, indeed, is the heart of imagination, since an essential feature of the imaginative person is being both disposed and able to think up various possibilities (White 1990, 185). In Ennis's list of abilities we find such items as formulating alternative solutions, considering alternative interpretations, seeking other possible explanations, thinking up questions to elicit possible meanings, designing possible experiments, and so on. As far as I can see, Ennis (1987) makes no explicit mention of imagination, though he does say that his current definition incorporates "creative elements" (11). The sorts of activities he mentions, however, do call for imagination. All that is needed is to bring the connection into the open.

Some commentators, however, take the view that there is a fundamental incompatibility between those ideas that are central in the modern critical thinking literature and those ideals that we associate with imaginative inquiry. Laura Duhan Kaplan (1991) argues that critical thinking texts and courses tend to teach political *conformity*, contrary to the expressed intention of teachers and authors.[6] Her conclusion is that the whole conception of critical thinking, and the movement inspired by this conception, is deficient if we are concerned, as she puts it, about "the ability to envision alternative events and institutions" (369). I take this to mean, although again it is not made explicit, that the student's imaginative capacity is impaired by courses and texts in critical thinking. To learn conformity is, after all, to have one's eyes closed to other possibilities. It is also clear from Kaplan's (1991) endorsement of critical pedagogy as "a means of awakening the student's awareness that the world contains unrealized possibilities for thought and action" that the notion of imagination is implicit in her argument and fundamental in her scheme of values (362).[7]

The nub of her objection is that critical thinking merely teaches students to practise certain skills with respect to given and fixed alternatives, whereas students ought to be encouraged to "create alternatives, not merely to choose between them" (ibid., 364). Her case is supported by reference to a few texts in the general area of critical thinking (Toulmin, Rieke, and Janik 1979; Kahane 1988; Kelley 1998). None of her claims, however, is at all persuasive. In discussing David Kelley's approach, for example, she objects that teaching should not assume that choice exists among clear-cut options, determined by the author or teacher. But it is surely obvious that critical thinking can show, and must allow, that *none* of the options presently before a thinker is defensible; some other option will have to be found. Reflection on the fallacy of many questions, for example, is one way in which students may come to appreciate how options can be arbitrarily excluded; and this lesson can be generalized for use in other contexts (Flew 1975, 99).[8] Awareness of other fallacies, such as oversimplification, the black-or-white fallacy, and begging the question, can also awaken in students an appreciation that a context or argument can be rigged or unfairly circumscribed, closing off other avenues.[9] One of the basic lessons in critical thinking is that alternatives may have been arbitrarily denied and consequently that we have to *imagine* other possibilities; these points are commonly made in critical thinking texts and this very insight can be applied to the critical thinking text in which the fallacies are described.

Kaplan (1991) observes that most major and many minor life choices do not present themselves as opportunities to select among clear-cut options. Surely, however, students can learn to distinguish between the context of teaching and the context of ordinary experience. They can practise their skills on the examples offered, and recognize that, once learned, such skills can be employed in other contexts and even turned against the very examples on which the skills were honed,[10] or against the teacher's views, real or apparent.[11] On the assumption that students have some capacity for independent, critical judgment,[12] we need not be concerned that the examples we choose may be inadvertently slanted *if* the students are not only permitted but encouraged to assess the merits of these examples.

In her classic and still useful primer on clear thinking, Susan Stebbing (1939) offers the following cautionary word to the reader, touching on this point: "I ought to avoid making elementary mistakes in logic, since I have been thinking about the conditions of sound reasoning and have been trying to teach logic for years. But eager haste to establish a conclusion may lead me to make elementary blunders.... Naturally I cannot provide an example of my own failure in this respect; to have recognized the error would be to have avoided it" (47–8). The invitation to apply the skills and techniques *to the book itself* is quite explicit.

Every good author and teacher concerned with the development of critical thinking will ensure that a similar self-referential doubt is cultivated. We can readily imagine that we have committed errors even if we cannot imagine what they are; and we can encourage our students and readers to try to imagine alternative positions to the ones we confidently defend. Would any self-respecting teacher of critical thinking disagree with Stebbing (1939) when she remarks, "I do not hope to succeed in escaping bias either in my selection or in my exposition of these examples" (75)?[13] Even more pointedly Stebbing observes, "It may even be that you can find in this book some evidences of my having used crooked arguments. Certainly I am not aware of having done so, but in that I may be self-deceived. I cannot hope to have avoided altogether the defects of twisted thinking" (89–90).

Another text rejected by Kaplan (1991) as seriously deficient is *An Introduction to Reasoning* by Toulmin, Rieke, and Janik (1979).

Kaplan's opinion that this book "teaches reasoning in the sense that we say the Sophists in ancient Athens taught reasoning" (366) seems unlikely in the extreme given that distinguished philosopher Stephen Toulmin is its senior author. Still, stranger things have happened and, as Carl Sagan remarks, one's skepticism imposes a burden, i.e., a responsibility to find out. Kaplan's interpretation of the book is that it teaches students to adopt those reasons that are socially acceptable, in her words "how to behave in the courtroom, the health spa, the realtor's office, and the office party, in order to be accepted as a member of the petty bourgeoisie" (367). Again, the alleged lesson is conformity and the result is the supposed demise of imaginative speculation about alternatives.

An examination of *An Introduction to Reasoning* reveals that Kaplan's reading of the book is a complete misrepresentation. As one might have predicted, it is not the authors' view (how could it be?) that a good reason is whatever is generally thought to be a good reason in a particular social situation. Why would one need to study critical thinking if it were the case that informal socialization would suffice? Their point is the quite different one that the appropriateness and necessity of giving and searching for reasons vary from one context to another: "The trains of reasoning that it is appropriate to use vary from situation to situation" (Toulmin, Rieke, and Janik 1979, 7). It is made perfectly clear that appeals to "well-founded" authority may be challenged and supposed authority cannot be taken for granted. Moreover, to say that reasons "relevant" to a certain situation must be given is not to say that what is traditionally and socially *regarded as* relevant *is* relevant. It is explicitly acknowledged that such reasons may be disputed (Toulmin, Rieke, and Janik 1979, 8). The notion of relevance is itself controversial. Similarly, the distinction between what appears to be quite acceptable and proper and what is acceptable and proper is always clear. What is not clear is how Kaplan could have so completely misinterpreted this book.[14]

Of course, any text can be presented and taught in an uncritical manner and in such a way as to discourage creative thinking; but there is no reason to believe that the books reviewed here present critical thinking as an exercise in conformity. In the hands of an unimaginative teacher, they might do precious little to foster critical and imaginative reflection, but that is true of any text and is merely a reflection on the way in which the material is approached. There is no reason, moreover, to conclude that the conception of critical thinking in these books is one which excludes imagination. The connection, however, between critical thinking and imagination needs to be made more explicit in general accounts of critical thinking so that any tendency to drift into a mechanical and formulaic approach to "critical thinking" is averted.

One final point about imagination and critical thinking. One hears much less these days about brainstorming. Perhaps it is yet another example of a practice that is occasionally useful but by no means the panacea which enthusiasts once proclaimed. The general idea at work is that judgment should be deferred as ideas are being produced so that those involved will not be inhibited by the concern that their ideas are foolish or irrelevant. It may indeed be that the technique is sometimes effective, as researchers have claimed, but whether or not imaginative suggestions have been produced can be determined only by judging their merits *at some point*, and this requires critical assessment. The great danger is that simply being prolific in producing ideas (regardless of their merit) will be equated with being imaginative. Nevertheless, the strategy of getting our ideas on the table before deciding too quickly that they are not worth mentioning seems sensible. This does not mean, however, that we have only to play down critical reflection to allow our imaginations to flourish. That is, once again, to set up a dubious dichotomy.

Believing in Imagination

In addition to resisting the false dichotomy between imagination and critical thinking, teachers who value imagination need to reject the suggestion that our imaginations cannot overcome allegedly insuperable barriers resulting from our gender, race, ethnic background, or life experiences. One view that has enjoyed wide appeal is that those who have not directly and personally experienced certain events cannot really understand what it is like to have those experiences, and thus one's right to contribute to policy decisions about such matters is called into question. It is alleged that without personal experience, we simply do not know what we are talking about. Those who do not have direct, personal experience cannot contribute to a critical discussion on the issue in question. This has already translated into proposals for restricting the teaching of certain courses and topics to those who belong to certain groups, and it is sometimes suggested that members of certain groups should not address certain topics at all (Hurka 1989). These views are no longer as widely endorsed as they were only a decade ago, but it remains important to appreciate the underlying confusions.

The effect of this view, which is also perhaps the intent, is to silence opinion and dismiss certain suggestions without benefit of serious examination. If someone does not, and cannot, understand an issue, it is scarcely sensible to pay attention to what he or she has to say about it. The thesis is that people understand only if they have personally experienced the matter in question (for example, the oppression suffered by minority groups in societies which discriminate against them).[15] It is asserted more than argued that we simply cannot imagine what such experiences are like if we have not had them ourselves; if it is grudgingly conceded that one might have an abstract, intellectual grasp of the experience, it is strongly denied that any genuine imaginative and sympathetic awareness at the emotional level could occur.[16] This view flies in the face of all ordinary experience that tells us that by means of appealing to similarities in our own experience with those experiences we have not directly had, we *can* enter imaginatively into those other situations.

Some people, moreover, have the ability to assist us by virtue of their capacity to create and present a vivid and striking imaginative world we can enter vicariously. Imaginative teachers can help students do this too.[17] It is not difficult at all to show that direct, personal experience is not a prerequisite for understanding. In many cases, we know that the person in question did not, in fact, undergo the experience he or she describes. Consider, for example, Hortense Calisher's (1983) achievement in portraying life in a space shuttle on an extended mission. Her lack of direct experience here seems to have been no bar whatsoever to her imagination. By her own account, she went to the library for a very short time and read some NASA publications: "When the book was published, John Noble Wilford, who is head of the science news for the *New York Times*, came to interview me. He asked me how long I had researched, I told him what I had done, and he said he couldn't fault me on what was there. I think you just put yourself in any environment that you write in" (Straub 1988, 66).

In other cases, we know that the individual did not have the experience in question because it has never occurred. We are convinced, nevertheless, that he or she has given us some idea of what that situation might be like and feel like. In some cases, what we could not previously imagine becomes imaginable through someone else's gifts. A devastating virus capable of destroying rice, wheat, barley, oats, and other basic food crops has so far not infected the world, but can anyone doubt that John Christopher (1970) has given us a sense of that world, its social and moral characteristics, if such a calamity were to occur? Nor is it plausible to suggest that the author must have had some familiarity with famine conditions and their effects on human beings as civilized society gradually gives way to anarchy. Quite simply, he was able to imagine various possibilities and present them with great plausibility. Endless examples of similar imaginative works could be given, but it is enough just to mention books such as Golding's *Lord of the Flies* and Huxley's *Brave New World*, and to note that science fiction would effectively disappear as a genre on this view, for the position to collapse into absurdity.

Teachers should reject this alleged limitation on imagination not just because it is false but because such a belief may be self-fulfilling and may deter them from attempting imaginative work. Barriers to the imagination arise easily enough. We hear of customs and lifestyles very different from our own and declare that we simply cannot imagine anyone living that way. We hear of a new scientific notion and find it unimaginable. It may indeed be psychologically impossible for us to imagine these things because everything we have ever learned has built up the conviction that *only* what we already believe is possible. If we do not use our imaginations, if we are not encouraged to try to imagine certain things, if our imagination is not given full rein as children, then it may be that we cannot imagine what we might otherwise have been able to imagine.[18] If we are led to believe that we cannot imagine certain things, we may not *try* to imagine them with the result that, in time, we indeed cannot do what we might otherwise have done.[19]

It is important for teachers to believe in the value of imagination in their own work, whatever subject they are teaching. Imagination can characterize our efforts in teaching any subject, and we need to put behind us the idea that a concern for developing the imagination is the prerogative of teachers in certain areas and other teachers need not concern themselves. The view persists, however, that some subjects are especially connected with imagination, and the favourite candidate is literature.[20] The difficulty involved in ridding ourselves of this view can perhaps be illustrated by noting that while Robin Barrow (1990), for example, recognizes that one can exercise imagination in *any* context, he insists nevertheless that history and literature have special value in the development of imagination. Of course, literature has the power to help us connect imaginatively with other people, to imagine other times and places, and in so many ways to stimulate our imaginative abilities. Why, however, would literature or history be more likely to develop philosophical imagination than imaginative philosophy? Russell (1979) argued persuasively that basic scientific information can stimulate the imagination if people will take the time to reflect on it. He wanted people to ponder the fact, for example, that the largest star measures six hundred million miles across. Is there any reason to think that history would do more than science to develop our imaginations in this direction? It surely will not do to say that imaginative mathematics feeds the imagination only in respect of mathematics. All imagination takes some form, and literature and history will satisfy some and not others.[21]

Teachers who believe in the value of the imagination in education should also resist the suggestion that the term "imaginative" cannot in any reasonably strict sense be applied to the activities and ideas of young children (Barrow 1990, 87–8). Barrow is surely right to insist that the word is bandied about loosely in much educational theory, and that the necessary connection with relevant standards of quality is often absent. Nevertheless, just as he properly allows that what we considered as imaginative at an earlier period of history would not necessarily count as imaginative today, so too the application of standards in connection with the work of students needs to take into account the child's level and knowledge. An unusual and valuable suggestion from a five-year-old counts as imaginative even if it would not count as such if uttered by an adult.[22] This is simply because what counts as unusual is a reflection in part of what the child knows (Groarke agrees and illustrates the latter two points in this volume). We need to keep this in mind as teachers so that we are encouraged to continue looking for and promoting such ideas in our students.

Teachers with Imagination

Teachers need to use their imagination in many ways in their work. If they are not to be trapped in narrow and negative views, they will need to entertain the possibility that either/or choices can be challenged and overcome. They might try to imagine ways in which they can do justice to critical thinking and cultural literacy, to knowledge for its own sake and vocational studies, to competence and creativity, to moral rules and moral thinking, and so on. Fanaticism on either side of these divisions in educational theory encourages teachers to take refuge in whatever fortified position they can, and the idea of an imaginative resolution is lost. For example, in the conflict over whole language versus more traditional approaches to the teaching of reading, the atmosphere was, at times, so hostile and the respective positions so uncompromising that it took an effort of the imagination to conceive that there might be "a new order of conceptions" (Dewey 1965, 5).

The central role of imagination in the kinds of cases just mentioned will be missed if we think of the imagination only as entering into the formation of utopian visions. Nicholas Burbules (1990), for example, anxious to point out the dangers of utopianism, reminds us that the capacity to imagine and describe better possibilities is not itself a way of attaining these objectives. He remarks that "utopian thinking avoids the tragic sense by substituting our imagination for our sense of reality" (472). The imagination, however, comes into play not only in conceiving of ideals and visions, but also thinking of the means by which these goals might be achieved or approached. Burbules also indicates that there will be inevitable tradeoffs between competing ideals in the real world, and the implication may be that our imaginative horizons will have to be limited. However, we should remember that the imagination will play a vital role in coming up with creative compromises when such conflicts occur.

Again, a vital imaginative capacity involves the teacher's grasping and sharing the perspective of the student coming to a new subject that may seem impossibly difficult or uninteresting.[23] It is important for the teacher to try to appreciate the difficulties and frustration students may experience, and all too easy to forget them in practice.[24] The teacher, we may hope, now well understands the material and perhaps no longer even recalls similar problems he or she may have encountered when the subject was first studied. It may take an imaginative leap to place ourselves in a certain situation, even if we once occupied that situation. Louis Arnaud Reid (1962) observes that one great benefit of student teachers studying a new subject during their professional program is that they are thus being placed in much the same situation as the children they will teach, allowing them to gain a new sense of their students' perspectives (194). Imaginative teachers are able to think of various reasons why students might have difficulty grasping or appreciating the material, and this puts them in a position to look for imaginative solutions. There is no point to merely informing the student that the solution to a problem is obvious if the student does not find it obvious; there is nothing to be gained by merely asserting the value of the work if the student does not appreciate its value.

Related to this, teachers need to be able to see what their students are getting at even though their questions and comments are often poorly phrased, awkward, and hesitant. It is a common complaint by students that their teachers "missed the point" they were trying to make, and dismissed an idea too quickly. The teacher needs to consider the possibility that the student has a valuable point to make, albeit clumsily expressed, and also to wonder if there may be a further, deeper meaning for which the student is reaching. In an interview with Magee (1982) Isaiah Berlin notes, for example, that children frequently raise questions that contain the germs of philosophical ideas, and are often told to stop asking silly questions (15).[25] They need teachers (and parents) with an imaginative grasp of the possible meanings in their questions—philosophical or otherwise—and with the ability to respond in such a way that the sense of wonder is not destroyed. Teachers need imagination if they are to be able to recognize imaginative ideas coming from their students.

Teachers also need to be able to see possibilities for the future in the behaviour and interests of their students. Of course, judgment also enters into this, especially when it is a matter of recognizing a teachable moment.[26] As Dewey (1956) notes, however, "other acts and feelings are prophetic; they represent the dawning of flickering light that will shine steadily only in the far future. As regards them there is little at present to do but give them fair and full chance, waiting for the future for definite direction" (14–15). It takes some imagination to see the potential indicated by such "flickering light," but it needs to be recognized if the opportunity for development is to be provided. We know, unfortunately, how easy it is in practice for children in school to be labelled and streamed in such a way that, in the end, teachers simply *cannot* imagine *any* promising future for them. One thinks here of Jill Solnicki's (1992) impassioned plea to her department head whose cynicism is overwhelming: "How can it be that you've never seen past their 'unclear, incorrect sentences' to the expressiveness in their writing, the humour, the insight, the God damn humanity?!" (209). Educators, Dewey (1965) observes, more than other professionals, are concerned to take a long look ahead (75). This forward-looking perspective often takes the form of imaginative insight.

Imaginative teachers are capable of seeing unexpected possibilities in teaching moments. Eisner (1985) illustrates this with great clarity when he observes that teachers need to be inventive and innovative as they deal with unpredictable contingencies, and in creating ends *as they proceed* (176). Max van Manen (1991) also stresses the importance of teachers knowing how to improvise, knowing at once what is the right thing to say (160). Some writers, however, have misconstrued the need for improvisation and interactive decision-making as meaning that imaginative teachers must avoid intending at the outset to achieve a specific result in teaching. Ruth Mock (1970) speaks of the teacher who "intends, unimaginatively, to obtain a predetermined result" (86).[27] The teacher who has a goal in mind, however, is not thereby prevented from seizing an opportunity which comes along. Once again, an unnecessary dichotomy looms before us, this time planning versus improvisation. Eisner (1985) is much closer to the mark when he comments that "the exclusive use of such a model of teaching (i.e. predetermined ends) reduces it to a set of algorithmic functions" (177). The crucial term here is "exclusive."

On a related matter, there is currently a popular view that if children are to write imaginatively and honestly, they *must* choose their own topics. If the teacher assigns a topic, the students' own imagination is compromised. Moreover, imaginative writing must not be constrained by conventional norms such as correct spelling (see, for example, Graves 1983). Clearly, there is much to be said for the student trying to identify a worthwhile topic; this is itself an imaginative exercise. Much more needs to be done to encourage students to identify for themselves the problems they wish to work on, as Eisner argues

(1991,14). We need to stop short, however, of the absurd situation where a teacher is afraid to suggest possible topics. There is no point in teachers being more mature, Dewey remarks (1965, 38), if they throw away their insight. Similarly, it would be foolish to be so obsessed with correct spelling that one missed the imaginative ideas that students are producing, as Jill Solnicki (1992) points out. On the other hand, the possession of basic writing skills, including spelling, means that students are able to concentrate on their ideas.

There is sometimes a temptation to think that imaginative teaching must necessarily involve the kind of unusual, innovative strategy that succeeds sometimes precisely because it is so unusual that it captures the student's imagination. John Keating, the charismatic teacher in the film *Dead Poets Society*, comes to mind. As with courage, the dramatic examples may dominate our conception of imaginative teaching and blind us to other forms. Imagination, however, can be displayed in teaching that follows commonly employed methods such as instruction, discussion, and question-and-answer sessions. If these approaches are not imaginative, imaginative variations may well be introduced.[28] In the course of teaching in these ways, the teacher can show his or her imagination in the examples, cases, references, analogies, connections, metaphors, allusions, and diagrams introduced. Tired examples give way to fresh ones that open up the issue for teacher and student alike. These possibilities for imaginative teaching, however, are ignored by those who take the simplistic view that classroom teachers who value and emphasize creative learning will "minimize to the extent possible their own talk in class" (Massialas and Zevin 1983, 235). There may be good reasons why, on occasion, teachers should minimize their own talk but this is not a general guideline for imaginative teaching. It is the quality, not the amount, of talk that matters. Some teachers show their imagination by being able to think of another way of explaining a point or demonstrating a principle when other teachers would be defeated.

The impossibility of reducing teaching to rules and routines suggests that teachers will need imagination to think of ways to satisfy conflicting needs and claims *in their own teaching situations*. There is no ready-made rule to follow which will satisfy the demands of authority and freedom in education, however, and Russell (1971) is surely right to insist that teachers will simply have to *find* a way of exercising authority in the spirit of liberty (102). Tact, sensitivity, and judgment will be required here, but also imagination and critical reflection. Like Russell, Dewey (1976) sets himself against recommending methods and strategies to be "slavishly copied" in other contexts (319). Moreover, fundamental educational principles, such as the freedom of the learner, do not carry self-evident implications for practice either; they need interpretation in one's own situation (Dewey 1969, 20). They do not constitute answers so much as problems, and solutions will be found only by those with the imagination to break out of traditional ways of thinking and to adapt familiar ideas to the unique situations in which they find themselves: "No teacher can know too much or have too ingenious an imagination in selecting and adapting...to meet the requirements that make for growth in this and that individual" (Dewey 1986, 199).

Imagination and Accountability

If we favour a conception of liberal education that seeks to nurture a wide range of desirable human qualities, then the development of imagination will surely rank among our central aims. It is our imaginative capacity, combined with critical thinking, that enables us to break out of the confinement that results from stubborn and settled ways of thinking, too ready acceptance of the familiar, and a host of factors which prevent us from looking at things differently and thinking of other possibilities. It may be an exaggeration to say, as Mary Warnock (1996) does, that helping students exercise their imagination is the teacher's *only* serious function, but it is certainly one of the central tasks and rarely given the attention it deserves (147). If students are to be helped to sustain and develop a sense of wonder, to entertain alternative interpretations and explanations, and to cultivate a willingness to engage in imaginative thinking, they must first see these attitudes, habits, and dispositions exemplified in the way their teachers approach issues and problems in their classroom interactions. To take imaginative ability seriously as an aim of education means taking it seriously as a virtue in teachers.

Encouraging imaginative ability in teachers and fostering imaginative work in student teachers will require that supervisors and teacher educators have a rich and appreciative grasp of the many forms imaginative teaching can take. These include the ability to improvise, to recognize a teachable moment, to find a memorable example, to see where something might lead, to notice connections where things seem fragmented and isolated, to suggest the right assignment, to discover the merit in what is haltingly expressed, to think of an effective compromise, to put oneself in the shoes of one's students, to set a problem that is challenging but not overwhelming, and so on. The teacher with imagination is someone who can entertain the possibility that he or she is mistaken, that there are alternative positions which may well turn out to be right, and that his or her own knowledge is really quite limited. Inquiry begins with wonder and the person who is puzzled considers that he or she has much to learn (Aristotle *Metaphysics*, Book 1, ch. 2); in this way a connection emerges between imagination and certain intellectual virtues, especially humility, open-mindedness, and self-criticism. If we can give appropriate weight to such virtues in our account of good teaching, it may help to offset any tendency towards interpreting teaching as no more than the authoritative, rehearsed, and skillful transmission of established knowledge.[29]

Evaluating the performance of teachers is crucial if we are committed to having students encounter teachers who meet the highest standards of excellence. We need to be able to recognize and encourage those teachers whose work is admirable, and offer support and further training to those who need to improve. As the demand for accountability in teaching becomes ever more insistent, however, imaginative qualities run the risk of being overlooked and crowded out by a preoccupation with demonstrable mastery of particular behaviours and content knowledge. Douglas Anderson (2002) depressingly notes that "we seem currently in the midst of a movement toward mechanical pedagogy" (33). With teaching increasingly being turned into a script specifying—in precise and bewildering detail—the content, approved methodology, and duration of lessons, attention becomes centred on readily observable teacher behaviour that conforms to the script; more nebulous and subjective qualities such as imagination and critical ability are ignored and our conception of good teaching is diminished.

To consider what imaginative teaching involves is to appreciate immediately that it cannot be reduced to a checklist of observable behaviours, steps, or methods. The literature is full of examples of approaches, however, which promise to train teachers to be effective and efficient in ways that can be directly observed and accurately measured. In a climate where schools are regarded as being in crisis, such promises are extremely tempting. When precision becomes our watchword, it is easy to forget Aristotle's wise observation that the same degree of precision should not be demanded in all inquiries. To limit "good teaching" to that which can be documented in terms of hard evidence ("data") means that the exclusive focus will be on those aspects of teaching that can be exactly measured and objectively reported. The real and important difference between imaginative and unimaginative teaching is in danger of being lost unless those who supervise teachers and student teachers continue to believe that the distinction matters and can be identified in practice. Supervisors must be willing to exercise a keen sense of judgment to recognize and encourage those imaginative suggestions, ideas, and approaches that stimulate the students' sense of wonder.

Teachers need to be mindful of the ways in which the curriculum, assignments, and tests can work against the fostering of imagination in their students. In connection with the curriculum, for example, we can become so concerned about "engaged time" and counting the minutes spent on what is thought of as serious business, that wonder and imagination are undermined (Eisner 1991). A concern to cover the ground may mean that students have little time to wonder about the meaning and significance of what they are learning. The curriculum ought to engage students in the kind of inquiry that opens their minds to unanticipated possibilities, but too often it operates as a constraint. Richard Dawkins (2003) reports meeting excellent science teachers in the United Kingdom who felt unable to spend adequate time on the theory of evolution—"the staggering, mind-expanding truth"—because it only warrants a brief mention in the syllabus they are expected to follow (58). In a similar vein, Douglas Anderson (2002) recalls visiting a school that had a three-inch-thick binder to set out the 5th grade curriculum, replete with instructions on how to conduct discussions and how many minutes to spend on each topic (36). These are anecdotes, of course, but ones that turn up with disturbing frequency.

Regrettably, too, student assignments and activities are sometimes little more than busy work, such as the dull and deadly worksheets that still make an appearance. To use Passmore's (1967) distinction, such work consists of mere exercises that ignore the kind of problems that would invite imaginative and critical responses (206). Again, as Eisner (1991) reminds us, student learning is frequently dominated by tasks that demand the acquisition of conventional knowledge and skills rather than tasks that allow for distinctive and unique responses (16). If, by contrast, teachers can suggest questions, dilemmas, puzzles, projects, and investigations that are interesting, provocative, and novel, in which students have to use what they know in unspecified ways, they may challenge the students and excite their imagination. Such assignments make more demands on teachers, of course, because evaluating this kind of student work requires judgment and interpretation, and takes considerably more time to assess, and there is no simple, objective standard to appeal to if one's judgment is challenged. Nevertheless, if the goal of fostering imaginative work is important in education, teachers must allow for assignments that make it possible.

In discussing tests, Dawkins (2003) condemns what he calls "today's assessment-mad exam culture" which, he argues, undermines the joy of true education (60). Eisner (1991) points out that familiar assessment practices militate against the development of the imagination. Teachers need to avoid being so locked into particular anticipated responses that they cannot entertain some other answer to the question posed.[30] Standardized tests, for example, which permit only one correct response deprive students of the opportunity to articulate an idea they have, and also prevent teachers from trying to look imaginatively at the students' responses (see Eisner 1991: Sobocan, this volume).[31] If the tests we employ allow no scope for imaginative and critical responses, we can hardly claim that our aims of education take such ideas seriously; we show by our actions that we prefer conformity to innovative thinking, safe and prudent responses to courageous speculation.

The final word must go to John Passmore (1980), who did so much to make the cultivation of the imagination in conjunction with critical thinking a central aim of education: "To teach in a way which emphasises at once the need to be careful, to be critical, and to exercise the imagination is extraordinarily difficult....But the teacher cannot be satisfied with any lesser ambition....Imaginativeness, disciplined fancy, lies at the very centre of a free society" (163–4).

Notes

1. There are, of course, some notable exceptions. See, for example, Warnock (1976), and the various contributors to Egan and Nadaner (1988).

2. It would not be fair to say, as Egan and Nadaner do (1998, Introduction), that philosophers in general have viewed imagination as "a damaging intrusion upon logic" (xi). The point is rather that philosophers have been clear that imagination and logic have different roles to play. Even Ryle (1963) is said to have "helped assign low status to nondiscursive forms of thought in education" (xi). It was Ryle, however, who showed us that there are many different sorts of behaviour which we can perform imaginatively; one of his favourite examples was the imaginative and intelligent behaviour of the circus clown. It is hard to reconcile such an example with a "bias for strict order" or a reduction of productive thinking to testable propositions, as Egan and Nadaner allege (xii). If Ryle also saw a darker side to imagination, he saw no more than is true of any virtue or excellence.

3. For a sense of the interest in creativity at that time, see Freeman, Butcher, and Christie (1968).

4. I agree with Robin Barrow (1988) that the term "imaginative" cannot merely refer to unusual ideas or practices. The praise implicit in the term excludes the bizarre, the absurd, or the incoherent (unless, of course, the context makes these appropriate). In excluding them, however, I do not believe we have to build in the criterion of effectiveness, by which Barrow means "conducive to a good solution to or resolution of the task or problem at hand" (1988, 85). Often, proposed solutions may have great intuitive plausibility and generate much interest and excitement before they are eventually shown not to work. Why would we not regard those who advance them as imaginative?

5. Perhaps this is the place to dissociate myself from the view of Kieran Egan (1991) that John Dewey, in stressing the importance of building on the child's everyday experience, somehow generated pedagogical principles which neglect imaginative activity. It is clear enough, surely, that Dewey included imaginative activity *within* the everyday experience of the child: "Even when a person builds a castle in the air he is interacting with the objects which he constructs in fancy" (Dewey 1965, 44). The environment, Dewey insisted, is whatever conditions interact with an individual to create the experience.

6. Her claim is partly empirical, of course, though it would seem that the burden of her argument is that the very conception of critical thinking is at fault. An empirical case, in any event, could not plausibly be made in terms of two or three examples.

7. Kaplan refers to Maxine Greene (1983). "Critical pedagogy" is used here in its technical sense to refer to a movement inspired by the work of Paolo Freire.

8. Other examples of the "many questions" fallacy from the literature would include the following: (1) "Is God one person or three?" (White 1970, 186); (2) "Why must countries having a dictatorship of the proletariat practise democracy towards the people and impose dictatorship on the enemy?" (Dearden 1988, 174). Of course, White and Dearden are giving these as *examples* of the fallacy. Kaplan (1991) actually commits the fallacy herself when she invites the student to ask, "If 'guilt by association' is a fallacy, why do we usually use it successfully to make decisions?" (369). Do we? Furthermore, any logic course surely will make it clear that there is a difference between validity and truth.

9. Having mentioned the usefulness of studying fallacies, I should add that I have not been convinced by the current onslaught on this important aspect of the development of critical thinking skills. I provide some reasons in Hare (1982).

10. Kaplan (1991) seems unaware that she does just this herself! In charging Kahane (1988) with indoctrination, she speaks of evaluating his work by "using the questions he teaches students to ask of conservative politicians" (366). But if these questions raised by Kaplan really are critical, it seems that Kahane has been successful after all.

11. Philosophers are not reluctant to say that this is one of their fondest hopes. See, for example, R. Hare's remark about educators being pleased when students disagree with them (Hare 1964, 47–70).

12. It is not clear that Kaplan (1991) shares my optimism, because she quotes with approval Friedrich Pollock's pessimistic appraisal of "the average citizen" who succumbs to the pressure to accept the issues as defined (Pollack 1976, 229).

13. She means "hope" in the sense of "expect." Clearly she *wishes* to avoid bias.

14. Kaplan (1991) criticizes critical thinking for not encouraging students to go on to ask about the forces which have shaped the views of those we convict of being illogical. This is false. Consider the following from a primer on critical thinking:

> It is perfectly legitimate, at least from the standpoint of sound thinking, to raise and to pursue questions about interests and motivations. In particular it is innocuous, and it can be illuminating, to do this when the original issues of truth and validity have been settled....Yet it will not do— notwithstanding that it is all too often done—to offer more

or less speculative answers to such consequential questions
as a substitute for, rather than as a supplement to, the direct
examination of whatever were the prior issues. (Flew 1975,
63)

To apply this point to the present case, having shown that Kaplan's (1991)
argument is faulty, we could now go on to ask about the forces and motives which lie behind her work. That, however, is not germane to our
concerns here.

15. Even here, of course, it is easy to forget that people may have had at some
    point in their lives experiences remarkably similar to those normally as-
    sociated with other groups (Hare 1979). Hare's point is that, as a prisoner
    during the Second World War, he had worked "in conditions not *at the
    time* distinguishable from slavery" (109).

16. Walkling (1990) rightly condemns "a cultural solipsism which, as an ex-
    planation of the world, cannot even account for how persons are mutu-
    ally intelligible across cultures" (87).

17. Peter McGlynn, the schoolteacher in a short story by Mulkerns (1961),
    was able to bring Spain alive to the students even though he had never
    traveled.

18. This is not to say that there is no sense in which we *cannot* imagine certain
    things. Feynman (1964) makes the point that "whatever we are *allowed*
    to imagine in science must be *consistent with everything else we know....*We
    can't allow ourselves to seriously imagine things which are obviously in
    contradiction to the known laws of nature" (20). Feynman is speaking
    here of what is intellectually impossible *given certain assumptions*.

19. A point made memorably by Spinoza:

    > For no one under-estimates oneself by reason of self-hate,
    > that is, no one under-estimates himself in so far as he imag-
    > ines that he cannot do this or that. For whatever a man imag-
    > ines that he cannot do, he imagines it necessarily, and by that
    > very imagination he is so disposed that in truth he cannot do
    > what he imagines he cannot do. (*Ethics* Part 3, def. 28 trans.
    > Andrew Boyle)

20. One well-known instance of this view in the literature is in Nowell-Smith
    (1958, 8). A similar view had appeared in The Harvard Committee
    (1945), in which it was held that "in literature [the student's] imagination
    is stirred with vivid evocations of ideals of action, passion, and thought"
    (60).

21. Whitehead (1965) gets the point right when speaking of imagination

being disciplined by science: "Of course it involves only one specific type of imaginative functioning which is thus strengthened, just as poetic literature strengthens another specific type....we must not conceive the imagination as a definite faculty which is strengthened as a whole by any particular imaginative act of a specific type" (47).

22. Sometimes, indeed, their suggestions are imaginative by any standard. See, for example, some of the remarks of children reported by Ann Margaret Sharp in "What is a 'community of inquiry'?", in Hare and Portelli (1988).

23. Similar comments could be made about the teacher recognizing that students may see school itself as intimidating.

24. Dewey (1965) thought that the teacher "must...have that sympathetic understanding of individuals as individuals which gives him an idea of what is actually going on in the minds of those who are learning" (39).

25. Perhaps this negative reaction will prove less common as the philosophy for children movement convinces more and more teachers that even young children really can raise and consider serious philosophical questions (see Lipman 1988).

26. For an excellent discussion of the need for teachers to exercise judgment, see Anderson (2002).

27. It certainly reads as if it is this very intention which condemns one as unimaginative.

28. Eisner (1958, 179) makes the point, too, that the possession of familiar repertoires allows the teacher to notice emerging ideas in the classroom, thus permitting imaginative work.

29. One is put in mind of Whitehead's (1959, 37 and 96) famous definition of the teacher as "an ignorant man thinking," and also of his account of the function of the university as the imaginative acquisition of knowledge. A footnote to Aristotle perhaps?

30. This point is made in an amusing way by Calandra (1972, 4–6).

31. Nunn (1947) also reminded us that "it is fatally easy to condemn as contrary to beauty, truth or goodness what merely runs counter to our conservative prejudices" (42).

References

Anderson, D. 2002. Creative teachers: Risk, responsibility, and love. *Journal of Education* 181(1): 33–48.

Barrow, R. 1990. *Understanding skills: thinking, feeling and caring.* London, ON: The Althouse Press.

———. 1988. Some observations on the concept of imagination. In *Imagination and education*, ed. K. Egan and D. Nadaner, 79–90. New York:

Teachers College Press.

Burbules, N. 1990. The tragic sense of education. *Teachers College Record* 91(4): 469–79.

Calandra, A. 1972. Angels on a pin. In *Myth and reality*, ed. G. Smith and C. Knicker, 4–6. Boston: Allyn and Bacon.

Calisher, H. 1983. *Mysteries of motion*. New York: Doubleday.

Christopher, J. 1970 [1956]. *The death of grass*. Harmondsworth: Penguin.

Dawkins, R. 2003. *A devil's chaplain*. Boston: Houghton Mifflin.

Dearden, R. 1988. Controversial issues and the curriculum. In *Philosophy of education: Introductory readings*, ed. W. Hare and J. Portelli, 167–75. Calgary: Detselig.

Dewey, J. 1986. The need for a philosophy of education. In *John Dewey: The later works, 1925–1953*, Vol. 9, ed. J. Boydston, 194–204. Carbondale: Southern Illinois University Press.

———. 1985. How we think. In *John Dewey: The later works, 1925–1953*, Vol. 8, ed. J. Boydston, 105–352. Carbondale: Southern Illinois University Press.

———. 1984. Construction and criticism. In *John Dewey: The later works, 1925–1953*, Vol. 5, ed. J. Boydston, 125–43. Carbondale: Southern Illinois University Press.

———. 1976. The university elementary school. In *John Dewey: The middle works*, Vol. 1, ed. J. Boydston, 317–19. Carbondale: Southern Illinois University Press.

———. 1965. *Experience and education*. New York: Collier Macmillan.

———. 1956. *The child and the curriculum*. Chicago: University of Chicago Press.

Egan, K. 1991. Relevance and the romantic imagination. *Canadian Journal of Education* 16(1): 58–71.

Egan, K., and D. Nadaner, eds. 1988. *Imagination and education*. New York: Teachers College Press.

Eisner, E. 1991. What really counts in schools. *Educational Leadership* 48(5): 10–17.

———. 1985. *The educational imagination*, 2d ed. New York: Macmillan.

Ennis, R. 1987. A taxonomy of critical thinking dispositions and abilities. In *Teaching thinking skills: Theory and practice*, ed. J. Boykoff Baron and R. Sternberg, 9–26. New York: W.H. Freeman.

Feynman, R. 1964. *The Feynman lectures on physics*. Reading, MA: Addison-Wesley.

Flew, A. 1975. *Thinking about thinking*. Glasgow: Fontana/Collins.

Freeman, J., H. Butcher, and T. Christie. 1968. *Creativity: A selective review of research*. London: Society for Research into Higher Education.

Golding, W. 1954. *Lord of the Flies*. London: Faber & Faber.

Graves, D. 1983. *Writing: Teachers and children at work.* Portsmouth, NH: Heinemann.

Green, M. 1983. The humanities and emancipatory possibility. In *The hidden curriculum and moral education,* ed. H. Giroux and D. Purpel, 384–402. Berkeley, CA: McCutchan.

Hare, R. 1979. What is wrong with slavery? *Philosophy and Public Affairs* 8(2): 103–21.

———. 1964. Adolescents into adults. In *Aims in education,* ed. T. Hollins, 47–70. Manchester: Manchester University Press.

Hare, W. 1982. Review of McPeck's *Critical thinking and education. Canadian Journal of Education* 7(4): 107–10.

———. 1979. *Open-mindedness and education.* Montreal: McGill-Queen's University Press.

Hare, W., and J. Portelli, eds. 1988. *Philosophy of education: Introductory readings.* Calgary: Detselig.

Harvard Committee. 1945. *General education in a free society.* Cambridge, MA: Harvard University Press.

Hurka, T. 1989. Should whites write about minorities? *The Globe and Mail,* 19 December, A8.

Huxley, A. 1932. *Brave new world.* New York: Harper & Brothers.

Kahane, H. 1988. *Logic and contemporary rhetoric.* Belmont: Wadsworth.

Kaplan, L. 1991. Teaching intellectual autonomy: The failure of the critical thinking movement. *Educational Theory* 41(4): 361–70

Kelley, D. 1988. *The art of reasoning.* New York: Norton.

Lipman, M. 1988. *Philosophy goes to school.* Philadelphia, PA: Temple University Press.

Magee, B. 1982. *Men of ideas.* Oxford: Oxford University Press.

Massialas, B., and J. Zevin. 1983. *Teaching creatively: Learning through discovery.* Malabar, FL: Robert F. Krieger Publishing Co.

Mock, R. 1970. *Education and the imagination.* London: Chatto and Windus.

Mulkerns, V. 1961. The world outside. In *Man and his world,* ed. M. Ross and J. Stevens, 272–80. Toronto: J.M. Dent.

Nowell-Smith, P. 1958. *Education in a university.* Leicester: Leicester University Press.

Nunn, Sir Percy. 1947 [1920]. *Education: Its data and first principles.* London: Edward Arnold.

Passmore, J. 1980. *The philosophy of teaching.* London: Duckworth.

———. 1967. On teaching to be critical. In *The concept of education,* ed. R. Peters, 192–211. London: Routledge and Kegan Paul.

Pollock, F. 1976. Empirical research into public opinion. In *Critical sociology,* ed. P. Connerton. New York: Penguin.

Reid, L. 1962. *Philosophy and education.* London: Heinemann.

Russell, B. 1979. On keeping a wide horizon. *The Journal of Bertrand Russell Archives* 33–34: 5–11.

———. 1971 [1916]. *Principles of social reconstruction.* London: Unwin Books.

Ryle, G. 1963 [1949]. *The concept of mind.* Harmondsworth: Penguin.

Sagan, C. 1987. The burden of skepticism. *Skeptical Inquirer* 12(1): 38–46. Available online: http://www.positiveatheism.org/writ/saganbur.htm.

Solnicki, J. 1992. *The real me is gonna be a shock.* Toronto: Lester Publishing, Ltd.

Spinoza, B. 1959. *Ethics.* London: J.M. Dent.

Stebbing L. 1939. *Thinking to some purpose.* Harmondsworth: Penguin.

Straub D., ed. 1988. *Contemporary authors.* New Revision Series, Vol. 22. Detroit: Gale Research.

Toulmin, S., R. Rieke, and A. Janik. 1979. *An introduction to reasoning.* New York: Macmillan.

van Manen, M. 1991. *The tact of teaching.* London, ON: The Althouse Press.

Walkling, P. 1990. Multicultural education. In *Handbook of educational ideas and practices,* ed. N. Entwistle, 82–90. London: Routledge.

Warnock, M. 1996. The neutral teacher. In *Philosophy of education: Introductory readings,* 2d ed., ed. W. Hare and J. Portelli, 139–48. Calgary: Detselig.

———. 1976. *Imagination.* Berkeley, CA: University of California Press.

White, A. 1990. *The language of imagination.* Oxford: Basil Blackwell.

White, J. 1970. Indoctrination. In *The concept of education,* ed. R. Peters, 177–91. London: Routledge & Kegan Paul.

Whitehead, A. 1965. *A philosopher looks at science.* New York: Philosophical Library.

———. 1959. *The aims of education.* London: E. Benn.

Chapter Seven

The Critical in Arts-Based Inquiry: What Is It and Can It Be Assessed?

Cornelia Hoogland

*E*motion, passion, imagination, and caring have been acknowledged by some within the field of critical thinking to be components of a critical attitude (Siegel 1988, 40). This signals a change in position from the one that viewed the "reasonable person as one without emotion, and as one who 'turns off' her emotions while engaging in reason" (ibid.). Such an attitude, says Siegel, is untenable. Bailin et al. (1993) write that "creativity and critical thinking are frequently depicted as opposite sides of a coin: creativity is equated with creating or generating ideas, actions or objects, while critical thinking is equated with evaluating ideas, actions or objects" (6). Bailin et al. go on to argue that "thinking critically and being creative are profoundly interrelated" (ibid.). Creative thought (which I use interchangeably with imaginative and/or metaphoric thought) is also embodied in many of the identifiable skills and dispositions that make up critical thinking in *The Ontario Curriculum* (1999 and 2007 [revised]).

In this chapter I first examine how artistic processes can be conceptualized as a critical activity that shares functions with critical thinking. I do so by presenting these processes as they are found in arts-based inquiry, a form of scholarly inquiry that includes both cognitive and affective meaning-making and approaches. Indeed, I believe that artistic forms, rather than being ungoverned or unrestrained by logic (as they are commonly conceived to be), are composed of forms and conventions that can and do function critically. The methodology

151

of such inquiry encompasses a variety of phenomena, which include questions at the beginning of inquiry, aesthetic attention, the formation of a problem or research question, data collection in its various forms, the editing and shaping (and reshaping) of the work, and the final performance/product. This examination of arts-based inquiry depends upon at least three areas of study: (1) the "field" of imaginative inquiry, (2) some of the processes involved in arts-based inquiry from the point of view of my own writing, and (3) imagination's evaluative capacity.

In section two of the chapter, I will illustrate the implications for critical thinking and creative thinking in an examination of the processes of arts-based inquiry that informed my recent literary work *Cuba Journal: Language and Writing* (2003; for another discussion of this work see Hoogland 2004). Placing my own literary work in the context of critical thinking is a productive exercise because it puts poetry in the context of research activity, with the hope of convincing educators and theorists to take the concept of imagination seriously. If theorists such as Bailin et al. (1993) believe imagination has a capacity for critical thought, then it seems appropriate that the concept be fully investigated and subsequently presented to teachers to inform their teaching and evaluation. My hope is to broaden the discussion of critical thinking, and of literature as well. Of course, I respectfully leave to theorists the task of evaluating my account of imaginative thinking and writing for its usefulness to their areas of study.

In section three, I argue that creative writing (imaginative writing) embodies many of the identifiable skills and dispositions that make up critical thinking, at least as they are enumerated in *The Ontario Curriculum* (1999 and 2007 [revised]). I hope to alert the reader to potential areas of commonality between the creative processes of arts-based inquiry and the critical processes of critical thinking and to discuss how arts-based inquiry can be best assessed by teachers and students in the classroom. In the course of that discussion of portfolio assessment, I hope to contribute to an understanding of the questions about critical thinking and assessment that motivated this volume.

An underlying claim of this work is that, wherever possible, human insights (knowledge) should be informed by direct, sensory experience. Arnheim (1969) says that "the cognitive operations called thinking are not a privilege of mental processes above and beyond perception but the essential ingredients of perception itself" (13). Ideally, the language that we use to compose even our most reasonable thoughts will reflect or embody that sense of physical engagement with the world.

Critical Thinking and Arts-Based Inquiry

Discussion of the relationship between the artist (or creative thinker) and the critical thinker—between the processes of arts-based inquiry and critical thinking—begins with understanding something of the nature of critical thinking. One of the key contributors to critical thinking (and to the controversies surrounding this subject) is Robert H. Ennis. He writes, "critical thinking is a process, the goal of which is to make reasonable decisions about what to believe and what to do" (1996, xvii). Most critical thinking theorists in this volume believe that the critical thinking process encompasses a set of skills or dispositions, or both.[1]

The skills emphasized by critical thinking theorists include both the ability to carefully interpret communications and arguments and the ability to evaluate and analyze information. In the latter case this implies, in particular, the ability to recognize bias, insufficient evidence, assumptions, and credibility (Pinto, Blair, and Parr 1993; Scriven and Fisher 1997; Groarke and Tindale 2008). Because critical thinking involves the construction as well as the analysis of reasoning and knowledge, critical skills include the ability to ask well-formulated questions and to support one's own interpretations, judgments, arguments, and answers with evidence or good reasons (Siegel 1988; Paul and Elder 2005).

In both the analysis and construction of arguments, critical thinking almost always requires analyzing and deciding the strength of the reasons for one's conclusions and appeals to authority; knowing when a reason is relevant; knowing when there are enough reasons to adequately support a conclusion or interpretation, i.e., having the ability to make valid, sound, or plausible inferences; qualifying conclusions appropriately; and attending to objections and other arguments or perspectives (Siegel 1988; Johnson and Blair 1995; Ennis 1996).

Creative or imaginative thought, on the other hand, is often described as the capacity to think of things that are at present unseen and unconsidered and that do not necessarily follow from logical or straightforward (reasonable) thought. Imagination is the ability to leap beyond the borders of conventional thought and to explore outside the box. Green (1995) states that imagination is the ability "to look at things as if they could be otherwise." Egan (1997) extends this definition considerably by explaining the difference between received images and concepts, and their incorporation into one's understanding:

> Imagination is what enables…transcendence, and is consequently necessary to education. It is important because transcending the conventional is necessary to constructing one's sense of any area of knowledge; accepting conventional representation is to fail to make knowledge one's own, is to keep it inert rather than incorporate it into one's life. (48)

It is the intersection of moving from received concepts and images to making them one's own, and thereby potentially furthering those concepts or images, that I wish to discuss. More specifically, I intend to discuss answers to the following questions: What are the processes and attitudes involved in generating new thoughts and novel ideas? Can people trust their perceptions and their emotions when they are taught not to? And lastly, how does imagination fit into critical thought?

The "Fields" of Inquiry

For the majority of informal logicians, argumentation theorists (mainly philosophers), and educators, critical thinkers have not only skills, but also one or many critical thinking dispositions, also referred to as habits of mind, tendencies, or character traits. A critical thinker is someone who consistently tries to understand others' opinions (Facione 1990, 25); "honestly evaluate[s] alternatives" (Hatcher, this volume); formulates or seriously explores alternative explanations or multiple views (Ennis 1996; Hatcher 2000; Hare, this volume); is fair minded and admits what he or she does not know (Paul and Elder 2005); is open minded (Case, this volume); and is reflective and self evaluative (Paul and Elder 2005; Hoagland 1995).[2] Ennis (1996) captures some key aspects of these dispositions when he says that critical thinkers are thinkers who care both about developing ideas and about other people in that they care about "getting things right," and about "the worth and dignity of others" (xviii). He argues that to be good at critical thinking, critical thinkers must care in the sense that they "discover and listen to others' views and reasons...[and] take into account others' feelings and level of understanding" (9).

Fair-mindedness and caring, as described above, involve empathy. Humans cannot choose between one act and another, and certainly cannot care, without being emotionally involved. Empathy is an emotional, imaginative process. We feel with, or for, somebody else. We try to see things from his or her point of view. We cannot do this without extending beyond our own frame of reference and incorporating the new framework into our own. Once otherness is within us, so to speak, we can begin to experience it, to tease out how we feel about it, how it feels to us. Siegel (1998) writes that a critical thinker is one who is "appropriately moved by reasons" (32). This is an imaginative act.

Other critical thinkers have more openly conjoined imaginative thought and critical thinking. I have already mentioned Bailin et al. (1993). Egan (1992) links imagination and rationality when he says that "the ability to hold alternative conceptions in the mind" (an imaginative act) "and assess their adequacy or appropriateness" (a critical act) "would seem a necessary component of any sophisticated rational activity" (42). Both activities are worthwhile and, it would seem, mutually supportive (Sobocan in this volume, for example, supports such a claim). To my knowledge, most discussions of imaginative acts within critical thinking end there. It seems to be enough to say that students should, and do, think imaginatively within critical thought. The problem, as I understand it, is that whereas critical thinking is taught, rather than assumed, in schools and most certainly at the university level, imaginative thinking is not.

Let me explain. To make reasoned calculations, students are taught to avoid arbitrariness, are given criteria by which to evaluate an argument or make a judgment, or shown the means by which to create criteria of their own. They are taught how to avoid generalizations and how to support their arguments. Once students have moved beyond the elementary grades, however, they are rarely taught, or even encouraged, to consider topics imaginatively or, put differently, to consider topics from aspects of the psyche other than the rational, everyday ones. For instance, Grade 12 history teachers usually do not ask students to fantasize the events of the war of 1812. Imaginative thought initially takes learners in directions startlingly opposite from the stated curriculum outcomes or goals (in the history example above, imaginative thought would presumably lead students away from the facts of war). Frye (1990) gives a more thorough explanation, saying that ordinary consciousness (i.e., the facts) "is only one of many possible psychic elements" that comprise our responses (22). The metaphoric language of all explorations of thought (what if, let's suppose, etc.) is the most primitive mode of thought and speech in that "the distinction between the emotional and the intellectual has disappeared" and "subject and object are eliminated, in that everything is potentially identifiable with everything else" (ibid.). Imaginative thought and expression, as used in the metaphoric language of poems and stories, depend "on a half-voluntary, half-involuntary, integration of the conscious will with other factors in the psyche, factors connected with fantasy, dreaming, let's pretend, and the like" (99). Fantasy indeed. Try passing dreaming by a critical thinker.[3]

Through its often convoluted route, imaginative thought does eventually settle into a form, be it a poem or story. Frye (1990) says that the metaphoric language of which these genres are composed is valuable because it brings to consciousness, within a temporal sequence of events, complex situations and ideas. And if it is a good, thought-provoking work, it brings attention to itself as a mode of expression that has to do with "a more open-ended world, breaking apart the solidified dogmas that ideologies seem to hanker for" (22). In other words the vestiges of the convoluted pathways of imaginative thinking persist in the critical thinking process.

The dilemma raised here is whether curriculum makers and educators, understanding the implications of imaginative thought, will pay it more than lip service. This issue goes far beyond the confines of this monograph, or even the concerns of my critical thinking colleagues. But let me put aside my momentary doubts, and assume that critical thinkers do want to include imaginative thought among their concepts. How might they, or we, start to think imaginatively? Allow me, from my perspective, to try to explain. I will first present imaginative thought as I experience it—as moving from (and between) perception and language (in other words, intensely close-up)—and then I will broaden the lens to place imaginative thought within literary conventions, methods, and genres.

Much like the feminist theorist who observes the world through the lens of gender and power, so the artist (in my case, the writer) experiences the world in tiny bites and through certain sustained desires. Those experiences include isolating discrete lines and phrases, trying them out (loud), letting them drum in the head all day, and trying to pick up associations; making notes and eavesdropping on conversations at the next table; continually creating metaphors (how can this be understood in terms of that?); alerting oneself to the context in which an experience is happening (as I walk, head bent, thinking about how I feel, dry leaves scratch the sidewalk). Inevitably, the image—that I am only half-aware that I am looking for (leaves)—is the image that distinguishes itself from the river of data swirling past. The image in turn informs me about my feelings; what I see is inextricably connected to language. "Oh," I say to myself, "I'm sad. I didn't know that I missed my dog." These events may happen over the course of a day or a month. Both in terms of time and approach, they are remarkably different from the more linear activity, for example, of making two lists to determine the pros and cons of a particular viewpoint. It is as if my soul casts its line into the world, and fishes for the external image that resonates with, and expresses, the inward experience. And if I hook an image as it leaps out of the river, my writerly net of conventions is ready. The whole thing is a miracle.[1] Every time.

To reduce the above paragraph to a personal, subjective observation of one person's feeling of sadness would be most unfortunate. But I believe that is how imaginative thought has been traditionally perceived; as wildly free-flowing, impulsive, non-directional, and above all, personal. I argue that the above paragraph is about thinking as well as about articulating experience. Thus, it is more useful to note, for instance, that perception itself is potentially verbal, as illustrated in the phrase, "I wonder if," and might be formulated in the above paragraph as, "I wonder about these leaves." Frye (1990) says that "any perception that leads directly to reflection must be a verbalizing impulse from the beginning: the ordering of words does not suddenly appear in the middle of the process" (7). The implications for the connection between sensory input and thinking for this present discussion are large. At the least it questions the origins of thought (how humans create thoughts). If the above acts of aesthetic attention—observation and perception—are conceived of as a way of thinking, or a means of knowledge, it may follow that they should be taught not just within the context of artistic practice or inquiry processes but also, as Bailin et al. (1993) suggest, seriously within the context of a critical thinking process.

In the above discussion, I have tried to show how imaginative thought works at the level of thought and perception. I have framed it within the need for educators and theorists to take imagination seriously. I would now like to set it within a larger framework of conventions, methodology, and the structure of *Cuba Journal*, an individual work of art.

Cuba Journal: A Case Study

If imaginative thought enables us to think beyond conventional concepts, as Egan (1999) suggests, then we can consider in detail its evaluative possibilities.[5] I would like to push this further by suggesting that it is the seemingly non-rational, non-linear aspects of these imaginative acts that enable us to weigh and evaluate. At first glance this seems contradictory, but it is such imaginative acts that enable people to step outside conventional concepts, to see from different points of view. I hope to show how *Cuba Journal* enacts such evaluation through entering an imaginative landscape in which writers play with nonsense, fantasy, leaping (rather than linear) movements among thoughts, emotional through-lines, point of view, trustworthiness of the narrator, metonymy, metaphor, and sideways or associative thinking.

Poetic works interrupt the usual condition—the daily routine of life—to reinvigorate us. They estrange the familiar and, conversely, make the strange familiar. Poetry does this at the level of language; interrupting the expected or dominant (usually linear) order of words to wake us not just to the wonder and mystery of life, but to its reality. Poetry taps into the vigour of language and uses that energy to alert humans to their experiences in the world (this flower, that building), or as Egan (1999) says, integrates conventional thought with our experience. This energy is palpable, and useful in not only questioning, but also in comprehending and evaluating human experiences in the world. It helps us (and our students) sustain interest in our work.

The framework for this case study includes an introductory account of *Cuba Journal* and an account of the four stages of arts-based inquiry and the dispositions and skills that accompany each stage. The four stages are (1) Originating impulse: Finding the artistic problem; (2) Aesthetic attention: Data collection and reformulating the problem; (3) Editing and evaluation: Creating a work of art; and (4) Performance: Understanding genre and context. I hope that the case analysis will illuminate more concretely how the critical aspects of my own artistic journcy are related to critical thinking as I have discussed it above. I do not claim that all creative works are critical (self-absorbed and undisciplined writing exists in all genres), and imaginative writing is no exception. In any event, there is no one way forward; advances in human thought have always been sporadic and unpredictable and the same holds true for our personal journeys into artistic and/or scholarly mature thought.

What is Cuba Journal?

Let me begin by describing something of the origins and content of *Cuba Journal*. These origins are signalled by the hand-written journal entries on the front and back pages of the book. In the process of its creation, and of its achieving its own voice or style, the book tried on many genres, and so exists at the intersection of a variety of them: fiction, poetry, travel writing, and journal writing. Each new version of the book informed the final work, shaping it in genre-specific ways. The final product/performance of the work aims to let the reader/listener hear a personal journey—with its human (human includes critical) themes, dilemmas, and concerns—in poetic form.

In *Cuba Journal* a number of the story lines are cast competitively along gender lines. Will the stereotypical male dominate? Will the myth of the Latin lover be played out? Will, and should, the narrator fall for Ernesto, the linguistics student? Other conflicts range in intensity, from native–tourist relations, to what the revolution means today. Is Castro's revolution still alive or have socialist ideals changed in light of tourism, market economies, and the incredible pressure on Cubans to obtain the advantaged American dollars? Fundamental themes of love and power, as well as high stakes, danger, problems, and tensions partly compose good works of literature; these have not changed since we started writing down stories. What I want to highlight here, however, is the story's (or poem's) form. I want to draw attention not just to what the work says, but to how it says it. Both involve critical elements.

For instance, a reading of the first page of *Cuba Journal* might go something like this (I have placed quotes from *Cuba Journal* in italics followed by parentheses that contain the reader's imagined response):

> *Two things happened* (Events suggest a story, the text is asking whether I want to hear a story) *to me* (The events happened to the narrator) *that made me reconsider* (The narrator changes—there is character growth in this story) *the turbulent vastness of language that can be spoken, scratched in dirt, bloodied onto walls, written, stuttered, gestured, sung* (There are actually many stories here—some dangerous, some embarrassing.). *The first event* (Here we go...what happens next?) *was misreading a sign* (An unreliable narrator? Who is telling this story?) *hammered into a tree in the gully behind Julie's grandparent's place* (Who is Julie? Even though we don't know her, we have a sense of the setting for this story, and that's good, we want to know where we are). *I read "No Writing," when the sign actually said something else entirely* (This is weird, is this narrator weird?).

Within the next three pages the reader learns the mystery of the No Writing sign, is introduced to memoir writing and feminist ideas, and spends one full day (page) in the gully where, within the context of an actual physical world, the ideas of language and writing are given fuller play. On page five a more conventional story (characters, plot, and place) is outlined and a second "event" is related—it appears that the reader can trust the narrator to keep her promises—but then again, "falling into the ocean," although an event, is not normally associated with learning about language. A puzzle is introduced: How is falling into the ocean like learning how to relate to, or understand, language?

My travel to Cuba, and the performance of my findings in *Cuba Journal*, are a form of research. My aim in writing and editing *Cuba Journal* was to gain a better understanding of Cuban–Canadian relations, gender relations, orality as literacy, writing as literacy, my literary foremothers, and something of the lives and desires of several Cubans whom I came to know. Perhaps more conventional methods of research could have achieved an understanding similar to that in the finished book, but I think not. The nature of what I could understand evolved from being in an artistic field and using the tools of my practice. This required that I be attentive to my surroundings, to myself in my surroundings (my physical experience), and to others within the framework of political and cultural, as well as language and artistic, concerns.

Originating impulse: Open-ended questioning

Because *Cuba Journal* is a book about travel, and because my work as an arts-based researcher has parallels with the best notions of what it means to travel, there is opportunity for metaphor here. In *The Tempest* (1942, Act I, Scene II, 282), Shakespeare's main character, Viola, lands on the shores of Illyria and asks, "What shall I do in Illyria?" Her first act is to question her purpose and name the place in which she has set foot. In this open-ended way, Viola invites response from the place itself. Her question embodies the spirit and form of artistic research.

But travelling comes in many forms and requires further definition. My travelling metaphor is based upon an alert and socially aware traveller. In reality, however, each traveller intersects with the place and culture to which he or she travels in accordance with the arrangements made prior to the travel. Backpackers have one experience; luxury hotel guests have another. Elderly or disabled travellers would each have different experiences in accordance with their particular situations.

So it is with different research paradigms that foreground certain kinds of questions and desired experiences, and devalue others. At the beginning of my own arts-based inquiry I ask, metaphorically speaking, "Where am I?" This open-ended quality distinguishes artistic inquiry from the predetermined questions and hypothesized outcome of conventional scientific inquiry (and perhaps a standard critical thinking process, although an attempt to think critically about an issue can involve the open-ended consideration of it). While the narrator of *Cuba Journal* calls herself a tourist, her adventure is set apart from the packaged and predictable tourist experiences in which a predigested experience is bestowed upon the guest.

My trip to Cuba in 1998 was structured as a series of informal meetings with people and visits to institutions—a family doctor, an outdoor education centre, a classroom teacher and her students, small towns—and not as a research trip. But the place and the people attracted me, and I wrote copious notes in my journal (collecting data). Given the open-ended nature of the artist's questions in the first stage, initial data collection is quite unsystematic. It is more like the meander that accompanies a critical thinker's first investigation of a topic rather than the focused examination of the logic of already specified reasons and conclusions. In its first manifestation as journal entries, *Cuba Journal* was spontaneous, erratic, and sporadic: literally all over the page, scratched while I leaned against my bicycle on the sides of roads, in restaurants, or in the plaza central.

But I felt strongly engaged with being on an island (my home is Vancouver Island), and with the ocean (also familiar). I believe that in the artful and industrious relationships Cubans have to place and work (such as their desire to achieve, and their ability to live by their wits and to make do and never give up) I recognize something of my parents' own immigrant disposition. The physical and emotional familiarity—affective reactions—might be compared to Ennis's caring disposition. I cared to deeply understand and get right what I understood about Cuba, its people, and my relationship to them.

These background emotional factors prepared me to really hear and try to carefully understand the significance of what happened next.

Aesthetic attention: Data collection and reformulating the problem

It was the questions of a young man in a small Cuban town in 1998 that grabbed my attention and gave me my focus.

"You are writing."

I look up, squint through the light shaft that falls around a young Cuban man poised in front of me.

"You are writing," he says.

"Yes," I say, holding up my journal to him. "I'm writing."
(Hoogland 2003, 31)

This apparently insignificant yet nevertheless challenging incident was the originating impulse of *Cuba Journal*. There were many questions that followed on the heels of the Cuban's simple yet jarring observation. What did this young man see as I bent over my black journal, chewing my pen, and writing? What are the effects of such acts? Where do they occur and not occur? Cuban society is highly literate, yet as I looked around (for the first time as it were), there was little evidence of text or signs in the square of the small town where I sat writing.

In this challenge to my foundational understanding of literacy I had found my artistic problem. I was mistaken about what I thought self-evident about writing, about Cubans, about...what else? I saw myself as an expert in the area of literacy and it was suddenly clear to me that I had taken my daily, literate actions for granted.

Perhaps being jarred out of complacency had to do with neither imaginative nor critical thought—at least not in any instrumentalized sense. Instead, it was my being present to an artistic inquiry that was important. I was open to experience, including re-evaluating my assumptions. Later, back home, I could critically weigh my experience, but here, in Cuba, critical looking was a matter of "look again, look more carefully." The formal evaluative aspects of arts-based research would appear in the editing process when I consciously incorporated a number of views of literacy, informed by questions such as, "If Cuban/Canadian notions of achieving literacy were vastly different, what other differences were making themselves known to me?" But in my role as a writer, the spirit of inquiry (disposition) opened me to self-doubt as well as perception. I began to notice the differences among the Canadian tourists, gender differences within the group, and the same considerations cross-culturally.

But mainly I continued writing in my journal, unaware of any larger patterns and significance. It was only when I returned home and was working with my notes (data) that I began to reformulate my core writing concerns. This stage of my work requires that I select the data (descriptions of sights, smells, experiences, events, people) for what will best illuminate my intentions about this particular work. Here the literacy issue would be identified, along with the travelling and swimming metaphors, as well as the rhythms of the work (which emulate the waves of the sea). Once I recognized literacy as a focus of my research, other foci became more obvious.

Editing and evaluation: Creating a work of art

Although the content stayed roughly the same, the various versions of the book required different aspects to be emphasized, reformulated, and realized. Once I was home, it also required library searches and much reading. Upon reworking, the journal entries became, as they often do, the hearts of poems. These heart-kernels called out for more detail, which I recollected or researched, focusing on correcting or detailing such things as dates, spelling, order of events, and generally ensuring historical, geographical, and political accuracy.

In the course of finding the foci and working my way to the final version of the book, I decided that I wanted these loosely connected poems to create a stronger plot line. This required connections that joined events, whether events-in-time, character development, or emotional shifts. The poems *flattened* (as it were) into prose-poems, a form more able to carry narrative continuity as well as tension.

Integral parts of the process of creating *Cuba Journal* were a caring disposition and an engagement in self-evaluation. Because I cared about my subject, I needed to know how I felt about my subjects. This required evaluating those feelings, as well as shaping them into what I felt was the inherent appeal of the book. What literary methods, strategies, and conventions could achieve my idea of what makes this particular work special to myself and to others? Evaluation of the data for patterns also led to selection of genre, informed the ordering of concepts, and shaped the material into themes, or said differently, synthesized the data.

Performance: Understanding genre and context

Art is about gathering our own, as well as getting other people's attention. Poets who say that they write poems to find out what they think and feel about a subject have found a way of getting and sustaining their own attention, and if the poem is successful, the attention of others. In stage three, the strategies chosen for the work were chosen to appeal to others by making the work mutually intelligible. If I write merely to satisfy myself, I will have a readership of one (perhaps two). The requirements of one's audience provide a critical framework within which the artist works. Poets are usually keenly interested in accessibility and the responses of their viewers or listeners.

In their account of critical thinking Groarke and Tindale (2008) emphasize the principle of communication that underlies critical thinking. The second principle they enumerate emphasizes that we must, in interpreting the performance of any "speech act" (including non-verbal speech acts), interpret "in a way that fits the context in which it occurs" (54). In performing speech acts critical thinkers have a corresponding obligation to the aesthetic dimensions of the subject or problem under investigation. The work of critical thinkers must also fit the context (and so audience) in which it occurs. In this regard performance from either field of inquiry can be said to involve a critical concern for intelligibility and context.

The main aspect of performance that informs my writing, however, is the material understanding that writers bring to language. Critical thinkers are taught that the purpose of language is to communicate, but for writers, words are alive. They are emotional and they connote worlds of meaning beyond their letters. (If, for example, within the context of a drama exercise I ask my students to say "I love you" to a classmate, some invariably cannot complete the task). Words are physical presences in our mouths and our bodies. When performance is part of the writing process writers pay close attention to words for meaning and sound. (Of course, sound is meaning.) As they write, poets listen to the stress they put onto each word and each phrase. This helps them decide where to pause, where to make the line-break, the appropriate use of punctuation, and where to scrunch the line in order to release it into the open field of the next line.

This discussion of *Cuba Journal* has in part been about language and modes of discourse, as well as what counts as critical language and as metaphoric language, and the larger frameworks within which the two can intersect. I have examined *Cuba Journal* for its metaphoric language and the literary conventions and structures that house it. I have tried to demonstrate the implications of including imagination and its metaphoric constructs into critical thinking. Although it would seem the two forms of discourse remain worlds apart, I believe that the discussion about portfolio assessment that follows might help to align the two fields in mutually supportive ways. Central to this attempt is the need for clarity about the disparate language modes that inform critical and creative thought.

In the opening section of this chapter I stated that one of my underlying claims is that human insights must be informed by direct, sensory experience. This is not to disparage critical thinking concepts such as abstract thought, mental processes, or principled thinking, but,

rather to take seriously Arnheim (1969), who said that "the cognitive operations called thinking are not a privilege of mental processes
above and beyond perception but the essential ingredients of perception itself" (13). Ideally, the language that we use to compose even our
most reasonable thoughts will reflect or embody that sense of physical
engagement with the world. This continues to be a major concern, but
one that goes well beyond the limited scope of this chapter.

Assessing Arts-Based Inquiry

Cuba Journal demonstrates many general cognitive capacities: spatial
reasoning (conceptual ordering of ideas), conditional reasoning (where
necessary I was able to adjust my thinking before I moved forward in
my writing), imagination and invention (I visualized new relational
possibilities among people), creative thinking (the diverse subject matters and contexts that I sequenced and balanced), and lastly, symbolic
interpretation (without understanding codes I could not have interpreted them).

　　If it is accepted that my research has parallels with the kinds of
research tasks required of students in schools, several questions arise.
How might teachers assess both the critical thinker and the artist in
terms of attentiveness or caring? How can teachers assess the care the
artist takes to attend to detail and nuance with respect to both context
(Groarke and Tindale 2004) and others (Ennis 1996; Ellett and Pitman,
this volume)? What is the best way to assess students' open-mindedness (in the sense that implies that they actively imagine alternatives
and engage in self-evaluation)?

　　In his article "Assessment Strategies for Secondary Classrooms," Case (2008) discusses portfolio assessment as a way in which
language arts teachers can assess more than the ability of students to
recall information. A portfolio is a self-selected, albeit limited, com-
pilation of work. It offers opportunities for reflection and revision by
students, and can be directed toward the construction or creation of a
culminating work or performance. I will talk about portfolios within
the language arts curriculum; however, the portfolio can be used in
other subject areas as well. The varied purposes the portfolio can serve
depend upon the individual needs of classes, teachers, and students.
Please note that this is an outline rather than a thorough elaboration of
portfolios and their assessment. Any one of the processes or attitudes
to which I refer is in itself a complex aspect of portfolio assessment

worthy of individual study and application.

Case and Stipp (2008) say that "portfolio assessment draws heavily on the practices of artists and designers, who carefully assemble samples that represent key characteristics of their work for use in demonstrating particular competencies to others" (393). The basic idea of portfolios—that students collect and shape the ideas gathered there into a theme or artwork that relates to both their personal experiences and their classroom learning—is roughly comparable to my journal writing, and later in my process, my more formal research, as well as reflection and reassessment over time. I believe that portfolio assessment can also be understood in terms of the four different stages of the arts-based inquiry process that I described above. I will support my understanding by referring to Ontario curriculum documents.

The Ontario Curriculum

The Ontario Curriculum (1999 and 2007 [revised]) echoes Ennis (1996) when it defines critical thinking as "the process of thinking about ideas or situations in order to understand them fully, identify their implications, and/or make a judgment about what is sensible or reasonable to believe or do" (Grades 1–8, Language Explanatory Notes). Along with judgment, students are expected to learn how to use many of the cognitive capacities I described as critical in my own arts-based inquiry. Among them are the capacity to

> [l]isten [or hear] in order to understand and respond appropriately in a variety of situations for a variety of purposes; use speaking skills and strategies appropriately to communicate with different audiences for a variety of purposes; and to reflect on and identify their strength as listeners and speakers, areas for improvement, and the strategies they found most helpful in oral communication situations. (Ontario Curriculum 2006)

The relationship between judgment (Ennis's critical thinking) and creative inquiry (*Cuba Journal*) emerges in *The Ontario Curriculum Achievement Charts* (2004) rubrics for evaluation purposes entitled "Thinking/Inquiry" where thinking is said to be "[t]he use of critical and creative thinking skills and/or processes" (6). This definition suggests that teachers are expected, in the course of judging both thinking and inquiry, to assess or evaluate critical and creative thinking in their students, and presumably, also to teach these diverse modes of thought. The evaluation of thinking and inquiry is explicitly broken down into "planning skills (focusing research, gathering information, organizing an inquiry); processing skills (analyzing, evaluating, synthesizing); and critical/creative thinking processes (inquiry, problem solving, decision making, research)" (*The Ontario Curriculum (Draft)* 2004, Grades 1–12 Achievement Charts). All of these components are easily associated with both arts-based inquiry and critical thinking as I describe them in this chapter.

Elsewhere in the curriculum, there is a difference in the quality of the verbs used to describe creative as opposed to critical thinking acts. The favoured verbs associated with creative acts and critical thinking can be seen in the lists below.

Creative acts	Critical thinking
imagine	react
invent	describe
alter	interpret
improve	judge
germinate	think
compose	understand
arrange	identify
edit	believe
elaborate	do
evaluate	question
	hypothesize
	infer
	analyze
	compare
	contrast
	evaluate
	predict
	reason
	distinguish
	synthesize
	detect

These groups of verbs suggest that the clearest distinction between the act of being creative and the act of critical thinking is precisely that noted by Bailin et al. (1993)—that the creative act generates data of some sort, and that the critical act applies skills to a specific task, an event, or an artifact already existing in the world. Also, both are implicated in evaluation.

Indeed, the only verb that appears in both the creative and critical thinking sections of the curriculum is "evaluate." This is a significant overlap, but many more cross-over verbs can be added, especially when one recognizes that the act of critical thinking may be the act of creating and constructing arguments or opinions and is not limited to the analysis of pre-existing arguments. Considered from this point of view, most of the verbs the Ontario curriculum uses to describe creative acts might be applied to critical thinking, including, "invent," "alter," "improve," "germinate," "compose," "arrange," and "edit." Because the creative process can be understood—as the above arts-based inquiry makes clear—as a process that in part includes identifying a problem, collecting data, and then refining one's answer to the problem through editing and self-evaluation or meta-cognition, most of the verbs the curriculum applies to critical thinking can in principle be applied to arts-based inquiry:

react	describe	analyze	interpret
judge	think	understand	identify
believe	do	question	hypothesize
infer	compare	contrast	evaluate
predict	reason	distinguish	synthesize
elaborate	detect		

In this document, two essential components shared by critical thinking and arts-based inquiry are "imagining" and "evaluating." In both cases, evaluation and especially self-evaluation (and the "editing" this implies) are the crux of a normative act that can be criticized or judged as successful or unsuccessful, as good or unconvincing. Both cases depend on the student's abilities to imagine and seek out alternative points of view, such as the perspectives of those with different values and beliefs, or thoughts that are newly invented as the result of the student's caring response to a conflict or problem. In both cases the process of inquiry is characterized by caring: both about other people and their views (most obviously, but not only, one's audience) and caring in the sense that implies careful interpretation and attention to detail. The critical thinker or inquirer (in my case, artist as researcher), furthermore, is disposed to use these skills consistently across contexts: the personal, social, political, and intellectual contexts in which they are located.

Originating impulse

The most surprising critical thinking verb used in the curriculum documents is "react." As any high school teacher or university instructor can confirm, intelligent reactions from students are valuable and hard-won commodities. Teaching students to collect relevant data and react critically or respond intelligently—obviously so integral to critical thinking—teaches them how to connect with the originating impulse, such as the one that motivates an arts-based inquiry. However, students must react to something or somebody. Endless possibilities for such an initiating artifact or problem exist; in the case of *Cuba Journal*, journal writing was a response to travel. In language arts, students react (or respond—a more holistic term) to aesthetic artifacts such as stories, plays, novels, and poems, which intend to elicit response. Their metaphoric language invites a response that reflects or embodies a sense of physical engagement with the world. The portfolio requires such rich prerequisites to inquiry to which students can respond by using a broad array of conventions such as notes, audio and video tapes, diaries, drawings, essays, poems, photos, doodles, computer downloads, blogs and wikis, and so forth.[6] Students should be encouraged to make contributions to the portfolio that make sense of their responses and of their artistic or critical problem, once they find it. Teacher feedback, especially in helping students find their research problems, is an integral part of portfolio assignments.

Aesthetic attention

Case and Stipp (2008) explain that portfolios allow for, among other things, reflection "in collaboration with peers,...[for] analyzing patterns or key features, [and] diagnosing strengths and problem areas" (394). Consistent student and peer reviews of various portfolio products and of the portfolio process itself enable students to experience and analyze reactions; to express and analyze their personal relationship to data; to include their sensory responses (sight, sound, taste, touch, and feel) to the data; and to consider other views (aspects of arts-based inquiry which are difficult to capture in standard tests). Portfolios can recognize the complexity of problems and can encompass more than one answer to a question or problem (see Pinto and Portelli, this volume), and certainly more than one view. As contributions to the portfolio are added over time, they can be used to assess students' dispositions as they (hopefully) show their careful reflection on their previous responses and developments.

Editing and evaluating

By making contributions to a portfolio over time (both older and newer versions of works are kept in the portfolio), students have the opportunity to improve or deepen their understanding. Students are "...expected to report (orally or in writing) on what they observe about their learning and to recommend a plan of action" (Case and Stipp 2008, 394). The reporting should always include evaluation of each stage of the inquiry or artistic process, and will include discussion on aspects of editing. Editing can improve the work (a critique[7] can inform the ways in which students can improve and shape their data, formulate themes, etc.) but also teaches self-evaluation through responses to feedback from teachers and peers. With peer evaluation as part of the portfolio exercise, Case and Stipp (2008) encourages respect for others' points of view (an important aspect of critical thinking that ought to be evaluated—see Ellett and Pitman in this volume). Students can listen, reflect, and use feedback to address problems or gaps in previous understandings and performances. Improving portfolio contributions moves the student beyond entry-level interpretation to critical interpretation and critical self-evaluation. A teacher can assess whether students care to fine-tune their work, and care to deepen their understanding, by noting when they take advantage of opportunities to respond to feedback, i.e., to improve previous entries. Thus, the reflections students and teachers engage in, both individually and as a group, are not limited to one-time responses, actions, and performances. Rather, students and teachers also reflect upon the learning process as a whole and, throughout the exercise, learn how to assess. This allows students to deepen their understanding of their processes and work.

Performance

Performance, as I have discussed above, is not just a presentation of learned material, but a reenactment that is in itself an opportunity for further reflection, discussion, and re-evaluation. In ways comparable to my earlier discussion of writing with an ear to performance, performance informs the processes of creating a portfolio. For instance, the student who wishes to perform her work using computer technology would be well advised to create a portfolio that suits new media's multimodal formats that highlight the oral and gestural modes.

Teachers can determine the extent to which the student has examined the thought process leading to creative decisions by asking students to write about or perform, or both, what they wanted the work to say (the problem or issue), why they chose a certain way to say it (the themes, genres, and methods chosen), the thinking that went into the processes of choice and revision, and how the performance furthers the content.

Since the portfolio is a developing work, the teacher must assess both individual assignments and the final performance. In this way, portfolio assessment engages teachers in ongoing self-evaluation of their own performance. Like the students, the teachers must revisit their own assumptions, values, and evidence by which they justify individual and overall evaluations of students' work, as well as engage in dialogue with their students about the best ways of assessing students' unique performances. In these ways, portfolio assessment requires that teachers be accountable—a matter that captures the spirit of expectations in *Ontario Secondary Schools, Grades 9 to 12* (1999), which states that "assessment and evaluation of student achievement thus provide teachers with an opportunity to think critically about their own methods of instruction" (34).

Conclusion

Unlike a standard test, the portfolio assessment allows students to deepen their understanding through the "critical" aspects of their inquiry; to shape the portfolio products toward a final performance or product (which may be located at an intersection of various genres); and to evaluate that final work in the context of its performance (for instance, attention to one's audience). This small foray into critical thinking will not lessen the disagreements regarding the extent to which we can validly test for reasoning skills or the extent to which we can assess critical thinking dispositions (Sobocan 2002; Pinto and Portelli, this volume). In fact, the problems of assessment will seem more difficult should imaginative, creative thought be valued as part of critical thinking.

I hope this discussion has been helpful in two ways: in showing strong connections between arts-based inquiry and critical thinking and in providing educators with one way to assess the skills associated with each. The key traits of a critical or creative inquiry experience are evidence of care and self-evaluation in the making of finished work, as well as an evaluation of the suitability of the form and the language through which students express their findings.

Notes

1. I took many of these textbook skills (Blair and Johnson 1995; Ennis 1996, particularly) as the same as those implied by the definition temporarily agreed upon by my co-contributors at the Sobocan "Testing Critical Thinking" symposium that inspired this book: "Skilled, active analysis, and evaluation, done with a strong emphasis on the identification and due consideration of alternative interpretations and points of view." All of the skills and dispositions listed here can also be found in more detail (among others) in many reasoning and critical thinking textbooks. They are also described in detail in a research report prepared for the American Philosophical Association entitled "Critical Thinking: A statement of expert consensus for purposes of educational assessment and instruction" by Peter A. Facione (1990), who canvassed the opinions of many experts, including some of the authors I cite here (see Giancarlo-Gittens and Groarke in this volume for more detailed content from the document, which they refer to as the "Delphi Report").

2. Of course this list is not exhaustive, but given the definition agreed upon, the papers presented, and the discussion at the conference, I am assuming that the authors cited would generally agree on these core skills and dispositions.

3. I acknowledge that Bailin et al. (1993, 6) seem to have a conception of critical thinking which can include dreaming; in other words, there may be allowances for dreaming as contributing to critical thinking.

4. A sense of the miraculous provides the energy to keep working. Learning is a dynamic, energizing activity, especially when the field of instruction includes one's experiences in the world, and is not limited to a textbook or a right answer.

5. Envisioning alternate realities, or modes of behaviour, or choices, is clear-

ly stated to be part of critical thinking (Siegel 1988; Ennis 1996; Paul and Elder 2005).

6. Computer-based applications (hypertext, flash, and other media; student blogs and wikis used in the construction of common documents) suggest forms of inquiry that offer radical opportunities to integrate imaginative and critical thought.

7. Critique includes both positive and critical (constructive) feedback.

References

Arnheim, R. 1969. *Visual thinking.* Berkeley, CA: University of California Press.

Bailin, S., R. Case, J. Coombs, and L. Daniels. 1993. A conception of critical thinking for curriculum, instruction and assessment. A paper commissioned by the Examinations Branch, BC Ministry of Education and Ministry Responsible for Multiculturalism and Human Rights in conjunction with the Curriculum Development Branch and the Research and Evaluation Branch. Victoria, BC: Ministry of Education.

Case, R., and S. Stipp. 2008. Assessment strategies for secondary classrooms. In *The anthology of social studies.* Vol. 2, *Issues and strategies for secondary teachers,* ed. R. Case and P. Clark, 383–97. Vancouver: Pacific Educational Press.

Egan, K. 1999. *Children's minds: Talking rabbits and clockwork oranges.* London, ON: The Althouse Press.

———. 1997. *The educated mind: How cognitive tools shape our understanding.* Chicago, IL: University of Chicago Press.

Ennis, R. 1996. *Critical thinking.* Upper Saddle River, NJ: Prentice-Hall.

Facione, P. 1990. *Executive summary critical thinking: A statement of expert consensus for purposes of educational assessment and instruction.* Millbrae, CA: Insight Assessment (ERIC Doc No. ED 315 423).

Frye, N. 1990. *Words with power: Being a second study of the "Bible and literature."* Markham, ON: Viking Press.

Groarke, L., and C. Tindale. 2008. *Good reasoning matters!,* 4th ed. Don Mills, ON: Oxford University Press.

Hoagland, J. 1995. *Critical thinking.* Newport News, VA: Vale Press.

Hoogland, C. 2004. An aesthetics of language. *Journal of the Canadian Association of Literary Studies* 2(2): 43–59.

———. 2003. *Cuba journal: Language and writing.* Windsor, ON: Black Moss Press.

Johnson, R.H., and J.A. Blair. 1995. *Logical self-defense.* Toronto: McGraw-Hill Ryerson.

Paul, R., and L. Elder. 2005. *Thinker's guide series: Critical thinking competency standards for education*. Dillon Beach, CA: Foundation for Critical Thinking.

Pinto, R., J. Blair, and K. Parr. 1993. *Reasoning: A guide for Canadian students*. Scarborough, ON: Prentice Hall.

Scriven, M., and A. Fisher. 1997. *Critical thinking: Its definition and assessment*. Point Reyes, CA: Edgepress.

Shakespeare, W. 1942. The tempest. In *The complete plays and poems of William Shakespeare*, ed. W. Neilson and C. Hill, 282. Cambridge, MA: Houghton Mifflin.

Siegel, H. 1988. *Educating reason: Rationality, critical thinking and education*. New York: Routledge.

Sobocan, J. 2002. Critical thinking: Two views. In *Proceedings of the fourth international conference on argumentation*, ed. H. van Eemeron, J. Blair, C. Willard, and A. Snoeck-Henkemans, 974–8. Newport News, VA: Vale Press.

The Ontario Curriculum. (1999 and 2007 [revised]). Grades 9 and 10: English. Online. Available from http://www.edu.gov.on.ca/eng/document/curricul/curr971.html#process.

———. 1999. Program planning and assessment guide, Grades 9–12. Online. Available from http://www.edu.gov.on.ca/eng/curriculum/secondary/grades.html.

The Ontario Curriculum–Grades 1-12: Achievement charts (Draft). 2004. Available from http://www.edu.gov.on.ca/eng/document/policy/achievment/index.html.

Chapter Eight

The Ontario Secondary School Literacy Test: Creative Higher-Order Thinking?

Jan Sobocan

$\mathcal{T}$he Ontario Secondary School Literacy Test (OSSLT) is designed to "prepare students with the knowledge and *higher-order thinking* skills they will need to solve increasingly complex problems and make decisions in a richly diverse, information-driven society" (Ministry of Education 2003a, 6 [emphasis added]). The test seems to substitute the concept "literacy" for the less fashionable 1980s phrase "critical thinking," at least to the extent that the "critical" in "critical thinking" represents "higher-order" thinking. In the Ontario Curriculum, whose professed goal is teaching students a skill set that will enable them to solve "increasingly complex problems" and "make decisions," the critical thinking that is implied includes creative thinking.

It is in view of these considerations that I set out to answer a number of related questions: What is the relationship between literacy and critical thinking? What is the relationship between critical thinking and creative thinking? And can an instrument like the OSSLT solicit and validly test for higher-order thinking, in particular, creative critical thinking?

Literacy and Creative Critical Thinking
In the Ontario Curriculum, "literacy" is defined as "the skills and knowledge in reading, writing, speaking, listening, representing, and

viewing that empower learners to make meaningful connections be-tween what they know and what they need to know" (Ministry of Education 2003a, 6). But when one reviews the OSSLT, the 2003 Literacy Report, and its complement document *Think Literacy Success: Cross-Curricular Approaches Grades 7–12* (Ministry of Education 2003b), it is clear that literacy involves more than making connections. In par-ticular, it comprises the skills students need to acquire and to critically assess the information given to them: skills that enable them to make good inferences and judgments (70). Such judgments require that stu-dents "assess different viewpoints and perspectives...and thin[k] criti-cally about important concepts, issues and ideas" (74). Literacy is thus interpreted as the ability to read and assess various types of texts criti-cally in order to make informed judgments about what to believe; to make better decisions at home, work, and school; and to speak and write persuasively (70).

In the supplementary documents provided for Ontario teach-ers and principals, instructors of all subjects are encouraged to foster higher levels of literacy in students in a variety of ways. They include ways of helping students learn how to critically digest various media, to review and reflect on information from a variety of disciplines in order to generate questions, and among other skills, to communicate opinions clearly (Ministry of Education 2003a, 7). Reviewing is decid-ing what the most important information is, and using this informa-tion to make reasonable inferences or to develop a persuasive piece of writing, or both. "Reflecting" implies developing key questions and generating questions for reflection (Ministry of Education 2003b, 12, 70), constructing arguments (giving relevant reasons for opinions), and considering alternative points of view or assessing various perspectives (41, 74). More generally, instructors are to help students understand the importance of—and how to ask—key questions when making judg-ments. Such questioning is said to help students learn how to "process information...to assess the importance and relevance of the informa-tion, and apply it in a new context" (74).

Many of these thinking activities are familiar to those taking reasoning skills courses at North American universities, as is evident in the critical thinking textbooks used to teach and test students in these courses (Gratton 2001). Reflection is often taken to be the heart of crit-ical thinking and the connection between it and literacy skills is made readily apparent by Ennis (1996), who provides an approach to critical thinking that focuses on reading and writing, and on interpretation and evaluation skills. The latter skills include identifying main ideas and issues, asking key questions, and constructing arguments (which implies the ability to provide relevant reasons, evaluate context, self-evaluate, and so on). His textbook content, like the content in the *Think Literacy* documents, provides examples and practice exercises that aim to teach students how to "make reasonable decisions about what to believe or do" (xvii). The skills generally regarded as the critical aspects of a thinking process are the skills involved in argumentation: the construction, interpretation, and evaluation of arguments and information as well as situations or contexts (Sobocan 2003). Many of these skills are also used in creative thinking. The ones I will discuss are detecting bias and hidden assumptions, considering alternative points of view, imagining authors' intentions and intended audiences, and making inferences.

Most contributors to this volume would likely agree that considering alternative points of view, ferreting out assumptions, and making good inferences are a few of the essential elements of a step-by-step thinking process used in the critical evaluation of arguments and information.[1] Such elements are incorporated in my fellow authors' working definition of critical thinking as "skilled, active analysis and evaluation, done with a strong emphasis on the identification and due consideration of alternative interpretations and points of view."[2] The component of this description that is most relevant to literacy education, and most obviously concerned with creative thinking, is the "consideration of alternative interpretations and points of view."

In the reading and writing sections of the 2007 literacy test, respectively, the students are asked to consider "all Canadians" in deciding whether it is good to have honourary citizens, and whether "every student should be required to take a Physical Education class every year of high school" (EQAO Educator Resources OSSLT 2007). Such judgments require consideration of a large range of views when one considers the diverse citizenry of Canada, or a population of high school students (also relatively diverse). For many critical thinking theorists, considering alternative views is part of a judgment of the quality of argument, but for educators it remains to be seen whether considering a range of views is to be evaluated as critical thinking, or as creative inquiry.

The significance of alternative points of view in creative critical thinking is evident in the role they play in the making of inferences or the development of arguments. As suggested in *Think Literacy Success* (Ministry of Education 2003a, 70–4) and in Ennis (1996, 365), persons who draw conclusions are thinking critically only when they have searched out and considered points of view other than their own. Hare and Hoogland (this volume) make precisely this point when they hold that critical thinkers must be able to imagine different perspectives or a variety of communication styles.

In many significant cases, critical thinkers must be able to imagine alternatives to the views presented to them because something that is presented as a fact is questionable; or because only one view of a controversial issue or ambiguous situation is communicated. This alternative viewing (which is implied whenever one detects bias) is an especially important aspect of the careful reading of a text, and an aspect of literacy that is described in curriculum documents as reading "between" or "beyond" the lines (Ministry of Education 2003b, 14).

In its account of literacy, the Ontario Curriculum states that higher-order thinking incorporates the way in which we process what we read, verbal reasoning, and written communication skills (ibid., 2–6). In the documentation on literacy, one can discern three broad categories of critical thinking that imply creative thinking skills: generating questions and ideas; developing opinions or constructing arguments; and visualizing and understanding unseen text (more on this below). In all three of the cases, the ability to creatively imagine and consider alternative points of view is a core element of literacy. I will therefore emphasize this core ability in turning specifically to the OSSLT (2003), and considering the extent to which the OSSLT does (or could) test for creative aspects of critical thought.

The Ontario Secondary School Literacy Test

In 1998 the Ontario government publicly announced the OSSLT as a diploma requirement that would be administered by the province's Education Quality and Accountability Office (EQAO). This particular performance or "achievement" test was first said to measure basic reading and writing skills to identify at-risk students. The test was implemented during the 2001–02 school year, when it was administered to Grade 10 students who had enrolled in Grade 9 in September 2000. The test takes five hours over two days, and is divided into reading and writing sections.

The OSSLT is described as a "useful quality assurance measure that shows the extent to which Ontario students are meeting a common, basic standard for literacy across the province" (EQAO 2001–02 Report of Provincial Results, 1). I believe the test attempts to measure much more than basic or minimum competency. This claim is supported first by what is implied by the government's definition of literacy, which is that the understanding and importance of literacy extends to a "notion of literacy as freedom" (Ministry of Education 2003a, 7). Second, as the reading and writing questions above indicate, literacy encompasses both basic reading and writing, as well as higher-order thinking (as in taking and defending a controversial position on what it means to be a citizen). Given the latter consideration, much more than a basic disciplinary understanding is also clearly required. Before considering further what level of thinking is tested, whether the test validly measures what it intends to measure or whether it tests creative higher-order thinking, I will briefly discuss some of the social and political consequences intended by EQAO with respect to the OSSLT, an aspect of test validity discussed by Ellett and Pitman in Chapter Five.

The EQAO has stated that the results of the OSSLT can be used, provided they are used efficiently and ethically, to give at-risk students the remedial support they need to graduate (Lipman 2004, 168). Those students who cannot perform the foundational reading and writing tasks necessary for learning are to be provided with the additional help they need to meet the standards set by the test. Students can achieve these standards by passing an additional test or by completing a literacy course. There are no OSSLT performance-based financial incentives for schools, and although students could take the test up to three times, the OSSLT was nevertheless often identified as a "high-stakes" standardized selection test (Murphy 2001, 146).

Although the stakes in Canada are not as high as in the United States (as Giancarlo-Gittens discusses in this volume), in a climate where the validity and usefulness of test results are consistently questioned (Gorrie 2004, for example) it is not surprising that the OSSLT has been generally criticized for being a waste of precious education monies. More specifically, the test is said to be unfair to those whose native language is not English and to those with a lower socio-economic status. A number of commentators have said that it employs inconsistent grading criteria implying invalid diagnoses of levels of literacy (Lipman 2004; Ricci 2004). Others have claimed that it compromises teacher autonomy (Runte 1998), that it creates undue stress for students, and that the money it costs would be better spent on books. These criticisms—the prevalent (and unauthorized) use of the test results to rank schools, and the persistent question of why the government spends $15 million annually on minimum competency testing—have convinced many that the test is not worthwhile. I take a different view.

I disagree with the widespread sentiment that there is nothing redeemable in the OSSLT or in accountability programs in general. In particular, I contend that the generalization that the test does not help serve to diagnose and improve student learning is a hasty one. Instead of rejecting the OSSLT entirely, and lamenting neo-conservative agendas and testing "regimes" in general, I believe it is more productive to try to improve the tests themselves. By doing so, perhaps accountability initiatives can move closer to helping teachers, schools, and boards not only diagnose at-risk students but achieve higher educational standards. In keeping with this, I will attempt to show that the 2003 version of the Ontario Secondary School Literacy Test does have significant potential, particularly for the testing of higher-order critical and creative thinking abilities.

In the discussion that follows, I examine some of the types of questions that the 2003 OSSLT uses to solicit critical thinking processes that include creative elements. This analysis will provide the basis for two general conclusions: first, a conclusion about the extent to which the test solicits creative higher-order thinking, and second, a conclusion about the extent to which standardized instruments of this sort might validly test such skills.[3]

The OSSLT: Critical thinking?

I asserted earlier that a core element of creative critical thinking is the ability to imagine, analyze, interpret, and evaluate alternative points of view. In examining the OSSLT tests, I will argue that it provides some significant opportunities for testing these abilities, though I am more interested in the potential for such testing than the details of the

OSSLT. The OSSLT is much too long to be systematically studied here, especially because its answer keys and rubrics are not publicly available. Rather than attempt a systematic study of the test, therefore, I will consider particular aspects of it that can illustrate its potential (and sometimes its failure) in testing and promoting creative critical thinking.

The OSSLT (2003) test format is comprised of a series of multiple-choice and short-answer questions in the reading section. The writing section asks students to write a summary, a three-paragraph opinion piece, a news-style report, and an information paragraph (Ricci 2004, 79). In his contribution to this volume, Groarke criticizes the use of multiple-choice questions in the *California Critical Thinking Skills Test*. Murphy (2001) raises similar concerns about multiple-choice questions. Such questions are problematic in a critical thinking test because they do not ask students to demonstrate the reasoning behind their answers, though it is this reasoning (not their answers) that most determines whether they are engaged in critical thinking. In many cases, critical thinkers may reasonably defend different answers to multiple-choice questions, especially when there is room for "reading between" or "reading beyond" the sentences on the page. What matters is the evidence they adduce for reading something in a particular way, not the reading itself.

As in the *California Critical Thinking Skills Test* (see Groarke, this volume) some of the multiple-choice items in the reading section of the OSSLT do not allow for "between" or "beyond" (critical) readings of the text. In one question, students are asked to select the best meaning of the word "swear" in a paragraph with which they are provided. In the paragraph a witness is asked whether she still believes, after discovering that the defendant has an identical twin, that she saw the defendant involved in a crime. The sentence begins "Can you still swear that the man you saw..." and test-takers are asked to define "swear" as (a) "trust"; (b) "curse"; (c) "think"; or (d) "claim." But one could reasonably argue that "trust," "think," and "claim" are all interchangeable with the term "swear" in the above case—perhaps in any case. In a test question of this sort, one cannot reasonably discern whether the student is thinking critically, particularly in "comprehending subtle meanings in texts" (Ministry of Education 2003b, 40). Such questions are not higher-order thinking items, because the test-taker is not given the opportunity to explain how he or she may be reading beyond the text. A grader, then, could only guess at the test-taker's reasoning. One could easily see how the question could be considered to go beyond minimum competency to "critical" thinking if the test-taker is asked to explain the difference in meaning.

Other questions in the OSSLT better measure the critical and creative skills that are an integral part of literacy. Parts of the reading section of the test ask students to "provide various interpretations of the situations described in each statement" (ibid., 41). Consider, for example, questions about the situation described in the courtroom scenario discussed above. Defence counsel is trying to discredit the testimony of a woman who claims to have seen a defendant drop a murder weapon in the dead of night. Though she has never worn glasses, and she saw the man under a streetlight, the defence lawyer has pointedly argued that the man she saw could be the defendant's twin brother (the defence points out the twin, who is dressed exactly like the defendant). One of the questions on the OSSLT is whether or not the witness is "believable." Students are asked to state "why or why not."

This is a question with creative potential because one may imagine reasons for alternative positions or answers to the question of whether this witness is reliable. She could be said to be believable because she has good eyesight; because the accused was directly under a streetlight; and most importantly, because there was no motive established for the twin. Yet another answer might be that it seems ludicrous that the twin would incriminate himself by appearing in the courtroom. An alternative view is that the witness is *not* believable: the similarity of the twins must raise a reasonable doubt in the minds of the jurors (even if there has been a clever collaboration). This range of possible answers does not exhaust the possible reasons for believing or not believing the witness. Reasons why she is or is not believable will be good grounds for creative critical thinking as long as they consider "various interpretations of the situation described in the passage."

Though this illustrates one way in which a test question can solicit creative critical thinking, one might criticize this question on the grounds that a student is given only three lines on which to write his or her answer. Such limited space inhibits a creative answer. To the extent that it is desirable to have questions that promote critical thinking, it would be best to have additional space for students to explicitly state reasons for "why or why not" the witness might be considered reliable and to choose from among them. In the current test, there is simply not enough space for students to be able to illustrate the requisite creative critical thinking—or even to construct a convincing argument that would support their beliefs or chosen answers. While the question allows for a range of answers or alternative views, the test structure itself does not ensure that students engage in the creative thinking that this question evokes.

It is not difficult to find other examples that illustrate the unrealized potential for creative critical thinking in the OSSLT. Consider a group of questions in the test's reading section about a public notice on water conservation entitled "Be Water Wise." The notice organizes information about water conservation according to various environments: home, farm, and along rivers. In relation to the presentation and classification of information, one test question asks why the title "Be Water Wise" is a good title, and provides one line for an answer. Another question asks test-takers to explain why it was a good idea to use boxes to frame the information. These two types of questions attempt to measure critical thinking by asking students to give their reasoning for their answers, and provide what could have been an opportunity for creative thinking. Yet the questions are formatted and asked in ways that limit *creative* critical thinking.

The above questions limit the development of an opinion (and in this way creative thinking) and the expression of alternative views. By assuming that both the title and organization of the piece in the question are "good," the questions leave no room for the creative thought that possibly this is not so—that there would be a *better* way to organize the text, for example. Similarly, the questions' design detracts from one of the tenets of good critical thinking: a position on qualitative matters such as these is never unequivocally true and any judgment or use of information, for that matter, should be evaluated in terms of *both* its strengths and weaknesses. One might, for example, argue that the title "Be Water Wise" is good in one way—it is catchy because of the alliteration. But one could also imagine someone arguing that the title falls short of the mark. For example, the public notice for water conservation was published during a period of drought, and one might point out that in these circumstances the title should convey the necessity of water conservation and the seriousness of the situation much more directly. Perhaps a title like "Don't Be a Water Waster!" would work better because of the persuasiveness of the rhetoric given an audience who tends to neglect reading past the headlines of news articles and government-issued brochures. Once again, an interest in creative critical thinking could best be promoted by a question format which would ask students to consider alternative points of view.

I have argued that most of the reading questions that I have briefly analyzed attempt to solicit creative critical thinking, but that ultimately the question format and wording prevent a valid test of it. To the extent that higher-order literacy requires that students "develop greater awareness that texts can be understood on more than one level" (Ministry of Education 2003a, 40), the reading questions on the OSSLT could do more to require students to imagine and analyze different points of view.

What about the writing portion of the test? The Ontario Curriculum documents suggest that good literacy teaching will place an emphasis on verbal reasoning and written communication skills and strategies for writing in a variety of forms (ibid., 9). Do the types of questions in the writing section adequately test such abilities, and if so, which ones? And do they pose questions that measure creative critical thinking? It is difficult to answer such questions in detail without the rubrics used to judge answers to the test questions but one can assess, to some extent, the content validity of the writing segment by considering how well the structure of the questions promotes a potential for creative answers.

The *Think Literacy Success* curriculum documents suggest that a key part of literacy is, in a writing context, "visualization" of "unseen text," "unseen text" being "the information that resides in the reader's head: ideas, opinions, essential background knowledge" (Ministry of Education 2003b, 56). This sort of visualization involves the consideration of views other than those that are literally presented, and is indeed creative, because the missing text and the corresponding point of view must be "imagined." Visualization can also be considered an aspect of critical thinking, because in order to imagine what is missing, students must generate key questions and arguments that would lead them to reasonable conclusions (about the author's intentions, about the logical structure of the text, about how other readers might interpret the passage, and so on).

Even in the reading section of the OSSLT, the type of creativity I describe is tested in questions that ask students to imagine the intended audience for a paragraph: an imagining that is the first step in visualization. Still more significantly, the writing section of the OSSLT includes questions that solicit opinion paragraphs, asking students to write a short argument on a topic with a specific audience in mind. Test-takers are instructed to support their ideas with evidence in the way of proof, facts, examples, etc. In this process, students taking the test must imagine how the audience in question will be persuaded. This imagining is creative in the sense that students must "*develop* content and opinions for *persuasive* writing" (ibid., 70 [emphasis added]). The "stepping inside the shoes of another" that this requires is a type of role-playing which is a paradigm of creative activity that requires higher-order thinking, but particularly when they must include in their answers the purpose for arguing one point or another, or for choosing a particular style of communication. In role-playing, imagining, and assessing various purposes and audiences, choosing requires both imagining (creative thinking) and seeking out good reasons (critical thinking). However obvious, I need to add that in these interrelated choices, the creative and critical elements of thinking are inseparable parts of the thinking process that informs good choices, and therefore, good answers to the questions asked.

More generally, the opinion writing required by the OSSLT illustrates the key features of questions that elicit and test creative critical thinking. First, such questions ask a test-taker to construct (rather than simply criticize) an argument. Unlike in the questions in the reading section of the test, test-takers are given more space in the writing section to reflect, review, and generate some questions. In keeping with the literacy documents' claim that literacy necessarily includes the analysis of text, the drawing of conclusions, and the assessment of different points of view (Ministry of Education 2003a, 40, 70), the writing section asks students to demonstrate such skills. In a question that asks whether Canada should "join" the United States, for example, students have the room to generate a question about, say, the meaning of "join" and can proceed to argue from that standpoint. If the scoring criteria are flexible, a student who exercises higher-order thinking might even entertain the possibility of answers based on different political orientations, or two or three ways in which Canada could "join" the United States.

The writing questions on the OSSLT, therefore, might be improved by including fewer questions that ask students to identify the main point of a particular paragraph or story. This sort of question inhibits creativity: students can choose only one answer, an answer that surely must be keyed as the only "passing" or "correct" answer. In soliciting and testing creativity, it is better to have students independently explore alternative points and conclusions, thinking that would involve higher-order activities like ferreting out an implicit premise or conclusion (or in Ministry of Education terminology, a "hidden" or "unseen" premise or conclusion).

Creation and Evaluation: At Odds?

In attempting to address whether the OSSLT has the potential to (or does) measure creative critical thinking, I have tried to offer some practical insights that may be considered in the design of future tests (particularly literacy tests). A quick look at the political and validity aspects of the OSSLT, alongside its associated documents, shows that the test is well intentioned and has the potential to accurately measure more than minimum competency critical thinking or literacy (perhaps, then, has potential for government money to be better spent). Still, an important question remains: How can the design, validity, and political consequences of such tests be improved to allow for answers that can be claimed to be creative, critical thinking?

As Hoogland points out in her contribution to this volume, it is often assumed that criticality and creativity are mutually exclusive. Received wisdom suggests that creativity cannot be measured in multiple-choice formats, and that it is not accurately measured by standardized formats (Ricci 2004, 80; Ryan 2004). I have agreed with some of the criticisms of multiple-choice questions. Multiple-choice questioning is problematic because it denies test-takers the opportunity to provide evidence of their own thinking, in particular the reasoning behind their choices of answers. And this is what matters when judging whether students are engaged in critical creative thinking.

It does not follow, however, that it is impossible to test for critical creativity in any formatted way. On the contrary, I hope that I have shown that standardized formats that ask for written answers (and possibly even multiple-choice answers supplemented with written answers) can do more than test for minimum competency in critical and creative thinking. I believe such question formats could lead to stronger inter-rater reliability and thus have potential to lead to the achievement of higher educational standards in Canadian classrooms.[4] I have already argued that many of the kinds of questions already contained in the OSSLT show how we might test not only critical, but also creative thinking outside of portfolio or authentic assessment formats— impossibly expensive and completely impractical testing formats to administer in a system of accountability.

If it is true that "[a]ccording to research, students who lack literacy strategies and skills need the...[a]ctivities that involve higher-level thinking, reasoning, and communication" (Ministry of Education 2003a, 8), then we would do well to construct test questions that ask students to imagine and consider alternative points of view, to develop opinions, to visualize, and so on. In constructing a test instrument that validly measures creative critical thinking, three rules of thumb should be followed. First, multiple-choice items should be avoided; if they are used, they should be combined with short-answer questions with sufficient space where students must *and* are able to justify their choice of answers. Second, questions should be constructed in a way that widens the range of answers that test-takers can give in response to a question. Among other things, this means that questions should not prejudice the issue with an explicit value judgment that some claim, remark, or discourse is good. Third, writing questions should be designed in a manner that pushes students beyond pre-set answers, toward the consideration of alternative points of view (and, ideally, beyond the typically polarized "why or why not" choice of answers).

This leaves open questions of grading in such contexts, and raises one last major concern about content validity. I have not looked at the scoring criteria of the OSSLT because I do not have access to them or to the specific grading procedures. One cannot make concrete suggestions about how to improve the test without access to the scoring key (if there is one for a pass/fail evaluation format). More generally, one might blame a failure to analyze, understand, and improve the test on the lack of transparency with respect to grading criteria and how grading team supervisors make decisions about disputed judgments.

When it comes to the grading of *creative* critical thinking skills, there are many general issues to address. First, it is a problem that scoring criteria tend to emphasize minimum competency skills such as the mechanics of spelling and grammar, both of which are rote cognitive capacities (Ricci 2004, 83). Second, and also related to scoring, the pass/fail rubric developed for grading the literacy test limits the range of accurate responses to one not-so-apparent accurate answer (Lipman 2004; Ricci 2004). The OSSLT is indeed a pass/fail test, but the critical thinking it demands implies many more discrete levels of competency (a critical thinker thinks beyond minimum competency, and a simple pass does not distinguish between low, minimum, and higher-order competencies). I thus fail to see how such a rubric and the standard it sets could help Ontario teachers diagnose and correct a specific lack of competencies in individual students and improve the quality of education generally (both expressed aims of the EQAO).

Though I have argued that the OSSLT has potential for testing creative critical thinking, scoring limitations render the test invalid as a measure of higher-order thinking skills. From the point of view of creative thinking, simplistic scoring criteria of this sort raise the most common concern educational commentators have expressed in discussions of standardized testing initiatives: that they encourage teachers to "teach to the test," which inhibits the exploration of alternative views and discourages independent thinking not only for test writers, but for evaluators and teachers alike (Runte 1998; see Giancarlo-Gittens, Hare, and Hoogland in this volume). As serious as these problems are, I think it would be a mistake to conclude that there should be no attempts to design more valid tests of critical thinking, and more importantly, of creative critical thinking. To the extent that better tests can be constructed, the Ontario system could benefit from testing of this sort.

Conclusion

Though many commentators have raised issues about the validity of tests that claim to improve education, there has been little, if any, analysis of standardized tests that attempt to measure creative critical thinking. In the place of careful discussion, I believe there has been a blanket and educationally unhelpful critique of government-mandated standardized or performance testing that has usually presented such testing as an unfortunate correlate of Tory or neo-conservative governance (see Moll [2004] for many such critiques). I have provided an alternative view—one that would embrace a need for accountability, and provide suggestions that might help turn existing tests into instruments that allow students to read, write, and think more critically and creatively, and so allow teachers more space to think and to "provide creative and relevant instruction" (Ministry of Education 2003a, 9).

Standardized testing does hold promise for testing parts of a higher-order thinking process, a process that includes creativity. We can and should develop tests that measure higher-order thinking skills and that test for the kind of creativity captured in literacy documents that go beyond helping develop abilities to "understand, think, apply and communicate in reading and writing" toward a level of effectiveness that would help our students have better relationships, become more discriminating as consumers, and perhaps then be more effective citizens (Ministry of Education 2003a, 6).

Notes

1. Ennis (1996) codifies this process as "FRISCO" (Focus, Reasons, Inference, Situation, Clarity, and Overview). Much of what is applied when using the FRISCO framework is outlined in the *Think Literacy Success: Cross-Curricular Approaches* document (Ministry of Education 2003b). There is too much that is entailed by "good" inference to be covered in the scope of this chapter.

2. Generally agreed to at The University of Western Ontario Workshop and Symposium organized to develop this book.

3. At this stage, I do not make any claim about the validity of the OSSLT in terms of inter-rater reliability. Because I do not have access to specific scoring criteria, I can only imagine what the limitations of current and potential scoring criteria might be.

4. For reasons other than what one might say in response to Ricci's (2004) critique, I believe that stronger inter-rater reliability can be achieved in the evaluation of answers to more open-ended question formats (or answers to essay questions). Space does not allow me to enter into such reasoning here, but Hatcher does deal with this subject more extensively in Chapter Eleven of this volume in relation to evaluating extended arguments.

References

Education Quality and Accountability Office (EQAO) Educator Resources OSSLT. 2007. Online. Available at http://www.eqao.com/Students/ Secondary/10/10.aspx?Lang=E&gr=10&Aud=Students.

Education Quality and Accountability Office (EQAO). 2001–02. *Ontario secondary school literacy test resource guide.* Online. Available at http://www. eqao.com.

Ennis, R. 1996. *Critical thinking.* Upper Saddle River, NJ: Prentice Hall.

Gorrie, P. 2004. Literacy test a write-off? *Toronto Star,* Sunday, February 15.

Lipman, P. 2004. The Ontario grade 10 literacy test and the neo-conservative agenda. In *Passing the test: The false promises of standardized testing,* ed. M. Moll, 166–71. Ottawa: Canadian Centre for Policy Alternatives.

Ministry of Education. 2003a. *Think literacy success: The report of the expert panel on students at risk in Ontario.* Toronto: Queen's Printer.

Ministry of Education. 2003b. *Think literacy success: Cross curricular approaches grades 7–12.* Toronto: Queen's Printer.

Moll, M., ed. 2004. *Passing the test: The false promises of standardized testing.* Ottawa: Canadian Centre for Policy Alternatives.

Murphy, S. 2001. No-one has ever grown taller as a result of being measured revisited: More educational measurement lessons for Canadians. In *The erosion of democracy in education: Critique to possibilities,* ed. R. Solomon and J. Portelli, 145–68. Calgary: Detselig Enterprises.

Ricci, C. 2004. Breaking the silence: An EQAO marker speaks out against standardized testing. *Our Schools/Our Selves* 13(2)#74: 75–88.

Runte, R. 1998. The impact of centralized examinations on teacher professionalism. *Canadian Journal of Education* 23: 166–81.

Sobocan, J. 2003. Teaching informal logic and critical thinking. In *Informal Logic @ 25 Symposium,* ed. H. Hansen and C. Tindale, CD-ROM. University of Windsor: Informal Logic.

PART THREE

Assessing the Teachers, Courses, and Programs

Introduction

The standardized critical thinking tests examined so far in this book are instruments designed to test the abilities of students. In attaining excellence in education, one might go further and assess the teachers, the programs, and the institutions that attempt to make higher-order thinking (a "quality education") a key component of their mission. Although the importance of critical thinking has been widely recognized, it is difficult to gauge the success of critical thinking courses. Evaluating schools and post-secondary programs is more difficult, in part, because of the huge expense of testing large groups of students over time.

One might avoid the expense of full-scale program evaluation by using standardized or summative assessments to evaluate specific aspects of courses or programs. But in that case, one must choose what aspects or criteria taught within the course or program are most central (and so should be tested). Even if one limits oneself to course evaluation, critical thinking involves such a wide range of skills and dispositions that it is difficult to create one test that reliably and validly encompasses it. Such issues are exacerbated in the evaluation of educational programs because it is a daunting task to decide what and when to evaluate, and to effectively evaluate all stages of a program.

In attempting to evaluate approaches to teaching courses, or programs and schools, it is difficult to know how to proceed. One way is to use the available tests to evaluate the quality of student learning and then to make limited conclusions about the overall quality of education in a given course, program, or school. Another way is to assess the quality of approaches to teaching critical thinking, or education programs designed at delivering critical thinking curricula. The chapters in Part Three look at critical thinking instruction from the point of view of experienced critical thinking teachers, and those who have developed and implemented innovative critical thinking approaches, programs, or curricula at various levels.

In Chapter Nine, Roland Case advocates a "tools" approach to critical thinking. His approach recognizes different kinds of intellectual resources that function as components of critical thinking—background knowledge, criteria for judgment, critical thinking vocabulary, thinking strategies, and habits of mind. Case describes these components and provides examples that illustrate how they can be incorporated into teaching and assessment practices.

In making background knowledge a key component of critical thinking, Case views critical thinking as discipline specific. In Chapter Ten, Gerald Nosich takes this view further and develops an approach to critical thinking teaching and its assessment that is intended for courses in specific subjects (rather than a stand-alone critical thinking course). His general reasoning assessments strategy is focused on teaching with what he calls "fundamental and powerful" concepts, and can be transferred to teaching within any discipline.

In Chapter Eleven, Donald Hatcher describes the Baker University critical thinking program. Designed to make critical thinking a central component of liberal arts education at Baker University, the program represents one of the most ambitious attempts to incorporate critical thinking within education. The resulting program is unique in many ways, especially because it has been the subject of an annual assessment for fifteen years. In this way the Baker experience provides not just an example which might be emulated but also fifteen years of assessment data that can be used in comparing and assessing other programs.

In the final chapter in this section, Frans van Eemeren and Bart Garssen introduce the "Pragma-Dialectical" approach to critical thinking. Developed in Amsterdam, this approach has become one of today's most influential theories of argument (in many fields, argumentation is a central part of the critical thinking exercise). In pragma-dialectics, argumentation is seen as an attempt to reconcile differences of opinion between two opposing parties, hence the "dialectics." Van Eemeren and Garssen not only describe pragma-dialectic theory and its teaching methods, but explain how to use pragma-dialectics to evaluate their students' critical discussions in the classroom.

Chapter Nine

Teaching and Assessing the "Tools" for Thinking

Roland Case

*I*n this chapter I explain and defend an operational conception of critical thinking built around the metaphor of intellectual resources or "tools." This conception was developed in 1993 in collaboration with Jerrold Coombs, LeRoi Daniels, and Sharon Bailin (see Bailin, Coombs, and Daniels 1993, 1999).[1] We use the term "operational" to refer to the elements, or building blocks, that guide educators in embedding critical thinking into curriculum and instruction, not to an account of the concept or meaning of critical thinking.

In offering this account I am cautioned by Carol Channing's wry comment when asked what she wanted for her birthday: "Don't give me a book," she quipped. "I've already got one." All of those reading this chapter already possess an operational conception of critical thinking—perhaps many have even developed their own. They may not want another. In light of this understandable reluctance to entertain yet another conception, I will begin by contrasting the dominant versions currently in play with our "tools" conception and suggest why this newer account is preferable. I will briefly explore the nature of these tools and conclude with their implications for classroom instruction and assessment.

Two Ways of Operationalizing Critical Thinking

Prevalent conceptions of critical thinking perceive it as a set of thinking competencies variously identified in terms of ambiguous notions such as abilities, skills, processes, procedures, or mental operations. Despite their differences, these approaches identify the "characteristics" of a critical thinker or the "elements," "aspects," or "dimensions" of critical thinking partly, if not exclusively, in terms of an identifiable list of tasks or functions that must be successfully completed. Marzano et al. (1988) identify eight thinking processes (including concept formation, problem-solving, decision-making, and research) involving twenty-one core thinking skills (including defining goals, setting goals, inferring, and predicting). Scholars within this tradition operationalize critical thinking in terms of constituent competencies—things that a critical thinker must be able to successfully carry out or accomplish.

There is not space here to articulate particular concerns about the various "constitutive competencies" approaches to critical thinking, especially because various authors use these terms differently and in overlapping ways. My colleagues and I have written about some of the epistemological confusions associated with many of these approaches (see Bailin, Coombs, and Daniels 1999). I want to focus on their lesser appreciated, pedagogical limitations.

Explicating critical thinking in terms of a finite list of "complex" competencies and dispositional traits typically leaves educators with inadequate or misleading advice about how to promote critical thinking. By definition, these conceptions tell us what a thinker should be able to do, and what he or she should be inclined to do, but not what developing these competencies and dispositions might require. Typically, the recommendations for teaching are general and predominantly methodological: educators are encouraged to engage students in a repeated practice of critical thinking "skills" across a variety of contexts.[2] However, this fails to tell teachers what they should teach students to develop these abilities or successfully undertake these processes. Especially inadequate is advice on how to remediate the spotty "transfer" of these supposedly generalizable skills or processes. What is needed is a variety of tools (e.g., varying strategies, criteria, and commitments) that are helpful in enhancing proficiency and in extending the domains within which a person can successfully draw inferences.

In addition, an emphasis on general abilities and skills is easily misconstrued in a way that creates the impression that critical thinking is about basic competencies rather than skilful analysis. Having the ability to play chess means little more than knowing the rules; it says little about the quality of play. As Blair points out in this volume, it is not basic abilities of this sort that are the aim of critical thinking. When educators read that thinking involves the "skill of analysis" they should understand this to mean that thinking requires "skilful analysis;" and that the "ability to draw inferences" should mean much more than the capacity to do so. Unfortunately, these distinctions are commonly missed and educators adopt a "dumbed-down" version of critical thinking in which enabling resources are inadequately addressed.

These misrepresentations of the qualitative requirements of good thinking are evident in the tendency to distinguish "higher-order" and "lower-order" thinking. Properly understood, there is no direct or necessary connection between "higher-order" operations and critical thinking, and no necessary disjunction between "lower-order" operations and critical thinking. Whether or not students are thinking critically depends more on their intentions and the qualities that characterize their thinking as they carry out a task, than on the specific nature or type of mental operation. The mere fact that students are analyzing does not mean that they are doing it critically. If students blindly accept assumptions, leap to fallacious conclusions, and rely on inaccurate statements, one would be hard pressed to describe their "analysis" as exhibiting critical thinking. Conversely, the so-called "lower-order" operations, such as comprehending or remembering, need not consist of mere rote transfer of information but can be occasions for critical thinking.

Critical thinking is thus a way of undertaking any intellectual activity—by approaching it in a critically thoughtful manner. Success in the particular endeavour will depend on possessing the tools relevant to the task. We cannot teach students to be good analyzers or predictors, per se, but we can help them acquire the diverse intellectual resources needed to analyze or predict successfully in various contexts.

Accordingly, I want to unpack critical thinking in a way that identifies the varied intellectual resources or tools (the "enabling resources") that would assist or enable someone to successfully complete the range of tasks involved in thinking critically. Put another way, enabling resources refer to the knowledge and commitments that make it possible for someone to develop competence in the tasks that constitute good thinking. Enabling resources are not simply more specific sub-competencies (e.g., the ability to draw inferences can be sub-divided into the ability to infer deductively and inductively) but consist of the knowledge and affects which enable someone to successfully draw various kinds of inferences. In this respect, enabling resources are elemental: they cannot be divided into more basic elements.

As far as I am aware, the informal logic movement offers the only prevalent operational conception of critical thinking largely in terms of enabling resources (notably, in terms of principles and concepts). A major limitation of this account, recognized by its own proponents, is that informal logic addresses only a small part of the range of tools needed by critical thinkers (see Blair and Johnson 1991, 50).

There are, of course, widely accepted conceptions of critical thinking, such as those put forward by Robert Ennis (1996) and Mathew Lipman (1991), which are "hybrids"—that is, they delineate critical thinking partly in terms of enabling resources (notably, criteria and strategies) and partly in terms of dispositions and competencies (sometimes dividing general competencies into more specific sub-competencies).[3] Naturally, the attention to enabling resources is welcomed. Unfortunately, only some competencies are unpacked in terms of enabling resources and, even when they are, the enumerations rarely capture the full range of tools that competence in the specified task would require.

The "Tools" Conception in a Nutshell

In opposition to attempts to conceive of critical thinking as a limited set of constitutive competencies, I am suggesting an open-ended array of intellectual resources or tools that are drawn upon or employed by a critical thinker. Although the specific tools will depend on the nature of the challenge facing the thinker, promoting critical thinking is largely a matter of helping students master an ever broadening repertoire of five types of intellectual resources: background knowledge, criteria for judgment, critical thinking vocabulary, thinking strategies, and habits of mind. I briefly discuss each of these below.

Background knowledge

Background knowledge is knowledge of the relevant information about a topic required for thoughtful reflection. Although it should be obvious that one cannot think critically about a topic knowing little or nothing about it, many accounts of critical thinking fail to identify background knowledge as one of their building blocks. Instead, it is presumed that thinking skills or operations are independent of the content areas to which the skills are to be applied. Properly understood, relevant background knowledge is not separate from any skill, but part of what is required to be skilled.[4] Consequently, to be able to think critically about a range of topics, individuals need to acquire information relevant to those topics. This speaks strongly for embedding the teaching of critical thinking within the teaching of curricular content.

Criteria for judgment

Criteria for judgment are appropriate criteria or grounds for judging the reasonableness or merits of the options presented by a thinking challenge. To think critically is to engage in deliberations with the intention of making a reasoned judgment. And judgments inevitably are made on the basis of criteria. The root shared in common by "critical" thinking and "criteria" is instructive: thinking critically is thinking in light of or using criteria (Lipman 1988, 45). For this reason, an important category of tools is awareness of and concern for the relevant criteria for judgment. These criteria are far more numerous than the handful of intellectual standards suggested by Elder and Paul (2005). Rather they include a myriad of context-sensitive criteria spanning the diversity of intellectual tasks found in the curriculum, from what makes a good argumentative essay, a sound solution to a business problem, or a thoughtful question, to the qualities of a reliable scientific experiment, an accomplished artistic performance, or effective lecture notes.

Critical thinking vocabulary

"Critical thinking vocabulary" refers to concepts that expressly address distinctions foundational to thinking critically—for example, knowledge of the difference between "conclusion" and "premise," "cause" and "correlation," or "cause" and "effect," and knowledge of various informal fallacies. Theoretical and pedagogical attention to these concepts has been a key component of the informal logic movement.

Thinking strategies

Thinking strategies include procedures, heuristics, organizing devices, algorithms, and models that may be useful when thinking through a challenge. Good critical thinkers draw upon a large variety of strategies to work their way through the challenges facing them. This category of tools is most closely aligned with what others call skills, although we believe they are better viewed as strategies. Looking for counter-arguments is a general strategy, yet it is not a broadly generalized skill (developing a persuasive counter-argument often requires contextual knowledge and situation-specific criteria). Thinking strategies may be very elaborate, such as following a comprehensive decision-making model (for example, when tackling a complex problem, begin by identifying the issue, then consider the consequences, research each option, and so on). Alternatively they may be very focused strategies addressing a specific task (for example, to gain clarity about a statement rephrase it in your own words, ask others for clarification, or graphically represent the problem). There are literally thousands of strategies—in various forms (procedures, models, algorithms, graphic organizers, and other types of heuristics)—that guide individuals in working through the challenges they encounter.

Habits of mind

Although more commonly described as dispositions (as Giancarlo-Gittens refers to them in this volume), we prefer the term "habits of mind" to refer to the intellectual ideals or virtues to which a careful and conscientious thinker will be committed. A commitment to these virtues orients and motivates thinkers in habitual ways that are conducive to good thinking. The characterization offered below is representative of the intellectual virtues important in thinking critically:

- ❖ *Initiative*: To think without prompting from others (not waiting to be told everything)
- ❖ *Inquisitiveness/curiosity*: To explore matters and not take everything at face value
- ❖ *Critical-mindedness*: To evaluate information when it is important to do so
- ❖ *Open-mindedness*: To be open to views other than one's own, especially to contrary positions
- ❖ *Fair-mindedness*: To judge ideas on their merits and not simply enforce personal interests and biases
- ❖ *Independence of mind*: To resist pressures to adopt opin-

ions merely because they are popular

❖ *Intellectual work ethic*: To persist in thinking through problems in a careful manner

❖ *Circumspection*: To be tentative in one's belief until there is sufficient evidence or complexity to warrant a more definitive position

❖ *Empathy*: To imagine sensitively the experiences and feelings of those in situations different from one's own and in different historical contexts

❖ *Tolerance of ambiguity*: To live with ambiguity and not require black-or-white answers

❖ *Self-reflection*: To ensure that one's beliefs and actions are well grounded

❖ *Respectfulness*: To engage respectfully in discussion with others

❖ *Humility*: To not take oneself too seriously (i.e., to be able to laugh at oneself)

❖ *Consultation*: To seek several sources of information, solicit expert opinion, and confer with others

❖ *Attentiveness to detail*: To take careful note of non-trivial particulars

❖ *Flexibility*: To alter tactics or approaches when needed

Significantly, there are "schools" of thinking that focus on each of the five kinds of tools that we identify. McPeck (1981) and Hirsch (1988) argue that sound thinking is best served by promoting student mastery of the subject matter of the disciplines. Perkins and Salmon (1989), Siegel (1988), and Norris and Ennis (1989) believe that a central ingredient of good thinking is thinking dispositions, which are closely related to what we have called "habits of mind." Lipman (1991) and Paul (1988) are prominent advocates of the centrality of criteria for judgment (also called intellectual standards). The informal logic school of thinking stresses two categories of tools: those criteria for judgment reflected in the formal and informal rules of logic (e.g., the rules of class, conditional, and probabilistic reasoning) and what we call "critical thinking vocabulary." The final category of tools—thinking strategies—is arguably the most widely espoused dimension of critical thinking. Much of the literature on promoting thinking skills is a matter of teaching strategies for carrying out various operations.[5] The existence of these different camps suggests that our five categories of tools represent a more complete synthesis of the range of critical thinking building blocks than is found in any single account.

Teaching and Assessing the Tools

I now want to turn more directly to how critical thinking, understood as I have conceptualized it, can be taught and assessed. It should be obvious that nurturing critical thinking is a *long-term evolutionary goal*—critical thinking proficiency develops gradually as individuals acquire and enrich a vast repertoire of intellectual tools. Consequently, promoting critical thinking requires incremental, collective effort—no single course can do it. Our efforts are, as Tyler (1969) suggests, like dripping water on a stone: "In a day or week or a month there is no appreciable change in the stone, but over a period of years definite erosion is noted. Correspondingly, by the cumulation of educational experiences profound changes are brought about in the learner" (83). Clearly, educators must take the long view when nurturing critical thinking: it is a kindergarten-to-university challenge.

Tools must be developed and assessed in realistic or meaningful contexts because the context determines the tools that are needed.[6] The choice of contexts and the range of tools to be taught and assessed will depend on the kinds of tasks that we want students to be able to do. There is no generic skill of inferring to be exercised. Rather, there is a desirable range of contexts for drawing inferences in history, biology, geometry, literature, and other subject areas. Students will need to acquire the requisite tools to meet these challenges. Embedding critical thinking in the teaching of curriculum content means that students are more likely to acquire the subject matter that they are supposed to learn and that critical thinking is more likely to be an ongoing classroom activity.[7]

The pedagogical value of conceiving of critical thinking as the competent use of contextually relevant tools is best seen through examples of teachers attempting to help their students work through particular critical thinking challenges. An important function of the tools approach is to help teachers identify what students need to be taught to enable them to undertake a given task in a critically thoughtful manner. To illustrate the instructional value of our model, I discuss two examples of teaching students the tools needed to ask effective questions. I begin with teaching primary students to think critically about developing "powerful" questions.

Developing powerful questions[8]

As part of their social studies curriculum, Tami McDiarmid's kindergarten to grade three class was to learn about the significance of Remembrance Day (November 11). In fostering appreciation of this event, Tami invited her students to think of questions they might ask of a classroom guest who was to speak about his World War II experiences. Left to their own devices, many students would likely have asked rather trivial or irrelevant questions. Tami sought to support her students in thinking critically about the questions they might ask by focusing their attention on four tools: some critical thinking vocabulary, criteria for judgment, a thinking strategy, and background knowledge.

A few days prior to the visit, Tami re-introduced key vocabulary by reminding her students that they had previously talked about two kinds of questions: "weak" questions and "powerful" questions. Armed with this distinction, the class discussed what powerful questions "look like or sound like"—or, to use our terminology, they discussed the criteria for judging powerful questions. Tami recorded the following student-generated criteria.

Powerful Questions

- ❖ give you lots of information
- ❖ are specific to the person or situation
- ❖ are open-ended—can't be answered by yes or no
- ❖ may be unexpected
- ❖ are usually not easy to answer (McDiarmid, Manzo, and Musselle, 2007, 115-9)

Next, Tami made use of a thinking strategy—brainstorming—that her students had already learned to use. Brainstorming is a useful strategy to help with the generation of ideas. In itself, it does not invoke critical thinking. In fact, while brainstorming, individuals are discouraged from making judgments about the proffered ideas—the point is simply to generate as many ideas as possible. The critical thinking began in earnest when students, working in pairs, began to assess the brainstormed questions. Using the agreed-upon criteria as their guide, students discussed whether or not their proposed questions were likely to elicit a lot of information, were obvious or predictable, and so on. Some "weak" questions were rejected; others were modified to make them more powerful.

Tami had developed a fourth tool—relevant background knowledge—during the three weeks preceding the guest's visit by reading and discussing various children's stories involving the war. Without the knowledge acquired from these stories, many students would have been incapable of asking a thoughtful question. Here is a sampling of the student-generated questions asked of the World War II veteran:

- ❖ Why did you fight in the war?
- ❖ Do you remember some of your friends from the war?
- ❖ Which countries did you fight over?
- ❖ Where did you live during the war?
- ❖ Were there any women in World War II? If so, what were their jobs?
- ❖ What started the fighting?
- ❖ Why was Canada involved?
- ❖ What was your safe place? (McDiarmid, Manzo, and Musselle, 2007, 117)

Tami systematically aided her primary students in thoughtfully constructing questions by teaching four tools. Notice, *teaching* the tools is not the same as giving students the answers or doing the thinking for them. Tami did not indicate to students the questions they might ask; rather she helped them develop the intellectual resources they needed to thoughtfully complete the task for themselves. Not only were these students able to pose powerful questions aided by the tools their teacher helped them acquire, but their understanding of the subject matter—in this case the significance of Remembrance Day—was enhanced by the experience.

We can appreciate the contextual nature of teaching the tools and, by implication, the limitations of generic thinking models, by contrasting the tools Tami developed with those developed by a junior high school teacher as she helped students think critically about questions for an end-of-unit test in social studies.

Developing examination questions[9]

Karen Barnett, a junior high school humanities teacher, borrowing an idea from fellow teacher Bob Friend, had her students *create*, rather than simply answer, exam questions. Their task was to prepare an end-of-unit quiz consisting of six questions and an answer key focused on their study of seventeenth-century England. In supporting her students in this task, Karen provided three tools: background knowledge, criteria for judgment, and a thinking strategy.

The required background knowledge—knowledge of the focus of questions—was acquired by reading the relevant chapter in their textbook and by undertaking a variety of related assignments. When framing their six questions, students were instructed to consider four criteria:

* ❖ must be clear so that fellow students will understand what is required;
* ❖ should address a non-trivial aspect of the chapter content;
* ❖ can be answered within a half page (or twenty minutes); and
* ❖ must require more than mere recall of information.

Karen further supported her students' efforts by offering a thinking strategy—the use of "question frames"—to help generate questions that went beyond mere recall of information. More specifically, students were invited to frame questions using prompts such as the following:

* ❖ Compare...with...
* ❖ What conclusion can be drawn from...?
* ❖ Decide if...was correct when...
* ❖ Predict what would have happened if...
* ❖ What was the effect of...?
* ❖ Decide which choice you would make if...

A list of the best student-generated questions was distributed to the class well before the test. Students were informed that their test would be drawn exclusively from their questions. The following questions were submitted by one of the students in Karen's class:

1. Compare the ideas of Thomas Hobbes and John Locke on government.
2. Do you think Cromwell was correct in chopping off the king's head, and what advantage did government gain over royalty because of this?
3. What were the effects of the civil war on the monarchy and the peasantry of the country?
4. If you were the king, how would you handle the pressures of government and the people?
5. Compare the power of the government in the early 1600s to the power it has today. What do you think would have happened if the people hadn't rebelled against the king?

We can see the contextual nature of the tools involved in posing effective questions by contrasting the two situations. The required background knowledge in one case was knowledge of World War II; in the other, it was knowledge of the civil war period in seventeenth-century England. Karen's sample "question frames" offered a thinking strategy—a complementary strategy to brainstorming—to help students generate questions. Karen's articulation of the criteria—different from the criteria offered in the primary class—focused students' thinking on the features of good examination questions.

Significantly, teaching students to think critically about the questions they posed contributed to their understanding of the subject matter. The criteria that Karen set—notably that students ask non-trivial questions—required students to think about what was important about the historical period. So, too, did her inclusion of student-generated questions on the unit test. Because these questions went beyond mere recall of information, studying for the test required that other students think about the issues raised. Karen insists that had she posed the very questions her students had produced, she would have been bombarded with complaints: "How do you expect us to know this? You never told us the answers to this!" Instead, not only did students take seriously the assignment to create the questions—in some cases reading the textbook for the first time—they were more motivated to study for the test because the questions were posed by their peers.

The motivational value of critical thinking is important. Although not all students will welcome opportunities to think critically, more often than not, students would rather think about matters than regurgitate facts or apply undigested ideas. This is especially true when the issues or topics about which students are asked to think critically are meaningful to them.

Assessing the Tools

Another useful feature of the tools approach is the parallel between instruction and assessment. Assessment is a major obstacle for many teachers in their efforts to promote critical thinking. If there is no single correct answer to look for in student responses, it is often difficult to know what to assess. As our last two examples illustrate, students can still fully construct a large number of effective questions. Does this mean that virtually any question is acceptable? If not, on what basis should these questions be assessed?

The topic of assessment of critical thinking deserves more space than is available here. Let me say simply that the key consideration is not whether teachers agree or disagree with the conclusions students reach but rather the quality of the thinking that supports their answers. In assessing critical thinking teachers should look for evidence that students' answers competently embody the relevant tools. It may be unrealistic to assess students on the complete range of tools that a particular task requires. A more appropriate or valid approach is to assess only those tools that students were expected and instructed to employ in the task before them. Returning to the two examples of teaching students to pose effective questions will permit us to see what this looks like in practice.

Assessing thinking about powerful questions

In learning to pose powerful questions to the war veteran, Tami's students were expressly taught four tools, all of which might form the basis for assessing students' thinking. The actual questions could be evaluated on two criteria:[10] the criteria for judgment and background knowledge about World War II. The former could be assessed by looking to see how well the question each student posed met the agreed-upon criteria. (Alternatively, students might be asked to explain how their question satisfied each criterion.) Students' questions could be used to assess background knowledge by looking to see whether any question revealed factual errors. The teacher could circulate among the groups and assess their use of the brainstorming strategy by observing whether students readily volunteered questions and accepted all suggestions. Students' understanding of the conceptual distinction between weak and powerful questions could then be assessed by providing sample questions and asking students to identify which of them were weak, which of them were powerful, and why.

Assessing thinking about test questions

In the second example, Karen's students were provided with three tools to support their thinking about examination questions: a range of criteria for effective test questions, the "question frame" strategy for generating questions, and background knowledge on the historical period. The student-generated questions could be assessed on all three grounds: how well they satisfied the stipulated criteria for judgment, the extent to which the questions represented a variety of question frames and, to a lesser extent, how much knowledge of the period was implied by the questions asked. (A more appropriate source for assessing students' background knowledge would be the answer key that was to accompany each student's six questions.)

Because the focus of the second example was on posing test questions, no mention was made of the tools needed to help students think critically about their answer keys (and, by implication, about their answers on the actual end-of-unit quiz). It would be instructive to consider briefly what these tools might be. Obviously, there is no definitive list of tools for teaching students to answer exam questions thoughtfully. Often, the identified tools depend on the teacher's priorities for the assignment, the perceived needs of the students, and the demands of the curriculum. Still, I think that there will be considerable agreement on the sorts of tools that teachers would recognize as being appropriate.

A useful place to begin thinking about which tools to assess is to imagine a weak student's response to a sample question (poor responses are often more revealing than good ones). Consider the question, "What do you think would have happened if the people hadn't rebelled against the king?", and the following obviously flawed answer: "If the people hadn't rebelled they would have quickly forgotten their troubles and gone back to watching television." What relevant tools appear to be absent in this answer? The historical error of assuming the existence of television in the seventeenth century comes immediately to mind. Or, to put it in our terminology, the background knowledge is incomplete. The bald assertion that the citizenry would quickly forget their problems is vague, somewhat implausible, and not supported with any evidence. These deficits suggest gaps in understanding the criteria for judging a thoughtful response.

The historical error about watching television might suggest stressing the need for students to read the relevant chapter of the text carefully. In addressing the gaps in criteria for judgment, the teacher might explore with students the importance of a detailed (or specific) answer, that it be plausible and amply supported by evidence (or reasons). The specification of these three criteria for judgment might raise the need to teach critical thinking vocabulary: all students would not know the difference between *plausible* and *actual* outcomes. (An outcome need not be actual, or even likely, for it to be plausible.) The teacher might also try to nurture an *empathic* habit of mind. Empathy, in this particular case historical empathy, involves an appreciation of how others in different situations and contexts might feel about an event. If students were inclined to put themselves, metaphorically speaking, into the heads and hearts of those living in the seventeenth century, their answers to the questions might be more detailed and plausible. In casting about for thinking strategies to help students construct a thoughtful answer, teachers might recommend a "template" for their answers. For example, students might employ a three-point outline: (1) Briefly summarize the position taken; (2) Elaborate on what is meant or implied by the position; and (3) Offer several pieces of evidence to justify the position.

Imagining other hypothetical student answers, including ideal answers, might help to elaborate upon and refine the list of requisite tools. For example, the imagined exemplary answers might include refutation of possible objections to the stated position (attending to what Johnson, in this volume, calls "dialectical obligations"). Or, answers may include suggested alternative positions and evaluations of the relative merits of each (what Sobocan, in this volume, might consider to be a creative, critical response). If these are thought to be reasonable and appropriate expectations, additional tools might be introduced, including teaching the concepts of *argument* and *counter-argument* and revising the suggested three-point outline to add a new step: (4) Anticipate possible objections to the position and provide a counter-argument for each. Needless to say, there are other possible tools for teaching and, in turn, assessment. The point to appreciate is how varied the tools and much better students' answers will likely be if they have been taught to apply some of these tools to textbook and classroom learning.

I have attempted to make a case on conceptual and pedagogical grounds against framing critical thinking in terms of a finite set of generalized competencies and dispositions. In its place, I have argued for recognizing a substantial repertoire of five types of intellectual tools, nurtured incrementally in the context of a wide spectrum of curriculum-embedded thinking challenges. We believe this approach does justice to the challenges inherent in promoting critical thinking while enhancing the development of other educational goals.

Notes

1. When I use the word "we" in this chapter I am referring to Jerrold Coombs, LeRoi Daniels, Sharon Bailin, and myself, unless the context suggests another obvious meaning.

2. Raths et al. (1986) unequivocally state, "Here, then, is the first principle upon which a teaching for thinking program is based: *Children need to spend many, many hours practicing higher-order thinking skills if they are to become successful thinkers*" (xiv [emphasis in original]).

3. Most of what Robert Ennis calls critical thinking abilities are constitutive tasks. Many elements of these abilities are simply more specific abilities (such as designing experiments, interpretation of statements) but others identify what I refer to as enabling resources—largely thinking strategies and criteria (see Norris and Ennis 1989, 183–7). Lipman (1991, 22) includes criteria, thinking strategies, and cognitive skills. Other writers identify some of the tools I will discuss.

4. Consider the example of teaching students the so-called operation of analysis. We cannot effectively teach students *the* process or skill of analyzing for the simple reason that analysis of, say, a poem for its metre, rhyme, and symbolism poses a significantly different challenge than that posed by the analysis of an ore sample for its chemical properties.

5. The close connections between many researchers' conceptions of "skills" and strategies are evident in the statement that "philosophers have a general skill: the strategy of looking for counterexamples to test claims" (Perkins and Salmon 1989, 19).

6. Although I focus on the curricular contexts for teaching the tools, critical thinking cannot be learned independently of the broader forces operating within the classroom and the school. Consequently, it is essential to foster "critical" communities where teachers and students interact in mutually supportive ways to nurture critical reflection. This is especially significant for acquisition of the desired habits of mind which are likely to develop only if they are modelled and continuously supported. Building a community of thinkers is also instrumental in countering a tendency to view thinking as a solitary enterprise. There is a key difference between thinking *for one's self* and thinking *by oneself*. Good critical thinkers regularly engage in dialogue with others as a way of broadening their knowledge, testing their ideas, and securing alternative perspectives. Learning to contribute to and to make use of the wisdom of others can be learned only through participation in a critical community.

7. Curriculum resources developed by The Critical Thinking Consortium that teach subject matter through critical thinking can be found at http://www.tcz.ca.

8. This example is based on a lesson described in McDiarmid, Manzo, and Musselle (2007).

9. Based on a personal communication with Karen Barnett.

10. Notice my use of criteria in two contexts: I talk about *assessment criteria* and *criteria for judgment*. Assessment criteria are the grounds for assessing a student's work and, in the area of critical thinking, we recommend using all five tools as sources of assessment criteria. This implies that the tools we refer to as "criteria for judgment" are but one of the ways to assess critical thinking.

References

Bailin, S., J. Coombs, and L. Daniels. 1999. Conceptualizing critical thinking. *Journal of Curriculum Studies* 31(3): 285–302.

———. 1993. (September). *A conception of critical thinking for curriculum, instruction and assessment*. Victoria, BC: Examinations Branch, Ministry of Education.

Blair, J., and R. Johnson. 1991. Misconceptions of informal logic: A reply to McPeck. *Teaching Philosophy* 14(1): 35–52.

Elder, L., and R. Paul. 2005. Universal intellectual standards. Online.

Available from http://www.criticalthinking.org/page.cfm?PageID=S27& categoryID=68. Last accessed October 24, 2007.

Ennis, R. 1996. *Critical thinking.* Upper Saddle River, NJ: Prentice Hall.

Hirsch, E. 1988. *Cultural literacy: What every American needs to know.* New York: Vintage Books.

Lipman, M. 1991. *Thinking in education.* Cambridge: Cambridge University Press.

———. 1988. Critical thinking: What can it be? *Educational Leadership* 45: 38–43.

Marzano, R., R. Brandt, C. Hughes, B. Jones, B. Presseisen, S. Rankin, and C. Suhor. 1988. *Dimensions of thinking: A framework for curriculum and instruction.* Alexandria, VA: Association for Supervision and Curriculum Development.

McDiarmid, T., R. Manzo, and T. Musselle. 2007. *Critical challenges for primary students.* Vancouver, BC: The Critical Thinking Consortium.

McPeck, J. 1981. *Critical thinking and education.* Oxford: Martin Robertson.

Norris, S., and R. Ennis. 1989. *Evaluating critical thinking.* Pacific Grove, CA: Midwest Publications.

Paul, R. 1988. *What, then, is critical thinking?* Rohnert Park, CA: Center for Critical Thinking and Moral Critique.

Perkins, D., and G. Salmon. 1989. Are cognitive skills context-bound? *Educational Researcher* 18(1): 1–21.

Raths, L., S. Wassermann, A. Jonas, and A. Arnold. 1986. *Teaching for thinking: Theory, strategies, and activities for the classroom.* New York: Teachers College Press.

Siegel, H. 1988. *Educating reason: Rationality, critical thinking, and education.* New York: Routledge.

Tyler, R. 1969. *Basic principles of curriculum and instruction.* Chicago: University of Chicago Press.

Chapter Ten

Central Reasoning Assessments: Critical Thinking in a Discipline

Gerald Nosich

Most discussions of the question how (or whether) critical thinking can be assessed focus on the general skills that it requires: the ability to judge the evidence for and against a conclusion, the ability to identify assumptions, and so on. As important as this question is, a full account of critical thinking must also consider how it should manifest itself within specific disciplines and subject areas (history, English, biology, etc.).

In this chapter I describe some interrelated ways to assess critical thinking in a discipline.[1] I will describe one of these in detail, and the others I will just outline. Each assessment strategy focuses on reasoning through, and in terms of, the most central parts of the discipline or field in question, and might therefore be called a *central reasoning assessment*. Such assessments are holistic: they require both analysis and synthesis; they require students to frame, organize, and sometimes identify the problematic situation to be addressed, to bring to bear insights from the course as a whole, and to reason within the discipline. For a number of reasons, these assessments satisfy the underlying goals of teaching the discipline. (Arguably, they do this better than do assessments based on individuated skills.) I will therefore end the chapter with a discussion of the implications that central reasoning assessments have for teaching.

Fundamental and Powerful Concepts

The first assessment I want to describe involves fundamental and powerful concepts (I will use the abbreviation "f & p concepts" throughout this chapter). In a course in a discipline (and, I would argue, in a discipline itself) there is a small set of f & p concepts. By "f & p" concepts, I mean those concepts which, if I could get students to understand them deeply, would enable students to understand a great deal of the course. Examples might be the concepts of *social patterns* and *social forces* in sociology; *romanticism* in nineteenth-century Western literature, music, and art; *place* in geography; *managing, marketing,* and *finance* in business; *audience* in writing; and *what is justifiable* in ethics.

Fundamental and powerful concepts can be contrasted with concepts that have a narrower, more restricted application. *Cell* versus *mitochondria* is an example. *Cell* is a much more fundamental and powerful concept in biology (think of a general-education biology course) than *mitochondria* is. (*Homeostasis* is probably even more f & p). Students who achieve a good grasp of the concept *cell* will be able to think through and gain insight into a very large number of topics in biology. If they think those topics through using the concept *cell* (in a way that is clear, accurate, and relevant, and that identifies relevant assumptions, possible alternative explanations, etc.), they will be thinking critically in the discipline. In addition, a good grasp of the concept *cell* will help students to think critically about a huge range of topics they will encounter outside the course. By contrast, a student who achieves a good grasp of the concept *mitochondria* will not thereby gain insight into nearly as large a range of other biology topics.[2]

F & p concepts are *fundamental* in the sense that they underlie—logically underlie—a large number of other concepts in a discipline. By explaining restricted, narrower concepts in terms of more fundamental ones, students grasp (or re-create) part of the logical structure of the discipline. F & p concepts are *powerful* in the sense that they illuminate a large number of problems and situations in a wide variety of settings. Thus, they are not simply concepts to be thought *about*. Rather, they can better be described as concepts-in-use: as tools that are useful for thinking about other things.

A General Template for Assessments in Terms of Fundamental and Powerful Concepts

The basic form of a question using f & p concepts is as follows:

#0. Explain the following problematic situation [problem, question, event, situation, state of affairs, fact, argument...]. Do that by using the fundamental and powerful concepts of the discipline as the key parts of your explanation. Give good reasons to back up your explanation.

In accord with this general template, assessments in terms of f & p concepts ask students to reason their way through problems using the f & p concepts. In many contexts, the instructions can ask students to focus on situations, questions, states of affairs, events, arguments, almost anything in fact. In giving their explanations, students are required to give good reasons to explain why they analyzed the situation the way they did (though instructions to do so will not always be explicitly stated in the question itself, as I discuss below). It is important that the problem or situation to be explained is one that has *not* been explicated in this respect by the teacher or in the reading for the course. Otherwise, the question requires only that the student recall what the teacher or text has explained.

Variations in instructions
Assessments in terms of f & p concepts may be presented in a great variety of ways. This variation is one of the strengths of such assessment. Instructions for answering questions can vary according to

- ❖ how specific and well-defined the question is;
- ❖ whether the problematic situation is to be identified by teacher or student;
- ❖ whether the appropriate f & p concepts are specified by the teacher or identified and then used by the student; and
- ❖ whether critical thinking dimensions are explicitly included in the question or must be seen as relevant and introduced into the response by the student.

The following list contains five variations in the kind of instructions that can be given to students. Each calls for the exercise of different sets of critical thinking skills. (The sample questions use general-education biology as the discipline and *cell* and *homeostasis* as the relevant f & p concepts.)

#1. Questions that are specific, and well-defined, where both the problem or situation and the f & p concepts are *specified* by the teacher:

    a. Reason out the following problem using the concept of *cell* and *homeostasis*.

    b. Explain what is occurring in the following situation, and why it is occurring, using the concept of *homeostasis* as the key concept in your explanation.

#2. Questions that are specific, and well-defined, where the problem or situation is identified by the teacher, but where the f & p concepts to be used are left *unspecified* by the teacher:

    Reason out the following problem using the most appropriate f & p concepts.

#3. Questions that are moderately *well-defined*:

    Chapter 7 discusses "Deriving Energy from Food." Explain the most important ideas in that chapter using the concepts *cell* and *homeostasis*.

#4. Questions that are *not well-defined*:

    Respond to the following situation as seems appropriate (or: as seems appropriate biologically).

#5. Questions in which the teacher specifies *context*, but the problem or situation is to be identified (and then framed and reasoned through) by the student:

    Look around this room at this moment: identify a significant situation or state of affairs that is within the domain of the discipline. Explain it, using the most appropriate f & p concepts in the course. [Variants include "Look at: this video, this novel, this essay, this newspaper, your family situation, the world today, your future as you envision it...".]

One important assumption behind these assessment strategies is that the more parts of an answer that are supplied by students themselves (instead of being contained explicitly in the written instructions), the more authentic the assessment of critical thinking in the discipline (see the discussion that follows). For example, in #4 the instructions supply only minimal information, asking students to respond to a described situation "as seems appropriate," or "as seems appropriate biologically." Students will have to frame the problem themselves—decide what is appropriate to address. This is fitting because it is precisely what needs to be done by anyone who is thinking critically about a real situation in terms of biology.

The level of authentic assessment is increased in #5. The goal in that type of question is to do as little identification of the situation-to-be-addressed as possible. The idea behind this strategy is that for people to think biologically about events they encounter in their lives outside the classroom, they must first be able to recognize and select (from the stream of their experience) those situations they need to think about in terms of the discipline.[3] This crucial part of learning to think within a discipline is seldom assessed.[4] It involves a disposition to see the discipline as relevant to one's life beyond the school setting. For example, if my brother is diagnosed with cancer, and I am confused about what is happening to him, I have to *recognize* that I might gain clarity by thinking through the situation in terms of the concept *cell*.

In varying the level of authentic assessment, a teacher may also decide to include *more specific* instructions in the question. As a teacher, I might choose to add any of the following to the kinds of questions outlined in #1–5:

In your explanation, in terms of f & p concepts, you should exercise the following critical thinking skills:

- ❖ give good reasons to back up your explanation;
- ❖ identify two key assumptions you are making;
- ❖ identify at least one alternative explanation someone might give;
- ❖ identify the strongest objection someone might make to your explanation; and
- ❖ identify the part of your explanation that is most questionable.

The teacher need not refer to the above required elements of the explanation as "critical thinking" skills or abilities. But it is important to note that these more specific central assessment instructions highlight elements of critical thinking skills or tools as identified by many other authors in this volume (particularly Johnson, Sobocan, and Case).

Giving more specific instructions along these lines is particularly appropriate near the beginning of a course, when the goal is to teach students some of the elements that are necessary to address in thinking through almost any question in the discipline. In explicitly asking students to identify the key assumptions they are making, I teach them that the identification of assumptions is a crucial step if one's response is to qualify as a critical thinking response. By later omitting those explicit instructions in questions of the sort outlined in #1–5, I am requiring students to identify assumptions without being prompted to do so. That is an important way to help students internalize the necessity of critical thinking in responses.

Additional variations
Another, more advanced, assessment alternative recognizes that f & p concepts in a discipline are not automatically adequate for explicating all ideas in that discipline.[5] In view of this, an important critical thinking skill is deciding when (and to what extent) a problem or situation *cannot* be adequately explained in terms of f & p concepts.

   #6. A problem to be identified within a context is one that is (or seems) *not adequately explainable* via the f & p concepts.

   a. Identify a significant topic from Chapter 4 that cannot be explained using the concepts *cell* and *homeostasis*.

   b. Identify some situation that is within the domain of the discipline, but which you cannot adequately explain using the f & p concepts in the course.

   i. What questions would you need to answer for the explanation to proceed?

   ii. What further information would you need for the explanation to proceed?

iii. How would you research that information?

In this case, the sub-questions are possible add-ons that can be used to assess students' skills in identifying relevant follow-up questions and in mapping out a plan of research. Both of these are major skills in learning to think critically within a discipline.

One virtue of assessment in terms of f & p concepts (and the other central reasoning assessments below) is its ability to infuse central critical thinking into standard assessment questions in a course—for example, those in the exercises at the end of a chapter in a textbook—whether those original questions required critical thinking or not.

#7. Take a standard, specific critical thinking essay question and change it into one that requires deeper, more critical thinking in the discipline.

> [*original*]   "What ecological consequences would occur if humans, using a new and deadly fungicide, destroyed all fungi on earth?" (Audeskirk 1999, 389)[6]

> [*add-on*]   After you have answered the original question, explain your response in terms of the concepts *cell* and *homeostasis*.

#8. Take a standard, highly specific problem from the chapter exercises, one that involves recall of information or rote problem-solving skills, and transform it into one that requires deeper critical thinking within the discipline.

a. [*original*] "Diagram the internal structure of leaves. What structures regulate water loss and CO_2 absorption by a leaf?" (Audeskirk 1999, 479)

b. [*original*] "Oxygen is released to the atmosphere in the light-dependent reactions of photosynthesis when water is split to supply electrons to

   A. Photosystem I
   B. Photosystem II
   C. Calvin cycle

D. C$_4$ pathway

E. CAM" (Krogh 2000, 166)

[*Add-on* to a. and b.]: Explain your answer using the concepts of *cell* and *homeostasis*.

Note that questions of this sort can require any degree of discipline-based depth or precision that the teacher deems appropriate, so no loss of rigour is entailed by central-reasoning assessments.

A similar virtue is that, by using f & p concepts, assessments can be constructed that require greater levels of synthesis. Very much of critical thinking testing has always emphasized analysis at the expense of synthesis, but with no real rationale other than that analysis is easier to test for. In fact, all central reasoning assessments require students to assemble and comprehend the broad, large-scale structure inherent in a discipline. Consider the following questions:

#9. What follows is a list of 18 "key terms" from the end of Chapter 8. Organize the most important of those terms into a coherent overall scheme, using the concepts of *cell* and *homeostasis* as your foundation. Note any terms that do not fit within this organization and explain why they do not fit.

#10. The end of Chapter 12 contains ten review questions and six multiple-choice questions. After answering them, explain how the questions are interrelated, using the concepts of *cell* and *homeostasis*.

#11. Look at the Table of Contents of your biology textbook. Review the headings of the 16 chapters. Explain how those 16 headings form a coherent picture of life. Use the concepts of *cell* and *homeostasis* to organize your synthesis. Give reasons and alternative explanations when appropriate.

Scoring student responses

Student responses to central assessments can be scored using general elements and standards of critical thinking as well as those that are more discipline based. Thus, a response can be scored on

❖ the extent to which it is clear and accurate;

❖ the extent to which it is backed up by reasons, evidence, and supporting details;

❖ whether it focuses on what is most important in responding to the problem (in contrast to listing unimportant information or details);

❖ whether it takes adequate account of complications that may arise;

❖ how comprehensive it is;

❖ whether relevant alternatives are addressed; and

❖ the extent to which it takes adequate account of the assumptions, interpretations, and inferences being used in the explanation.[7]

Other Central Reasoning Assessments

Using f & p concepts allows one to construct assessments that focus on some central ways of thinking critically within a discipline. A number of other tools for assessing critical thinking in a discipline work in roughly the same way by

❖ addressing *the most central question of the course*;

❖ seeing the world (i.e., interpreting situations) from *the point of view of the discipline* (including domain, categorizing of that domain, and connections among those categories); and

❖ analyzing *the logic of the discipline as a whole*.

The central question of a course is the question that underlies the course as a whole. (I speak of *the* central question, but there can be several—though not many.) The central question in an educational psychology course could be formulated in this way: "How do students learn, and how can I help students learn?" In a biology course, it might be, "How do living things work?" or "How do living things get to be the way they are?" These kinds of overall questions often get lost in the abundance of details in a course—yet it is the question that shapes the entire course. To answer a central question in an essay requires students to organize a well-thought-out way of fitting the whole together and to bring to bear insights from the entire course.

Asking students to write a response to the central question of the course serves as an excellent pre- and post-test for learning to think critically within a discipline. The difference between student responses at the beginning and the end of the course should display not merely a greater amount of information, but a substantially different way of approaching, organizing, and reasoning through the central question. Again, it is essential in central reasoning assessments that the teacher not present his or her direct answer to the central question during the course—otherwise the students' "well-reasoned responses" at the end may simply be mirroring the teacher's answer.[8]

Machine-Scorable Central Reasoning Assessments

Assessments in terms of f & p concepts, as described so far, are open-ended questions, requiring shorter or longer written responses. The same is true of the other central assessments mentioned above. Many of these questions, however, can be adapted to become machine-scorable as multiple-choice or multiple-rating items. There are any number of ways to do this, the simplest being for teachers to construct various responses (either created themselves or taken from open-ended responses by students to previous assessments) to variations #1–11, and then to ask students to rate them according to critical thinking standards, such as those listed above for scoring student responses. The conversion from open-ended to machine-scorable items brings with it a significant loss of authenticity in assessment, but there are of course distinct gains as well, particularly the feasibility of assessing large numbers of students.

Assumptions about Learning: Implications for Teaching

Central reasoning assessments are far enough removed from standard practices of teaching and assessing that I want to address some of their salient features and the implications they have for teaching, particularly for the question of how one should structure the attempt to teach students to think critically in a discipline. These implications concern the shift in course focus brought about by f & p concepts, the increased responsibility placed on students, and the goals of teaching general-education courses.[9]

Focus

Central reasoning assessments require students to attain greater mastery of a small number of flexible, widely applicable, discipline-central concepts and ideas rather than a cursory understanding of a much larger number of concepts that are only more or less central. An assumption I make in this chapter is that there is a distinct benefit in building a course around f & p concepts for learning to think critically in a discipline. F & p concepts are concepts-in-use: they are not simply to be learned *about*, but to be internalized and used to think about other things (lenses, rather than merely objects). They are organizers that help to put parts together into a coherent whole so that the students will not get lost in the details. F & p concepts constitute the most central, versatile, and widely transferable part of the discipline at the general-education level.

This approach clearly has implications for teaching. Teaching a course using dozens and dozens (maybe hundreds) of concepts (bold-faced terms in the text or in handouts, for example) is the most standard way of teaching and assessing in a discipline. In these cases, teachers sometimes take it for granted that students will get both an overview and the logic of the whole by studying the parts.[10] For many students the emphasis on numerous narrow concepts promotes a scattered, disconnected, patternless way of seeing the discipline, with little awareness of what is central and what is peripheral.

Centering a course on f & p concepts can counteract this disconnectedness. So, in a sociology course, students might study the same topics as before—culture, society, family, deviance, sexuality, and so forth—but now the course would be structured around the f & p concepts of *social patterns* and *social forces*. The focus of the course would be on having students take every important topic and learn to identify the *social patterns* inherent in it; and then understand the *social forces* that bring it about. Assignments and projects would also require students to use those same f & p concepts to reason through situations they encounter in their lives outside the course.

Student responsibility
Central reasoning assessments place more responsibility on students, requiring them to organize concepts into a reasonable, synthesized hierarchy. In the usual format for classroom tests, by contrast, questions or problems (a) are usually defined carefully by the teacher or the text, (b) relate only to the chapter or unit currently being studied, and (c)

concern concepts that appear largely disconnected from one another. None of these needs to hold true in a central reasoning assessment.

Clearly, this shift of responsibility also has teaching implications. The idea is to change the way the discipline is taught by focusing on helping students in three ways. First, the students must gain a strong grasp of the f & p concepts. Second, they must use the f & p concepts to link more specific concepts together into a logic. Third, they must then use those f & p concepts to gain insight—discipline-based insight—into a larger range of problems (topics, situations, states of affairs, questions, points of view, etc.). The aim is for students to become more self-sufficient in thinking their way through a wealth of problematic situations using the same small stock of fundamental and powerful concepts. Teachers may well begin this process by taking well-defined problems and guiding students through the task of critically understanding them using the f & p concepts. As time goes by, teachers can play a less central role. They can begin to describe problems more sketchily; they can direct students to a setting (a case study, a video, a book, etc.), leaving the problem itself to be identified not by the teacher at all, but by the students. As the course progresses, the teacher's role becomes more focused on providing guidance and feedback. The students will be required more and more to identify the relevant situations themselves, to frame them as problems to be thought through using f & p concepts, to organize their approach to understanding the situation in terms of the discipline, and then to carry out the explication themselves.

Goals of general-education courses

Central reasoning assessments facilitate the underlying goal of teaching a discipline as a general-education course. An assumption in this chapter is that such courses should be taught so as to benefit the students who are actually in them. One consequence is that non-majors and those who will not be professionals in the discipline should be taught knowledge and skills in the discipline that will benefit them *as* non-majors and non-professionals. That is, the course should not be taught as if all students were majors, when in fact they are not. Thus the underlying goal of a course, stated most generally, is to help students learn to use the discipline to identify, frame, and get insight into problems, questions, and situations that they will likely encounter in their lives, ones that will be important—important to *them*—to figure out.

Keeping central reasoning assessments in mind gives instructors a teaching guide, other than a textbook, by which they can select what is essential to achieving course goals. One such goal, perhaps the most important one (at least to those who contributed to this volume), is to emphasize the essential features of critical thinking throughout the course and in the evaluation of students' understanding of a discipline. To help students attain thoughtful understanding, instructors may well need to de-emphasize sub-topics, isolated skills, and details that are time consuming and less essential to the course. The skills targeted in central reasoning assessments are those that are essential both to thinking critically in a discipline within the classroom and to using discipline-based reasoning to enhance one's life.

Notes

1. I want to thank Richard Paul and Linda Elder for ongoing discussion about central reasoning assessments and a big-picture vision of critical thinking in a discipline. I also want to thank Jan Sobocan for putting together the conference, and for her patience in dealing with my delays and second thoughts.

2. Clearly there are several other viable candidates for f & p concepts in a biology course for non-majors: *gene* is one. *Replication, errors*, and *differential reproduction* are three in evolutionary biology. There are also misguided f & p concepts that people often already use to shape their understanding. *Progress* and *survival of the fittest* (in the ordinary sense of the terms) are good examples in evolutionary biology. Many students use such concepts to interpret all of the presented evolutionary material in the course, thereby subtly misinterpreting "the whole" while still getting "the parts" right on exams.

3. A rather extreme illustration: #5 might be accompanied by a ten-minute clip of a Hollywood movie, only one or two aspects of which have serious biological implications, requiring students then to recognize those aspects themselves.

4. It is assessed at least partly in some fields; for example, in trials in medical education.

5. Thus, both taxonomy questions in biology and ethics-related biology questions are not readily explicable using the concepts of *cell* and *homeostasis*.

6. In calling this a critical thinking question, I am again assuming that student responses would have to include reasons, evidence, possible alterna-

tives, and so forth. I am also assuming that the teacher has not already answered this question in a class lecture.

7. For a fuller account of these elements and standards of reasoning, see Paul and Elder (2001, 95–102).
8. For an explication of the idea behind these central reasoning assessments, see Nosich (2009, 97–119).
9. There are larger-scale implications as well. One has to do with using a concept of critical thinking that is substantive enough to shape instruction in such a far-reaching way. Another has to do with the kind of institutional change that needs to be made to support a shift in teaching for critical thinking across the curriculum.
10. Textbooks may or may not be a rough measure of the number of concepts covered in a course. A sampling of twenty-three major introductory-level college textbooks, across the curriculum (including composition, literature and the arts, social sciences, education, natural sciences, business, information systems, and math), shows an average of over 650 "key" terms per book. They range from a low of 120 key terms (in a history text) to a high of more than 3,600 terms (in a biology text). Key terms in a typical text range from those as fundamental and powerful as *plate tectonics* and *continental drift* to those as specific and narrow as *barchanoid dunes*.

References

Audeskirk, T., and G. Audeskirk. 1999. *Biology: Life on earth.* Upper Saddle River, NJ: Prentice Hall.

Krogh, D. 2000. *A guide to the natural world.* Upper Saddle River, NJ: Prentice Hall.

Nosich, G. 2009. *Learning to think things through: A guide to critical thinking across the curriculum.* Upper Saddle River, NJ: Prentice Hall.

Paul, R., and L. Elder. 2001. *Critical thinking: Tools for taking charge of your learning and your life.* Upper Saddle River, NJ: Prentice Hall.

Chapter Eleven

The Institutional Assessment of Critical Thinking: A Fifteen-Year Perspective

Donald L. Hatcher

Sometimes good things happen accidentally. People inherit money from distant relatives whom they have never met. Some very lucky people meet the loves of their lives quite by chance. In education, too, good things may happen accidentally. Let me describe an instance of my own.

In the early 1970s, I was simultaneously enrolled in an introductory logic course and a seminar in Plato. One day, after having studied some of the standard deductive patterns of reasoning (*modus ponens, modus tollens, disjunctive syllogism*) in the logic class, I was working through one of the Platonic dialogues when I realized that many of Socrates's arguments followed the same patterns I had learned in the logic class. I discovered that it was easier to follow the arguments if I sketched them in formal notation in the margins of the book. This was a useful exercise because a significant part of our grade was determined by the quality of our outlines of the dialogues we read (my professor was committed to a fundamental principle of critical thinking: that students cannot adequately criticize what they have not first understood, and outlining what one reads is a good way to achieve this first end).

The accidental application of the simplest tools of formal logic to the arguments of Plato (and the arguments of many other treatises read in graduate school) suggested an idea. Perhaps, when these great thinkers and writers sat down to write an essay, they sketched their arguments in standard deductive form, and then proceeded to write. I hypothesized that this might explain why some writers were able to create such clear and powerful arguments, whereas others wrote in a way that seemed muddled and unfocused. If the great thinkers of old proceeded in this way, why not find a way to teach college students today to employ this method? It seemed to me that the essays of average college students would be greatly enhanced if they first sketched the arguments for their theses in standard deductive form and evaluated them critically before writing. This was ten years before I heard the phrase "critical thinking."

These simple ideas were the genesis of what became, years later, Baker University's Liberal Arts Program, an experiment in joining the disciplines of logic and critical thinking with instruction in written composition. This is an experiment supported by $1,000,000 in grant funding (sometimes one gets really lucky).[1] Judging by the assessment results, it is an experiment that is relatively successful when it is compared to many other attempts to teach critical thinking.[2]

My chapter in this book explains the development and operation of the Baker program and reports on our ongoing assessment efforts. Because our approach to teaching critical thinking was unique—with some skeptics saying we were not teaching composition, others claiming that we were not doing justice to logic and critical thinking—careful assessment has been an extremely important part of the program. In addition to providing evidence for the success of our approach, our model shows how easily assessment can be implemented, and provides fifteen years of data that others can use for comparison.

The ability to compare is one of the great benefits of standardized critical thinking tests. These assessments allow us to compare the educational outcomes of different attempts to teach critical thinking. Such comparisons are the best way for teachers of critical thinking to find ways of teaching critical thinking that work (and do not work), and such comparisons, in turn, can inform the development of our testing instruments. In keeping with the latter, one of the interesting aspects of the Baker history of assessing critical thinking is our ability to compare the results of the two tests that we used. From 1990 to 1996, we used the Ennis-Weir Critical Thinking Essay Test (E-W), and from 1996 to the present, we have used the *California Critical Thinking Skills Test* (CCTST). Although the results have been positive in both instances, they have not been the same.

The History of Baker's Liberal Arts Program

Baker University's General Education Program of fifty-plus college hours contains three specially designed courses required of all students: a two-semester freshmen sequence (LA 101 and LA 102) and a senior capstone (LA 401). The freshmen sequence, "Critical Thinking and Effective Writing" and "Ideas and Exposition," provides all Baker freshmen with instruction in formal logic and critical thinking skills, and shows how this knowledge can be used successfully in writing expository prose. The senior capstone seminar, "Science, Technology, and Human Values," asks each senior to choose a public policy issue brought about by current scientific or technological developments, and then to research, prepare, present, and defend a fifteen- to twenty-five-page position paper that argues for a specific public policy with respect to the issue. Topics include cloning, water-use policy, energy policy, reproductive practices, numerous medical issues, and defence policy, to name a few of over one hundred possible issues. A significant part of the paper includes a critical analysis and response to alternative policies or objections to the proposed policy. Students must consider the ethical consequences of each alternative under consideration.

The senior capstone, LA 401, began thirty years ago in 1979, and it was not long before the faculty members who were teaching sections of the course realized that many of our seniors were seriously challenged when we asked them to write a critical or argumentative paper. The primary difficulty was their lack of understanding logic: what arguments were, how one constructs them, and how one evaluates them. To address this shortcoming, we began planning the required freshmen critical thinking and composition sequence, LA 101 and LA 102, in 1988. This project was funded by two grants from the Fund for the Improvement of Postsecondary Education (FIPSE) provided by the United States Department of Education. It has since been supplemented with a series of four grants from the Hall Family Foundation. A good deal of the Hall Grant money has gone towards faculty development, dissemination, and assessment. Those in the Hall Family Foundation are committed to the idea that the Baker method of teaching writing and critical thinking needs to be circulated more widely in education.

Although the primary reason for developing the freshmen critical thinking and composition sequence was to better prepare Baker seniors for the LA 401 capstone experience, Baker faculty members believed, more generally, that critical thinking skills are the skills that students need if they are to evaluate alternative positions and write carefully argued papers for any of their courses.[3] The critical thinking and composition sequence thus provides all of our entering students with skills essential for success in their college courses. The teaching of these skills includes instruction in paraphrasing and summarizing difficult readings; logical techniques for evaluating the reasonableness of beliefs and arguments; and logical strategies for developing strong arguments to support students' ideas used in papers across the curriculum.

The Critical Thinking and Composition Sequence

What are the Baker freshmen courses like? For those who worked on the Baker project, getting clear on what exactly we meant by critical thinking was extremely important. We understood that our conception of critical thinking would greatly influence both the structure and content of the courses. We examined some of the standard definitions of critical thinking and were not enamoured with any of them.[4] We wanted a definition that would be as clear and concise as possible, so that both we and the unconvinced would know what we were talking about when we discussed the new sequence. The definition needed to be easy to explicate to students, faculty, and administrators, showing why critical thinking is an essential educational goal.

We wanted a definition that referred specifically to the criteria that should be used for critical judgment. Otherwise, one could not expect agreement over what counts as a reasonable position. The definition should imply that critical thinking has broad educational utility, that it is applicable to many disciplines. It should be obvious from the definition that students in art, literature, political science, or history can benefit from learning logic and critical thinking skills. The definition, moreover, should allow people to distinguish critical thinking from other cognitive activities such as creative thinking, problem-solving, and logical inference. It should provide enough guidance to faculty to allow them to construct tests and assignments to assess whether students have acquired the appropriate skills and dispositions.

Given all of these constraints, the definition we chose defines critical thinking as "thinking that tries to arrive at a judgment only after honestly evaluating alternatives with respect to available evidence and arguments."[5] Properly understood, we believed that this definition could provide the needed foundation for a course integrating instruction in logic and expository prose. That is, when a student is assigned a position paper, the process will include the honest evaluation of alternative positions before the position to be defended is chosen. This means getting clear on the arguments for each alternative, and then evaluating their strengths and weaknesses. The paper's thesis will be the position with the strongest support and weakest objections.

Our courses begin, like many other critical thinking courses, by explaining the nature and importance of critical thinking. The text *Reasoning and Writing: From Critical Thinking to Composition* (2006) gives a number of arguments, both practical and theoretical, for the value of critical thinking instruction. We show how many social problems, such as those resulting from prejudice against women and minorities, are the result of basing beliefs on insufficient evidence and hasty generalizations. In addition, many personal problems, especially among the young, stem from poor judgment or a failure to evaluate honestly the available alternatives before making a decision. We begin the course by reading Plato's "Allegory of the Cave" in an attempt to get students to recognize how many of their ideas are a function of values projected on the walls of their specific "caves" when they were young. This approach to the beginning of the course clearly supports Hare's position that the claim "critical thinking texts and courses tend to teach political *conformity*" is indeed fallacious (see Hare, this volume). It is difficult to free students from the effects of living in a specific culture, and its values and ideas, in a few classes, but we do try to convince them that becoming a critical thinker is in their own interest.

After showing the importance of what we are asking students to learn, we follow with instruction in how to read, paraphrase, and summarize difficult prose and how to identify the arguments it contains. Because many students come to college with weak reading skills, learning to read carefully, with an eye to the evidence and arguments for any claim, is an essential skill. To address this, we spend a good deal of time teaching students how to paraphrase and ultimately summarize what they read. The goal is to read an argumentative passage, identify the position (conclusion), and identify the reasons (premises) given in support of the conclusion (e.g., "Smith believes X because A, B, C, and D"[6]).

Once students can identify and summarize arguments, the next step is instruction in argument evaluation. To this end we employ the technique of Deductive Reconstruction.[7] That is, each of the arguments is put into standard deductive form—*modus ponens, modus tollens, disjunctive syllogism*, or some combination of these. The theory behind Deductive Reconstruction is the following: if the arguments are in a valid deductive form, then, for purposes of evaluation, the main question is whether the premises are reasonable or whether they need further support. Evaluating the level of support for the premises usually involves understanding inductive logic. We spend only three to four weeks—an unusually brief time compared with other critical thinking courses—studying deduction, induction, and a few of the more common informal fallacies. There are other methods for evaluating arguments, but we decided to focus on these because of their simplicity, transferability among other disciplines, and usefulness in constructing arguments that will ultimately form the backbone of students' papers (remember my experience with logic and the Platonic dialogues). Most students have little trouble mastering the techniques we teach, though faculty who are not trained in philosophy sometimes struggle with the material when they first begin to teach it.

The final weeks of the semester provide instruction designed to show how the tools of Deductive Reconstruction are useful in writing expository papers.[8] We teach students how to use some of the standard argument patterns (*modus ponens, modus tollens*, and *disjunctive syllogism*) to construct arguments in support of positions they might defend in a paper. For example, one way to argue *for* a position is to employ what we call a *modus tollens* strategy. Students begin by negating the position in question, show how this leads to unacceptable consequences, and conclude that the position in question should be supported. If we wanted to argue for teaching critical thinking to all students, such an argument might go something like this: "If we do not teach critical thinking, citizens will be easily duped by politicians. We do not want that in a democracy. Hence, we should teach critical thinking to all students."

In a spirit that embraces the honest evaluation of alternative positions, we ask students to construct the best arguments they can on both sides of an issue before deciding upon a thesis. Often, weak papers are the result of students picking a position, not because they have honestly evaluated the alternatives, but because it agrees with their deeply felt intuitions or "gut feelings." In such cases, students fail to recognize the extent to which they have been socialized by their culture to think in certain ways about specific issues—even though there may be good reasons for alternative conclusions. We use Plato's Allegory of the Cave to underscore this point.

After evaluating arguments for and against different sides of an issue, students construct theses and create their outlines for their position papers. They then meet with teachers to discuss an outline. The focus of the conference is the thesis and the strength of the arguments given in its support. If the outline is judged acceptable, the student begins writing a draft. This, too, is evaluated by the instructor. All papers follow the same four-part pattern: an introduction, clarification, and thesis; supporting reasons and arguments; possible objections and replies; and a summation and conclusion.

The second semester of the freshmen course asks students to apply these same critical thinking skills and strategies to five sets of readings and to write five additional critical papers. All papers include the same basic parts—thesis, support, counter-arguments or objections, replies, and conclusion (though not necessarily in this order)—and are composed in a manner that follows the same process students used in the first semester. Although all sections of the course use the same text as a basis for the first semester's paper, teachers are free to choose any set of readings in the second semester, on the understanding that all the papers follow the same process and are graded according to the same rubric. Given that instructors come from many different disciplines, finding one text that all teachers felt equally enthusiastic about proved to be an unrealistic goal. These critical thinking courses differ from traditional courses in a number of ways. Unlike most critical thinking courses, they teach students to use formal logic and critical thinking skills to argue for and critique positions in their papers. The time spent on writing, probably 70 percent, far exceeds the time spent on instruction in the logic necessary for critical thinking. The Baker courses differ from traditional composition courses in so far as they emphasize only one type of paper: the argumentative essay. In addition, grammar is taught only in the context of student writing assignments. For example, upon returning a set of essays a teacher might spend half a class period going over the points of grammar found wanting in the papers or (better yet) choose to meet with each student to explain the problems. Students must return their papers with all mechanical errors corrected before their grades are recorded.

Assessing the Baker Freshmen Courses with the E-W

In the fall of 2005, we began the fifteenth year of the freshmen program. Our assessment data continues to demonstrate that our approach is as good as or better than many more traditional alternatives to the teaching of critical thinking or writing.[9] With the endorsement of Stephen Norris, we began assessing the critical thinking element of the LA Program with the Ennis-Weir Critical Thinking Essay Test (E-W). Because the sequence integrates instruction in writing with logic and critical thinking, this test was deemed to be the most appropriate. It asks students to respond, in writing, to an eight-paragraph letter to the editor, stating whether the reasoning in each paragraph is good or bad and supporting their judgments with reasons (see Johnson, this volume, for a more detailed description of the E-W). The pre-test is given to all freshmen the first week of the fall semester. We tell them that we are part of a large research project and to do their very best. The post-test is given as part of the final exam the last week of the spring semester and counts for about 3 percent of the student's total grade.[10] This encourages students to take the post-test seriously. The data below indicates the outcomes for the pre- and post-tests for the six years that we used E-W.

Year	Pre	St.D.	Post	St.D.	Mean Gain	Diff in St.D.* (Effect Size)
90/91 (n=169)	6.3		12.4		+6.1	+1.11
91/92 (n=119)	9.4		12.2		+2.8	+0.51
92/93 (n=178)	6.8		12.6		+5.8	+1.05
93/94 (n=178)	8.1		14.1		+6.0	+1.09
94/95 (n=164)	7.5		13.0		+5.5	+1.00
95/96 (n=169)	6.9		12.9		+6.0	+1.09
Mean (n=977)	**7.5**	**+/-5.3**	**12.8**	**+/-5.7**	**+5.3**	**+0.97**

*St.D. used is 5.5, the average St.D. pre- and post-tests.

Comparison Groups Using the Ennis-Weir Test

	Pre	Post	Diff.	Mean Gain in St.D.
Standard Logic Class F94 (n=44)	11.2	9.5	- 1.7	- 0.31
Standard CT Class S92 (n=23)	12.1	13.7	+1.6	+0.29
Mean (n=67)	**11.7**	**11.6**	**- 0.10**	**- 0.02**

Comparison of BU Freshmen Scores to Senior Scores on Ennis-Weir

	Fr.	Sr.	Diff	Mean Gain in St.D.
Grads 1995 (n=119)	9.4	14.6	+5.2	+0.94
Grads 1996 (n=88)	7.1	14.1	+7.0	+1.27
Grads 1997 (n=80)	6.8	14.8	+8.0	+1.45
Grads 1998 (n=58)	8.8	19.1	+10.3	+1.87
Grads 1999 (n=42)	7.3	17.4	+10.1	+1.84
Mean (n=387)	**7.9**	**16.0**	**+8.1**	**+1.47**

Table 1: Comparison of Ennis-Weir Critical Thinking Essay Test pre- and post-test scores for Baker freshmen, 1990–1996

Our experience using the E-W as an assessment tool leaves little doubt that our approach to teaching critical thinking achieved significantly better outcomes than the two comparison groups. Anyone who claims that an approach to teaching critical thinking that integrates written composition cannot work is thus shown to be mistaken. The same can be said of anyone who thinks that the only way to teach critical thinking is by using the standard approaches found in most informal logic texts. A freshman gain of nearly a full standard deviation in critical thinking skills is an impressive gain, and much better than the gain in the comparison groups.[11]

One might argue that the comparison groups started out with higher pre-test scores, and so could not be expected to gain as much. There may be something to this argument but it hardly accounts for the standard logic classes getting worse. The critical thinking class did have a higher post-test score, but the effect-size gain of 0.29 is less than the literature claims is average (an effect-size gain of 0.5 standard deviation is considered average[12]).

Why did the freshmen in Baker's integrated, two-semester sequence do so much better on the E-W than the comparison groups who were taking the more traditional classes in logic and critical thinking? Educational research is notoriously uncertain and definitive answers would take more controlled experiments that carefully isolated as many variables as possible, e.g., teaching methods, textbooks, and teacher preparation. We have not been able to carry out an extensive program of research along these lines, but there are some obvious aspects of our freshmen sequence that may be causally related to the difference in performance between our students and the comparison groups.

Key characteristics of our classes are simplicity and the repeated application of the critical thinking skills we emphasize in our two-semester sequence. Almost everything covered in the sequence aims to develop skills for evaluating the arguments found in what students read and what they write. Such simplicity and repetition may make it easier for students to internalize the basic critical thinking skills and apply them successfully to the E-W. Beyond that, it is possible that traditional logic courses confuse students by trying to cover too much material: deduction (with proofs), induction, informal fallacies, and sometimes quantification theory. In the two-semester sequence, we devote only the first six weeks to the study of the principles of critical thinking and logic. Most of what students cover early in the sequence is then applied repeatedly to what they read and in writing their papers. The logical tools are seen as something that have obvious and immediate use in students' educations—not as just a set of skills needed to pass a test and then to be forgotten.

In part because of our emphasis on repetition, the time our students spend using the skills we teach distinguishes our approach from that experienced by the comparison groups. Looked at from this point of view, it is not surprising that a two-semester sequence, in which relatively simple skills are repeatedly practised for twenty-three weeks, yields better outcomes than broader, traditional one-semester courses in critical thinking or logic. Our experience provides evidence of the value of an "across-the-curriculum" approach to critical thinking, in which all instructors ask students to evaluate positions by the standards of evidence and argument appropriate to their discipline. If the same song is sung often enough, most students learn it. When different teachers play the game by different rules, then students have, in contrast, a difficult time deciding what is important and what is peripheral, and are less able to evaluate the rationality of a position.[13]

Another reason our students may have taken critical thinking more seriously than those in the comparison groups is our emphasis on the value of a logical critique to most of the things they read and write. If we are successful in this, then students will use the techniques we teach, not only in assignments for our courses, but in assignments for other courses, and in reading and writing other material every day. In such a context, it is plausible to suppose that they may be more inclined to learn the skills we teach.

During the time in which we used the E-W for assessment purposes, our research indicated that one-semester courses in critical thinking make a fairly small difference in students' abilities to think critically. In contrast, student performance is significantly enhanced by a two-semester sequence that teaches the logical tools needed for "the honest evaluation of alternative positions" and then requires that students apply this knowledge to expository writing.

Hopefully, other educators interested in assessing student critical thinking skills can learn from our experiment and share their assessment data with the wider educational community. Some may be reluctant to use the E-W because it is an essay test and time-consuming to grade, and because one might imagine that it would be difficult to achieve inter-grader reliability. But our experience shows that it is possible to achieve inter-grader reliability of 0.85 or better using well-trained student workers, and grading time can be reduced if researchers choose a random sample of the essays and grade only those, instead of grading all students' essays for assessment purposes. We learned the latter lesson too late to take advantage of it— after double-blind grading of 1,447 E-W essays (sometimes one is *un*lucky).

Assessing the Baker Approach with the CCTST

In the fall of 1996, we began to do pre- and post-testing with the *California Critical Thinking Test* Form A (the CCTST). One reason for the change was concern about the growing post-test gains of our seniors. By 1999, the effect-size gain by the graduating seniors was 1.84, and that seemed unreasonably high. We hypothesized that the material on the test must be public, and the seniors were using it to study for the test. The data for the eight years during which we used the CCTST follows.

Freshmen	Pre	St.D.	Post	St.D.	Diff.	Mean Gain St.D.
F96/S97 (n=152)	15.14	+/-4.46	18.49	+/-4.30	+3.35	0.75
F97/S98 (n=192)	14.50	+/-3.84	17.17	+/-4.40	+2.67	0.60
F98/S99 (n=171)	15.81	+/-4.60	17.90	+/-4.72	+2.09	0.46
F99/S00 (n=153)	15.91	+/-4.20	18.28	+/-4.30	+2.50	0.53
F00/S01 (n=184)	16.00	+/-4.20	18.52	+/-4.23	+2.37	0.51
F01/S02 (n=198)	15.30	+/-4.11	17.47	+/-4.44	+2.17	0.48
F02/S03 (n=221)	15.60	+/-4.1	18.2	+/-4.40	+2.60	0.57
F03/S04 (n=169)	15.40	+/-4.1	18.1	+/-4.60	+2.70	0.60
Mean (n=1447)	**15.10**	**+/-4.2**	**18.0**	**+/-4.30**	**+2.60**	**0.56**

Comparison Group[143]	Pre	St.D	Post	St. D.	Diff.	Mean Gain St.D.
1990 Test Validation Study (n=262)	15.94	+/-4.50	17.38	+/-4.7	+1.44	0.32
2000 University of Melbourne (n=50)	19.50	+/-4.74	23.46	+/-4.36	3.96	0.88
2001 McMaster University (n=278)	17.03	+/-4.45	19.22	+/-4.92	+2.19	0.49
2001 Monash University (n=174)	19.07	+/-4.72	20.35	+/-5.05	+1.28	0.28
2002 University of Melbourne (n=117)	18.85	+/-4.54	22.10	+/-4.66	+3.35	0.73
Mean (n=831)	**18.08**	**+/-4.59**	**20.50**	**+/-4.73**	**+2.42**	**0.54**

*The standard deviation used is always 4.52. That was the standard deviation used when the test was validated.

Comparison of Freshmen Scores to Senior Scores on the CCTST: Fall 2000–Spring 2004

Seniors	Freshmen	Seniors	Diff.	Mean Gain St.D.
Grads. 2000 (n=102)	15.2	19.4	+4.2	0.93
Grads. 2001 (n=79)	14.3	18.3	+4.0	0.88
Grads. 2002 (n=86)	15.8	19.2	+3.4	0.75
Grads. 2003 (n=65)	15.8	19.7	+3.9	0.87
Grads. 2004 (n=88)	15.9	20.2	+4.3	0.95
Mean (n=396)	**15.6**	**19.3**	**+4.0**	**0.88**

Table 2: Freshmen pre- and post-test scores using the *California Critical Thinking Stills Test*, fall 1996 to spring 2004

The CCTST is a professionally normed test. It is used to assess critical thinking course outcomes and gives users a clearer sense of what student scores mean relative to other schools' performances than that provided by the E-W. With the average gain of +2.6 points or 0.56 of a standard deviation for the freshmen year, we did better than the mean gain of 2.42 points, or 0.54 of a standard deviation, for the comparison groups. Again, it is generally understood that any effect-size gain over 0.50 of a standard deviation for one course is a strong performance, even though the gains were much smaller than those on the E-W. Most heartening are our mean scores (0.56), which were always higher than the mean of the test validation study (0.32). The McMaster and University of Melbourne courses both employed computer-assisted exercises, something our timeline for teaching the basic logic and critical thinking material prohibits. Because the justification for the freshmen sequence is to prepare students to write strong critical papers, we spend minimal time on textbook logic and critical thinking exercises.

The average gain on the CCTST from the freshmen to senior year has been +4.0 points, +1.4 points better than the +2.6 point average gain during the freshman year. This is a reasonable gain on a very challenging test with only 34 points. Studies show that students' critical thinking skills usually do not increase over 0.55 of a standard deviation over three years of college.

Obviously, the pre-test scores for McMaster University (17.03) and the University of Melbourne (18.85) were much higher than the Baker scores. This may be a function of three things: first, the students at those schools were taking the critical thinking courses as an elective or a course serving a major; if so, they may have been better equipped or more inclined to do well in such a course. Second, they were older than the entering freshmen at Baker with more college courses completed, and one might assume that experience with college-level course work would in itself enhance critical thinking skills (although I have no way of knowing whether this is so). Third, unlike the students at McMaster University and the University of Melbourne, those in the Baker program were not allowed to drop the course, which may have meant that weaker students stayed in the courses and lowered the post-test mean.

Some Thoughts about the E-W and the CCTST

What can we say about the different outcomes from the two tests we used to measure the effectiveness of our courses and our program? The differences in mean gain in standard deviation between the E-W and the CCTST are obvious.

Freshmen	Pre	St.D.	Post	St.D.	Diff.	Mean Gain in St.D.
E-W Mean (n=977)	7.5	+/-5.3	12.8	+/-5.7	+5.3	+0.97
CCTST Mean (n=1447)	15.1	+/-4.2	18.0	+/-4.3	+2.6	+0.56
BU Freshmen to Seniors						
E-W Mean (n=387)	7.9		16.0		+8.1	+1.47
CCTST Mean (n=396)	15.6		19.3		+4.0	+0.88

Table 3: Comparing the E-W and the CCTST

The effect-size gains on the E-W are nearly double those on the CCTST, even though all students who took each test have gone through the same program, using the same text, doing the same assignments. This raises an obvious question: Which one is more accurately measuring students' abilities as critical thinkers? The answer to this question may depend on how one conceptualizes critical thinking. If we think that a fairly deep understanding of deductive logic and the ability to test scientific hypotheses are both essential skills of any student who claims to be a critical thinker, then I would say that the CCTST is a more accurate measure. This is because numerous questions on the test require that students have a clear understanding of deductive validity (and much of what that concept entails) or how to test for the acceptability of a hypothesis or to falsify one. I cannot imagine students doing very well on the CCTST without a clear understanding of both deductive and inductive logic.

But many informal approaches to critical thinking adopt a conception which does not emphasize formal logic. If one adopts this kind of conception, then the E-W might be a better tool for assessing student progress in critical thinking. In deciding which instrument to favour, it is important to remember that the ultimate purpose of assessment is not only to measure students' performance against that of others or some pre-established norm, but also to see how well students are achieving the educational goals of specific programs, or reaching course objectives.

Beyond the differences in the scope of the two tests (differences one can see more clearly after reading Groarke and Johnson in this volume), one could argue that the act of taking E-W more closely resembles what we want our students as critical thinkers to do in real life: read extended arguments, evaluate their merit, and then articulate them in writing with a cogent critique. The act of taking the E-W is a more natural experience for students than meticulously working through the thirty-four questions on the CCTST, some of which are highly artificial (e.g., the question that asks one to "Consider the 'krendalog' relationship"). Yet the CCTST has the sort of questions, as Hitchcock (2003) and van Gelder, Cumming, and Bisset (2004) have shown, that complement computer-assisted exercises, exercises that can significantly enhance students' performances. Students can prepare by practising discrete logical skills that can be applied to the CCTST. Yet, because of its resemblance to real-life situations that call for critical thinking, one might argue that the E-W is in fact a better gauge of a student's ability to think critically in real situations.

Conclusion

No matter which test more accurately measures students' critical thinking abilities, it is important that more teachers of critical thinking choose a standardized test that has been professionally normed or used so widely that norms are available. Only when a large number of teachers do pre- and post-testing in their courses will it be possible to determine systematically which approaches to teaching critical thinking work and which do not.

Many teachers prefer to use personalized "in-house" assessment tests or portfolios, but they are problematic. To the extent that teachers rely on instruments of this sort, they will not be able to determine how their students are doing relative to other students in similar situations in other institutions. Research reports that use such individualized, and hence unfamiliar, tests and approaches cannot tell the wider circles of academe what works and what should be avoided. Creating one's own assessment test or grading portfolios is time consuming, in any case, and there is no way to know, without a lot of professional help, whether the test or portfolio approach is valid.

The data on two standardized tests collected by Hitchcock, van Gelder, and me allows us to establish what sort of an effect-size gain can be expected from a one-semester critical thinking course, or a two-semester sequence that combines critical thinking and composition. If the results are better than those reported in the current research, this is good news that should be shared with all. If the results are lower than the norm, this is a useful sign that one should begin to address deficiencies in an attempt to achieve better student outcomes. That is what assessment is really all about: improving student learning by finding out in a systematic way what students know or can do at the end of a course or program and responding conscientiously to the outcomes.

In my case, a project begun in 1988 that grew out of my experience as a student simultaneously enrolled in a course in logic and a seminar in Plato produced a unique approach to teaching critical thinking and writing, and probably provides the largest pool of assessment data available using two well-known standardized critical thinking tests. I hope that our approach at Baker to teaching critical thinking and our ongoing attempts to assess it will be of use to others faced with the challenges of teaching and assessing critical thinking.

Notes

1. After the original FIPSE grants of $168,000 to plan and set up the freshmen sequence, the Hall Family Foundation has supplemented the program with grants of over $850,000 since 1991.
2. We also assessed the writing outcomes using the Test of Standard Written English, and found that our students did better than students taking courses using more standard approaches to written composition.
3. Of course, it was also a good excuse to try out my theory about the relationship between knowledge of formal logic and good prose.
4. For a defence of the conception we finally agreed to use, see Hatcher (2000).
5. I would be remiss not to give credit to Connie Missimer for her influence on this conception of critical thinking. Connie convinced me years ago that critical thinking, like good scientific investigation, should always include the weighing of alternatives, whether theories, explanations, accounts, courses of action, or policies. Note also, that although we distinguish critical from creative thinking in the Baker program, the part of our definition which includes getting clear on and honestly evaluating alter-

natives does not conflict with much of what is said in Part Two of this volume about the nature of creative critical thinking. If one is to evaluate alternatives, one must first "imagine" them.

6. Of course in a complex argument, the reasons A, B, C, and D might themselves have reasons to support them.

7. While the use of Deductive Reconstruction dates back to my college days mentioned at the beginning of the chapter, this approach to critical thinking is also present in Nosich (1982) and Cederblom and Paulsen (2001). For a defence of deductive reconstruction, see Groarke (1999).

8. By expository paper, I mean any paper where the student must have a thesis and support it with evidence and arguments. The techniques we teach would be of little use to students whose writing assignments do not involve such a task, e.g., creative writing, reports, surveys of the literature, or accounts of historical events.

9. For a more complete description of the program, see Hatcher (1999a, 1999b).

10. Perhaps a better strategy to insure that students take both the pre-and post-test seriously is to tell them at the pre-test that some students do worse on the post-test, albeit not many, and the score used for points on the final exam will be the higher of the pre- or post-test.

11. Pascaralla and Terenzini (2004); the three-year estimate for CT gain was .55 mean standard deviation.

12. In addition to the work of Pascaralla and Terenzini, Norman, Sloan, and Wyrwich (2003) come to the same conclusion.

13. The approach I take with respect to teaching critical thinking is quite similar to that of Nosich (in this volume). That is, we share emphasis on reasoning assessment. Comparing the two approaches and definitions of critical thinking might, then, be a worthwhile exercise. Similarities between the two approaches are not surprising, since previously Nosich (1982), like our program, has taken a Deductive Reconstruction approach to critical thinking.

14. Both the McMaster University and University of Melbourne courses used computer-assisted instruction to supplement in-class work. I think their positive gains indicate that computer exercises have a positive role to play in enhancing critical thinking test scores. It would be interesting to see their gains if they used the E-W. For a full account and analysis of the McMaster course see Hitchcock (2003). See "How to Improve Critical Thinking Using Educational Technology" by Tim van Gelder (2001).

References

Cederblom, J., and D. Paulsen. 2001. *Critical reasoning*, 5th ed. Belmont, CA: Wadsworth Publishing.

Groarke, L. 1999. Deductivism within pragma-dialectics. *Argumentation* 13: 1–16.

Hatcher, D. 2000. Arguments for another definition of critical thinking. *Inquiry: Critical Thinking Across the Disciplines* 20(1): 3–8.

———. 1999a. Why formal logic is essential for critical thinking. *Informal Logic* 19(1): 77–89.

———. 1999b. Why we should combine critical thinking and written instruction. *Informal Logic* 19(2 and 3): 171–83.

Hatcher, D., and L. Spencer. 2006. *From critical thinking to composition*, 3d ed. Boston, MA: American Press.

———. 2000. *Reasoning and writing: An introduction to critical thinking*, 2d ed. Boston, MA: American Press.

Hitchcock, D. 2003. The effectiveness of computer-assisted instruction in critical thinking. In *Informal logic at 25: Proceedings of the Windsor conference*, ed. J. Blair, D. Farr, et al. Windsor, ON: OSSA.

Norman, G., J. Sloan, and K. Wyrwich. 2003. Interpretation of changes in health-related quality of life: The remarkable universality of half a standard deviation. *Medical Care* 41: 582–92.

Nosich, G. 1982. *Reasons and arguments*. Belmont, CA: Wadsworth.

Pascaralla, E., and P. Terenzini. 2004. *How college affects students revisited: Research from the 90s*. San Francisco, CA: Jossey-Bass.

van Gelder, T. 2001. How to improve critical thinking using educational technology. In *Meeting at the crossroads: Proceedings of the 18th annual conference of the Australasian Society for Computers in Learning in Tertiary Education*, ed. G. Kennedy, M. Keppell, C. McNaught, and T. Petrovic, 539–48. Melbourne: Biomedical Multimedia Unit, University of Melbourne.

van Gelder, T., G. Cumming, and M. Bissett. 2004. Cultivating expertise in informal reasoning. *Canadian Journal of Experimental Psychology* 58(2): 142–52.

Chapter Twelve

Putting Pragma-Dialectics into Practice

Frans H. van Eemeren and Bart Garssen

A Method for Critical Reflection
on Argumentative Discourse

However one defines "critical thinking," it is clear that arguing plays a central role. And arguing is a propensity that everyone seems to have—at least anyone who has acquired language. Whether educated or not, everyone uses arguments in almost every conceivable situation—in deliberations at work, in civil conversations, and in interpersonal "fights." One might easily conclude that everyone knows how to argue. This is the impression that might be gleaned from letters to the editor in the local newspaper or overhearing one's neighbours debating whose turn it is to take the dog out. The apparent ease with which people argue might be taken as proof that argumentation is something one does not need to learn. But those who have studied argumentative practice more carefully know better. They know that argumentative competence depends on a complex array of insights, dispositions, and skills.

These insights, dispositions, and skills are in many ways distinct and, as a rule, relative and gradual. They are distinct because argumentative competence involves (at the very least) analytic, evaluative, and productive qualities. They are relative in the sense that one may be competent in dealing appropriately with some argumentative "action types" (or aspects of these types), but much less competent in dealing with others (van Eemeren 2004). They are gradual in the sense that people possess these insights, dispositions, and skills to a greater or lesser extent.

One of the goals of the "pragma-dialectical" research program is the attempt to examine and improve argumentative practice, and hence critical thinking, in all of its diversity (van Eemeren and Grootendorst 2004, 31). Such improvement can be achieved by analyzing argumentative conduct in various kinds of practices (or "action types"), and developing well-motivated proposals for "structural" changes. Improvements in critical thinking can also be achieved through education. To enhance argumentative competence in the latter way we have established a long-term project at the University of Amsterdam that aims to teach and develop the argumentative insights, dispositions, and skills of our (and other) students.

We believe that critical thinking education should not—and cannot—consist only of the teaching of argumentative skills. Instead, the teaching of these skills needs to be integrated into a more comprehensive program which stimulates a critical attitude that fosters key critical thinking dispositions and systematic reflection on the theoretical insights that lie behind the teaching method. In our view, skills cannot be sensibly developed without reference to the insights that shape argumentation theory as a whole. Practically speaking, this means that our teaching methods reflect all the insights relevant to the analysis, evaluation, and production of argumentative discourse gained in the research conducted in the philosophical, theoretical, empirical, and analytical parts of the pragma-dialectical research program (van Eemeren and Grootendorst 2004, 9).

A pragma-dialectical approach to argumentation concentrates, in the first place, on the potential role that argumentation plays in resolving differences of opinion in accord with certain critical standards of reasonableness. In our education program, this is reflected in an effort to explain systematically how different types of argumentative discourses and texts can best be produced, analyzed, and evaluated. A useful point of departure in the present context is a review of the four meta-theoretical starting points that guide our work methodologically. In explaining these starting points, we will demonstrate how we employ them in dealing with the different aspects of argumentative competence. We will use them as a basis for an explanation of testing and assessment within the pragma-dialectical framework.

The Meta-Theoretical Starting Points
of Pragma-Dialectics

From the pragma-dialectical viewpoint, argumentation is a method of overcoming doubt about the acceptability of a standpoint or criticism of a standpoint. "Critical discussion" (the argumentative exchange by which a difference of opinion can be resolved) tests the tenability of the standpoint(s) at issue against reasonable attacks in the form of doubt or criticism. A difference of opinion is solved if and only if the protagonist, as a result of a critical discussion, gives up his or her original standpoint(s) or the antagonist no longer doubts its (their) acceptability. A critical discussion cannot guarantee that the protagonist and antagonist will no longer disagree. Rather, it is an instrument for managing disagreement. In its absence, the most powerful people simply have things their way or persuade others by coercion or other irrational means. After a critical discussion ends, a new discussion may start, so that the flux of opinions continues.

In determining what counts as a reasonable way of conducting a critical discussion, pragma-dialecticians examine argumentative discourse starting from four meta-theoretical principles, which can be described as follows.

1. *Functionalization.* All language activity is treated as a purposeful act. Verbal expressions used in argumentative discourse and texts are treated as speech acts which have "identity" and "correctness" conditions (van Eemeren and Grootendorst 2004, 52).

2. *Externalization.* The obligations that are created by the (explicit or implicit) performance of certain speech acts in a specific context of argumentative discourse (accompanying such terms as "accept" and "disagree") are understood as public commitments that accompany these speech acts (and not in terms of internal, private states of mind; see van Eemeren and Grootendorst 2004, 54–5).

3. *Socialization.* The public commitments that accompany speech acts are understood in terms of the interaction between a speaker or writer and other people. We distinguish between the different interactional roles played by the people involved in the exchange and we view the speech acts performed as parts of an

argumentative dialogue between the parties (van Eemeren and Grootendorst 2004, 56).

4.   Dialectification. Language activities are regarded as part of an attempt to resolve a difference of opinion in accordance with critical norms of reasonableness. Dialectification is achieved by regarding the speech acts performed in an argumentative exchange as speech acts that should be in agreement with the rules for conducting a critical discussion aimed at resolving a difference of opinion (van Eemeren and Grootendorst 2004, 57).

In this chapter, we want to show how they also can help to shape the practical estate, in particular developing a teaching program and tests needed to assess students' critical thinking skills and insight.

In our educational program, we begin by teaching students to apply theoretical insights to the analysis of argumentative discourse. A second part of optimal practice assesses discourse using the norms and criteria provided by the pragma-dialectical model of critical discussion. In this context, the rules for conducting a critical discussion allow students to reach well-considered decisions about those moves in discourse which should be considered reasonable and those which should be considered fallacious. In this way, they allow an optimal analysis and evaluation of a discourse, which can serve as a basis for the last part of students' optimal practice—producing a satisfactory argumentative speech or essay which plays a constructive role in argumentative debate.

The Analysis of Argumentation:
Constructing an Analytic Overview

In constructing an analytic overview of a critical discussion, pragma-dialectics identifies standpoints and arguments, determines discussion stages, reconstructs implicit premises, and analyzes argumentation structures and argument schemes. So understood, an analytic overview allows the systematic evaluation of an argumentative discussion.

Because argumentation is constructed as an exchange between two parties, the construction of an analytic overview begins with the identification of the dispute and the parties involved. The student-as-analyst must indicate standpoints at issue and the dialectical roles of the parties: who is the protagonist—the person obliged to defend a standpoint—and who is the antagonist—the person who doubts the acceptability of that standpoint and criticizes the protagonist's argumentation? (van Eemeren and Grootendorst 1992, 16).

Because an external point of view (i.e., externalization) is assumed, students are not taught to focus on the deeper motives arguers may have for putting forward a certain standpoint or expressing doubts. In principle, it does not matter if Jane Doe, the one party, is a Democrat and John Doe, the other party, a Republican. It does not matter that the argument may be psychologically motivated by personal grudges which are the result of a divorce. We teach students to focus on the publicly assumed discussion roles and the rights and obligations implied by the positions that the arguers have taken on.

Having identified the positions of the interlocutors, the utterances that count as standpoints, and the roles of the discussants, the students look at the various discussion stages. In the ideal model for a critical discussion we identify four stages: a "confrontation" stage, in which the difference of opinion becomes clear; an "opening" stage, in which the parties' procedural and substantive commitments are identified; an "argumentation" stage, in which the protagonist defends his or her standpoint by means of argumentation and the antagonist attacks this argumentation by asking critical questions; and a "concluding" stage, in which the parties determine whether the protagonist's standpoint has been successfully defended and who has "won" the exchange (van Eemeren and Grootendorst 1992, 35).

Each of these four stages has its particular sub-goal and various utterances that are relevant for achieving these sub-goals. In the classroom, it is important to point out very clearly that argumentative reality differs, by definition, from the ideal model of a critical discussion. In many cases, the opening stage is implicit, but even in these cases the starting points accepted by disputants are important and it is vital that the student-as-analyst establish the starting points that are accepted by each party. Students must also understand that even when, on the face of it, there does not seem to be a critical discussion (or a stage of one), except when it is clear that the higher-order conditions are not fulfilled, the discussion should still be understood and treated as critical. Distinguishing the stages in an argumentative exchange is often the crux of a good analysis.

After distinguishing the stages in an argumentative exchange, an analytic overview considers the arguments presented in the argumentation. This analysis is not as straightforward as the step-by-step rules that characterize most exercises in formal deductive logic, and requires the identification of explicit and implicit elements of the discourse. Students must learn to recognize linguistic cues that indicate arguments and standpoints. Speech act theory and the theory of conversational implicatures can help them reach well-motivated decisions about what is communicated in argumentative exchanges (van Eemeren, Grootendorst, and Snoeck Henkemans 2002, 37).

The next task in the analytic overview establishes the way in which the various arguments in the discourse or text are interrelated (what we call "the argumentation structure of the discourse" (van Eemeren et al. 1996, 16). Argumentation may consist of one argument, such as the following:

> 1   We should replace Styrofoam cups with paper cups.
>   [Why?]
> 1.1   It would be better for the environment.

Argumentation always aims at overcoming the (potential) doubt of an antagonist or anticipating possible critique of the standpoint. In this way it captures the spirit of "critical thinking" —much in the way Johnson (this volume) characterizes an aspect of the dialectical component of critical thinking.

Of course, much more complex argumentation structures are possible. They often contain "subordinate" argumentation:

> 1   We should replace Styrofoam cups with paper cups.
>   [Why?]
> 1.1   It would be better for the environment.
>   [How so?]
> 1.1.1   Paper cups are biodegradable.

In another type of complex argumentation, more arguments are put forward to defend the same standpoint. These arguments anticipate, or react to, criticism against the arguments from the standpoint expressed earlier, and they attempt to overcome this criticism by putting forward "coordinative" argumentation:

> 1   You're wrong. We shouldn't replace Styrofoam cups with paper cups.
>   [Why?]
> 1.1a   Paper comes from trees and we need to preserve trees.
>   [Why do we need to preserve trees?]
> 1.1b   Trees provide the oxygen we all breathe.
>   [Can't we use recycled paper for paper cups?]
> 1.1c   Recycled paper can't fill the need for disposable cups.

Instead of trying to anticipate the objections to an argument (and trying to parry these objections), an arguer may make a series of independent attempts to defend his or her standpoint. In this case, the separate attempts to defend the standpoint are by themselves (considered to be) conclusive. The argumentation structure is "multiple":

> 1   We shouldn't replace Styrofoam cups with paper cups.
>   [Why not?]
> 1.1   It would be bad for the environment.
> 1.2   It would be too expensive.

The standpoint defended by multiple arguments still stands if (only) one of the arguments is not adequately defended. In a subordinate structure, in contrast, subordinate arguments depend on the acceptability of higher arguments in the structure. If one of the latter is shown to be unacceptable (say 1.1), then a consideration of all lower arguments (1.1.1, 1.1.1.1, etc.) is unnecessary. Students are therefore taught to distinguish the different kinds of argumentation structures, and to take the corresponding obligations of the protagonist into account while considering (anticipated) criticism from the antagonist (van Eemeren, Grootendorst, and Snocck Henkemans 2002, 66).

Recognizing Implicit Elements in Argument

In preparing to evaluate argumentation, one must identify implicit elements in the argumentation to which the arguer is committed. Implicit premises are claims that support a standpoint without being put into words. Though they are not explicitly expressed, they still function as part of the attempt to convince others of the standpoint (van Eemeren, Grootendorst, and Snoeck Henkemans 2002, 49).

Put simply, an implicit premise is a bridging device between an argument and the standpoint that is being defended. An example is the implicit premise 1.2 (below), which can be reconstructed as the step necessary to go from argument 1.1 to standpoint 1:

> 1   John Irving's newest book isn't much.
> 1.1   It is not about real life.
> 1.2   (Good books are about real life.)

Why would 1.1 be relevant for standpoint 1 and a possible argument for this standpoint? 1.2 provides the answer. It is easiest to start with the so-called "logical minimum," which can be summarized as "if argument, then standpoint." In our example, the logical minimum is "If John Irving's newest book is not about real life, it isn't much." This addition makes the reasoning valid, but it seems that the arguer is committed to more, and may be taken to mean, more generally, that books are not very interesting if they are not about real life.

Making clear what is logically necessary is only one analytic step. The reconstructed implicit premise should, where possible, be more informative than the logical minimum. Sometimes a generalization is clearly implied. In other cases, the logical minimum has to be made more specific. Taking this next step is an instance of functionalization, which treats the implicit premise as a form of indirect language use which can be understood in terms of Gricean maxims and the Searlean analysis of indirect speech acts (which provide a theoretical motivation for reconstruction).

Usually the missing premise can be seen as a general rule or a rule-like statement on which the argument is based. Such rules rely on abstract pragmatic principles, which are called "argument schemes" in the theory of argumentation (van Eemeren et al. 1996, 19). In a critical exchange in which a certain argument scheme is used, critical questions that pertain to the specific relation between the argument and the standpoint become relevant. The dialectification of the argument schemes pairs particular schemes with matching "critical questions." Because these questions direct criticism, the choice of an argument scheme is decisive in determining the dialectical route the interaction takes (van Eemeren and Grootendorst 1992, 94).

The following example illustrates argumentation based on a "symptomatic" relation:

1   That restaurant is very expensive. [because]
1.1   It has three Michelin stars. [and]
1.2   (It is symptomatic for three-star restaurants to be very expensive.)

A real-life example taken from a Dutch newspaper is Janet Jackson's argumentation for the claim that her brother Michael cannot be guilty of sexually abusing minors: "His dedication to all kinds of child welfare organizations already shows that Michael can't be guilty." Apparently, Janet Jackson thinks that people who do charity work for children's organizations cannot prey on children.

Several critical questions are pertinent here. Does a dedication to welfare organizations show the claimed innocence? (Especially as some readers of the paper thought that this dedication *supported* the suggestion that Michael Jackson was guilty.) Does someone who acts admirably in one area always act appropriately in others? These are the kinds of questions to be asked when an arguer uses the argument scheme based on a symptomatic relation. Other sorts of critical questions are to be asked for other types of argument schemes. In teaching students to become better arguers, we show them how to identify the various types of schemes and how to ask and answer the critical questions associated with each scheme.

Evaluating the Argumentation

Once a full analytic overview of an argumentative discourse has been completed, the discourse can be evaluated. A pragma-dialectical evaluation aims to determine to what extent the various speech acts performed in the discourse can be instrumental in resolving a difference of opinion.

To ensure that a dispute can be brought to a solution, the parties involved must subscribe to certain basic principles for a constructive exchange of opinions. These "rules for critical discussion" are such that everyone who makes an attempt to convince others by means of argumentative discourse can be held accountable to the rules. A violation of one of the rules impedes the resolution of a dispute and is regarded as a fallacy—an obstruction to an adequate resolution of the dispute (van Eemeren and Grootendorst 2004, 162). Because each of the rules plays an essential role in the dialectical process of testing the acceptability of a standpoint against criticism, all of them are the result of dialectification. The following provides a brief overview of the ten discussion rules (van Eemeren and Grootendorst 2004, 190–5).

1. *The freedom rule*: Discussants may not prevent each other from advancing standpoints or from calling standpoints into question.

2. *The burden of proof rule*: Discussants who advance a standpoint may not refuse to defend this standpoint when requested to do so.

3. *The standpoint rule*: Attacks on standpoints may not bear on a standpoint that has not actually been put forward by the other party.

4. *The relevance rule*: Standpoints may not be defended by non-argumentation or argumentation that is not relevant to the standpoint.

5. *The unexpressed premise rule*: Discussants may not falsely attribute unexpressed premises to the other party or disown responsibility for their own implicit premises.

6. *The starting-point rule*: Discussants may not falsely present something as an accepted starting point or falsely deny that something is an accepted starting point.

7. *The validity rule*: Reasoning that in an argumentation is presented as formally conclusive may not be invalid in a logical sense.

8. *The argument scheme rule*: Standpoints may not be regarded as conclusively defended by argumentation that is not presented as based on formally conclusive reasoning if the defence does not take place by means of appropriate argument schemes that are applied correctly.

9. *The concluding rule*: Inconclusive defences of standpoints may not lead to maintaining these standpoints, and conclusive de-

fences of standpoints may not lead to maintaining expressions of doubt concerning these standpoints.

10. *The usage rule*: Discussants may not use any formulations that are insufficiently clear or confusingly ambiguous, and they may not deliberately misinterpret the other party's formulations.

These rules ensure productive critical discussions in a variety of ways. The freedom rule is designed to ensure that standpoints and doubt regarding standpoints may be freely advanced. The burden of proof rule is intended to ensure that advanced and doubted standpoints are defended against critical attacks (because a difference of opinion cannot be resolved if a party who advances a standpoint is not prepared to take on the role of protagonist). The standpoint rule does not allow a participant in a critical discussion to distort his or her opponent's standpoint or impute a fictitious standpoint to the other party (doing so is known as the "straw man" fallacy). And so on.

The rules of critical discussion can be violated in a variety of ways. The freedom rule, for example, can be violated by declaring a standpoint sacrosanct, by threatening an opponent ("It is up to you to have that opinion but there comes a time when I can't control my temper anymore"), or by attacking an opponent personally. One way to violate the burden of proof rule is by shifting the burden of proof ("War is under all circumstances wrong, you can prove me wrong"); another is by expressing the standpoint in such a way that it looks as if it does not require any defence, because it should be considered an established fact ("Everybody knows that taking vitamins can be very bad for your health"). The concluding rule can be violated—in the concluding stage—by the protagonist's concluding that a standpoint is absolutely true merely because it has been successfully defended, or by the antagonist's concluding from the fact that it has not been proved that something is the case, that it is not the case (*argumentum ad ignorantiam*). For example, "Now that we see that it cannot be proved that Ecstasy is harmful, we can conclude that it is absolutely harmless."

The rules of critical discussion are not algorithmic, but heuristic. They are not rules that automatically lead to a specific series of instructions that guarantee the desired result. Argumentation is, in the pragma-dialectical view, not a mechanical process, but a social activity aimed at convincing others of the acceptability of a standpoint by removing the other party's doubt. Together with the analytic overview, the rules of critical discussion facilitate a critical reflection on argumentative discourse. Though they do not, by themselves, guarantee that a resolution will be reached, they provide valuable assistance in the evaluation of argumentation. By adhering to the rules, arguers will run little risk of fallaciousness.

It is not, of course, sufficient for students to learn the rules of critical discussion by heart. They must be able to apply them successfully in practice. What is essential is that they understand how the principle of dialectification is put to good use in the rules for conducting a critical discussion. We believe that the ability to explain how each of the rules is necessary to foster this critical process is more important than the ability to sum up the traditional fallacies.

Testing the Pragma-Dialectical Skills

What do we expect from students who take a critical thinking course? What exactly should they be able to do? First and foremost, they should be able to analyze and to evaluate argumentative discourse. That means that they need to know how to make, well-considered decisions in constructing an analytic overview and in evaluating argumentative discourse in terms of the ideal model of critical discussion. In addition, they should be able to produce clear and dialectically acceptable argumentative texts and to engage in discussions and debates in a critical and reasonable manner.

We test our students' insights and their ability to analyze, judge, and participate in critical discussion in a number of ways. For practical reasons, the analysis and evaluation tests are generally integrated in one comprehensive test paper. Students are asked to create an analytic overview of a text and provide a critical commentary. In putting together their analysis, students have to give a full and systematic overview of a written piece of argumentation: an argumentative essay, a newspaper column, or a letter to the editor. Students are not given free rein in their analysis, but are expected to respond in a manner that illustrates their ability to complete a variety of tasks, all of which have been practised intensively in the program.[1]

First, the students must describe the dialectical point of departure. What exactly is the bone of contention in this case? Who are the parties in the dispute and what are their positions? Which discussion roles are taken on by the different participants? In making an adequate analysis of the dispute as a whole, students may be expected to disentangle a mixed dispute as a complex made up of two or more single disputes. The ability to do so is vital when they are involved in dialectical analysis.

Second, students must indicate how the four dialectical stages are represented in the text in question. Lines in the text are numbered, to allow them to indicate relevant lines readily and precisely. In doing so, they are expected to explain which indicators and linguistic cues the text and the context provide for determining the various stages.

Third, students must reconstruct the argumentation structure of the text. In explaining arguments and their relationship to each other, the students must explain the precise reasoning behind their analyses, and justify the choices that have been made in the analyses. In particular, they are to indicate the dialectical clues in the argumentation and its presentation that they have taken into account.

After analyzing the argumentation structure of the discourse, the students have to reconstruct unexpressed premises in the arguments. In each case, they are expected to begin with the associated conditional ("the logical minimum") and make that statement as informative as the context allows.

Fifth (and last in constructing an analytic overview), the students are expected to identify all the argument schemes that are used in each component of the argumentation. After students complete an analytic overview, they are expected to demonstrate their evaluative skills by assessing the discourse they have analyzed. Because pragma-dialectics teaches students an ideal model of a critical discussion, the main question here can be summarized as "How far is the text as it has been reconstructed in the analysis removed from the critical ideal?" The questions that need to be answered in this endeavour can, in turn, be summarized as "Are there any inconsistencies or violations of rules for critical discussion in the text?" and "If so, what are their consequences for the resolution of (or the failure to resolve) the dispute?" The tasks covered in the standard pragma-dialectical test we have just described are summarized in the standard pragma-dialectical test described below.

The standard pragma-dialectical test

A. Making the analytic overview

1. Describe the dialectical point of departure: the bone of contention in the text, the parties involved and their role in the discussion (protagonist/antagonist).
2. Typify the explicit or implicit dispute: non-mixed/mixed, single/multiple, combination.
3. Identify the way in which the dialectical stages are represented in the text: confrontation/opening/argumentation/conclusion.
4. Reconstruct the argumentation structure: single/multiple/co-ordinative/subordinative/combination.
5. Make the unexpressed premises explicit.
6. Identify the argument schemes that are used in the argumentation: causal/symptomatic/comparison.

B. Evaluating the argumentation

1. Identify the logical and pragmatic inconsistencies in the text.
2. Determine whether the arguments put forward belong to the set of acceptable common starting points.
3. Ask the relevant critical questions pertaining to the argument schemes that are used and check whether the arguments adequately support the (sub)standpoints.
4. Identify violations of the rules for critical discussion and characterize the fallacies that have been committed.
5. Give an overall assessment of the argumentative text and explain the extent to which the difference of opinion has been resolved.

Making an analytic overview and evaluating the argumentation on the basis of the rules for critical discussion are excellent preparation for the attempt to teach students how to improve their oral and written argumentative discourse. After students have learned how to produce the overview, the finer points of constructing an argumentative essay can be taught and, along with them, the most advantageous way to present their arguments. At this stage, we focus on questions such as the following: Where can I best put my standpoint—at the very beginning of the text, at the end, or somewhere else? How can I best present my argumentation? What is the best order in which to present the arguments that back up my standpoint? Which of my premises need to be explicit and which should remain implicit? These questions also provide the general guidelines we use in assessing the students' written performances.

Finally, students can be tested on their performances in oral classroom debate. In this case, we expect them to demonstrate that they are able to engage in a verbal discussion without violating the discussion rules. In the process of doing so, they are expected to identify the rule violations of others in a dialogue, and to react to these violations in an appropriate way. The main goal of these verbal assignments is to test the students' inclination and capability to engage in critical discussion in a reasonable way.[2] The rules for critical discussion that are solicited by the test questions are, in fact, the same criteria that are used to judge the students' performances. In this way, the learning outcomes of the Pragma-Dialectics program is amenable to testing, in particular non-standardized testing.

Conclusion

Our commitment to the pragma-dialectical theoretical framework leaves room for different types of educational programs with varying degrees of intellectual sophistication. Our teaching and testing methods have been used successfully in many different kinds of educational contexts in the Netherlands and other countries, including the use of the method in high school classes and university-level academic argumentation courses, and in general composition programs for non-experts as well as specific courses for lawyers and other professionals. All of these courses vary in scope and difficulty according to the level, needs, and wishes of the students. What remains constant is the educational focus on making well-reasoned decisions in analyzing and evaluating argumentative discourse, and in producing argumentative texts. Because such decisions are central to critical thinking, its teaching and testing can be based on a critical reflection on argumentative discourse that is grounded in pragma-dialectical theory.

Notes

1. This style of analysis shares similarities in format to the Ennis-Weir Critical Thinking Essay Test (particularly the kinds of skills it attempts to measure) and with the style of learning and testing that Baker University's General Education program promotes (see both Hatcher and Johnson, this volume).

2. When we say "capability to engage in critical discussion in a *reasonable* way," here, we refer specifically to our aim to measure inclinations. This aim is quite similar to the kind discussed by Giancarlo-Gittens (this volume), with the exceptions that in her test description she refers to inclinations as "dispositions," and that we test these dispositions in a non-standardized format.

References

van Eemeren, F. 2004. "Mind the gap": Reconciling the pursuit of success with the maintenance of reasonableness. In *Argumentation and Cognition*, ed. T. Suzuki, Y. Yano and T. Kato, 1–8. Tokyo: Japan Debate Association.

van Eemeren, F., and R. Grootendorst. 2004. *A systematic theory of argumentation: The pragma-dialectical approach.* Cambridge, MA: Cambridge University Press.

——. 1992. *Argumentation, communication and fallacies: A pragma-dialectical perspectieve.* Hillsdale, NJ: Erlbaum.

van Eemeren, F., R. Grootendorst, and A. Snoeck Henkemans. 2002. *Argumentation: Analysis, evaluation, presentation.* Mahwah, NJ: Erlbaum.

van Eemeren, F., R. Grootendorst, A. Snoeck Henkemans, J. Blair, R. Johnson, E. Krabbe, C. Plantin, D. Walton, C. Willard, J. Woods, and D. Zarefsky. 1996. *Fundamentals of argumentation theory: A handbook of historical backgrounds and contemporary developments.* Mahwah, NJ: Erlbaum.

PART FOUR

Critical Thinking in an Era of Accountability

Introduction

*I*nevitably, methods of evaluation spawned by accountability movements (political movements) affect both teaching methodology and policy; teaching practice and the results of standardized testing, in turn, inform the future direction of policy as well as inspire various social and political responses. Each of the chapters in Part Four discusses this reflexive relationship among government platforms or initiatives (critical thinking and otherwise), teaching, policy, and society in order to explore the different program and policy options available to promote proper critical thinking education and assessment.

In Chapter Thirteen, J. Anthony Blair asks whether K–12 teachers are qualified to teach critical thinking. He argues that there are good reasons for thinking that this is not the case, and proposes some possible ways to rectify this situation. Ultimately he suggests a mechanism that might be used to assess teachers' critical thinking abilities and, by extension, Bachelor of Education programs for critical thinking content.

In Chapter Fourteen, Linda Kaser considers the politics of critical thinking in light of her participation in the development of the critical thinking curriculum and policies in British Columbia, a province notable for its concerted efforts to consistently promote critical thinking in schools. Kaser outlines the politics and the educational innovations that characterize her experience as an educational policy-developer in this area.

In Chapter Fifteen, Laura Pinto and John P. Portelli discuss the problems with high-stakes testing. Although such testing is more common in the United States than in Canada, they discuss some of the same themes that inform the Canadian experience. Pinto and Portelli outline an understanding of critical thinking from feminist and critical theorist standpoints and criticize attempts to implement high-stakes standardized testing of the kind that would interfere with the development of critical thinking dispositions. They offer suggestions for policy-makers with respect to critical thinking education and assessment that align with aims to prepare students for democratic citizenship. Pinto and Portelli also bring together issues of critical thinking and assessment with respect to what it might mean to foster a more democratic learning environment and, therefore, a better environment in which to test critical thinking.

Chapter Thirteen

Who Teaches K–12 Critical Thinking?

J. Anthony Blair

*D*ebates about the teaching and testing of critical thinking tend to assume a supply of competent critical thinking instructors. If such a supply does not exist (or cannot be produced), then it is difficult to see how students' instructional needs in this area can be met. In this chapter, I consider the capacity of K–12 teachers to serve as critical thinking instructors. I begin by developing the hypothesis that most of those who would be expected to teach critical thinking in K–12 are not adequately qualified, without the help of those who specialize in critical thinking, to do so. The circumstantial case for this hypothesis seems strong enough to justify the time and resources that would be needed to test it. I then consider the prospects for K–12 critical thinking instruction on the assumption that the hypothesis would be supported by appropriate assessment instruments.

Let us assume something that I take to be uncontroversial: that critical thinking is a complex of skills or abilities (I do not distinguish between skills and abilities). To avoid a possible misunderstanding it is vital to note that the concept of skill or ability is ambiguous. The ability to speak a language is a skill, and the ability to read and write involves higher-order skills, but we distinguish between someone who is simply literate and someone we say is skilled in the use of a language, such as an accomplished novelist or poet. Anyone who has learned how to ski or play the guitar has acquired a skill, but someone who can ski or play the guitar is not thereby necessarily a skilled skier or guitarist. The words "skill" and "ability" can thus denote (1) the capacity to perform a function to a certain baseline competence, or (2) the capacity to perform it to a high degree of competence (see Fisher and Scriven 1997, 23). We might call the former a "baseline" competence skill and the latter a "high" competence skill.

In which of these two senses is critical thinking a skill? If the concept of critical thinking is to denote anything of interest, anything worth teaching, or any ability to be prized, it must denote a higher degree of competence than that implied by a mere baseline skill. Critical thinking cannot be something everyone learns haphazardly, like the ability to speak a native language. It is more like the ability to teach: most people can acquire it to a moderate degree, but it takes effort and practice to do so. Many who think they have the ability do not, and most do not excel at it.

Like any other high competence skill, critical thinking is not universally distributed throughout the population. It cannot easily be acquired simply by unconscious modelling or copying (if it could, most people would be skilled at it). If critical thinking is to be learned, it must be taught. Supposing that it is an ability which is desirable in our society, it is desirable—other things being equal—to promote its acquisition. And because teaching is the way to promote its acquisition, it is desirable, and even necessary, to provide explicit instruction in, and/or opportunities to deliberately copy, model, and practise critical thinking skills.[1]

If it is fair to expect teachers to possess a level of competence in what they teach that is above the target level for those they are instructing, then those who teach critical thinking should be atypical. They should not share the general population's low level of critical thought—the level that makes critical thinking instruction needed in the first place. But are there good reasons to think that K–12 teachers today think critically at the requisite level? Are K–12 teachers better at critical thinking than the average person? Are they sufficiently better to qualify them to teach critical thinking? This is an empirical question. Empirical testing that would provide an answer is desirable, but it has not been undertaken. In the absence of the empirical evidence such testing would provide, we can usefully speculate about the likely results of such testing, and consider the practical implications of such results.

What distinguishes K–12 teachers from the rest of the population, apart from their motivation to teach K–12, are their general
university education and the professional training in instruction they
receive in faculties of education. So the question becomes "Is there
any reason to expect that this education and training provide K–12
teachers with the critical thinking competence necessary to teach in
this area?" To reasonably speculate on the answer to this question,
we need to proceed with an understanding of what counts as critical
thinking, and then consider the extent to which undergraduate education or teacher education is likely to provide it.

Definitions of critical thinking vary, but many suggest that it
is thinking about thinking, or thinking about intellectual products and
processes. So understood, critical thinking is made up of analysis and
evaluation. It entails the recognition, interpretation, and analysis of
thinking, in the first instance, which is to be followed up with evaluation
that is achieved through the articulation and application of normative
criteria. An implication is that critical thinking is to be distinguished
from other intellectual activities such as decision-making and problem-
solving, because these are not critical thinking so much as they are the
intellectual processes about which it is possible to think critically (or
not). As Hoogland, Sobocan, and Hare have suggested in this volume,
this implies that critical thinking cannot be sharply distinguished from
creative thinking; thinking critically itself requires creativity (an ability
to conjure up counter-examples, for instance), and creative work such
as writing, painting, or composing requires critical thought—at least at
the editing, revising, or refining stage.

In considering whether K–12 teachers are qualified to teach
critical thinking, I will use the Fisher/Scriven (1997) articulation of
critical thinking, which I find compelling. It maintains that "critical
thinking is the skilled and active interpretation and evaluation of observations and communications, information and arguments" (21). In
this definition, "skilled" means skilled in the high competence sense—
signifying, at the very least, a minimal standard of quality beyond
what is required to merely engage in critical thinking. "Observations
and communications" and "information and arguments" include everything that goes into making judgments about attitudes and conduct.
And "active" implies not only that the critical thinker reacts but also
that he or she is proactive in thinking and investigating, possibly to an

extent that will result in the formulation of new critical thinking principles.

The Fisher/Scriven definition of critical thinking is consistent with many definitions in the literature.[2] Unlike some definitions, it has to my mind the virtue of not building the disposition to exercise critical thinking abilities into the very conception of critical thinking.[3] Another virtue is its recognition that critical thinking should not be conflated with the ability to analyze and assess arguments. The latter is the principal focus of many college- and university-level critical thinking textbooks and courses, but dealing critically with arguments is just one element of critical thinking, and the Fisher/Scriven conceptualization reflects that fact. This is a virtue because arguments are not the only processes and products of mind that may be thought about critically, however central their role in the life of the mind.

Understanding critical thinking in the Fisher and Scriven way, we may ask whether and to what extent it is taught in undergraduate university programs. I propose—for three reasons—that we leave out of consideration the dedicated critical thinking courses often offered by philosophy departments. First, their success in improving critical thinking competence is disputed. Second, in spite of their popularity, only a minority of undergraduates take such courses and there is no assurance that most K–12 teachers are among that minority. Third, it is plausible to suppose that high levels of critical thinking competence require discipline-specific background knowledge (and possibly discipline-specific principles of reasoning) which is particularly relevant to Grade 9–12 teachers who specialize in disciplines or groups of related disciplines. In view of the latter, what is particularly of interest is whether K–12 teachers possess sufficiently well-developed critical thinking skills in the disciplines they teach—to the extent that they are qualified to teach critical thinking in their subject areas.

The question to be asked is the extent to which it is likely that a history major will have acquired the ability to think critically about historical issues, or an English major will have acquired the ability to think critically about the interpretation and assessment of literature. More generally put, the question is whether a social science major will have acquired critical thinking skill about matters falling within the domain of the social sciences or whether a science major will have learned to think critically about experimental research and theory in science.

Any critical thinking instruction that might occur in K–12 should also include training in critical thinking (applicable to the various fields) that relates to the current issues of the day with which an informed citizenry should be familiar. Consider, for example, thinking about social policies in each of the portfolios of civic life—be it finance and economic well-being, healthcare, energy production and conservation, housing, transportation, foreign affairs, environmental protection, or any other. In these areas, critical thinking requires the integration of background knowledge and theoretical insights from a variety of fields, including history, economics, politics, sociology, literature, philosophy, and the various sciences. In view of this breadth, we should be interested in the extent to which university training produces elevated critical thinking ability in such applications. We need to consider both students' training in their major subjects and the material used in the various optional courses that are supposed to broaden their education.

If we use the Fisher and Scriven definition, the question is to what extent we may expect that undergraduate university courses teach the skilled and active interpretation and evaluation of observations and communications, information, and arguments—both in a student's field of specialization and in applying that perspective to practical matters requiring multi-disciplinary analysis and evaluation.

I can make some observations about students' abilities in the interpretation and evaluation of arguments because I have taught critical thinking and argumentation for thirty-four years. One of my courses in argument has prerequisites, so it is the second—sometimes the third—course devoted to critical thinking or argument interpretation and evaluation that my students will have taken. Despite this relatively extensive training in critical thinking, many of these students lack a clear understanding of the concept of argument when they begin, and relatively few of them are, at the outset, good at recognizing arguments and argumentation, let alone analyzing or evaluating them. By the end of the course, and with a great deal of practice, they have improved significantly, but only the better students—perhaps one-quarter to one-third of the class—have begun to be able to think critically about arguments at an advanced level. I would worry about asking the others to teach this aspect of critical thinking (that is, about arguments) to K–12 students.[4]

What is surprising, and alarming, given the ubiquity and importance of arguments in all corners of learning, is the low level of understanding of arguments, and facility with them, that students exhibit when they begin dedicated courses in this area. This suggests to me that they are not learning about arguments and their uses in other areas of their studies. It is surprising because these subjects require the understanding of contending hypotheses and theories, which seems to require an understanding and an appreciation of the force of the observations and evidence that tell for and against them, or in other words, the strength of the arguments for and against them (see Kuhn 1991). If the students do understand the use of evidence in history, psychology, economics, physics, or biology, in particular, they do not seem to have learned how to generalize that understanding. They do not seem to have grasped the common general principles at work in the reasoning of these different domains.

My experience is admittedly anecdotal, but it is consistent for over thirty years of annually changing populations. It leads me to expect a similar situation in other areas of critical thinking. I do expect that the better students who take several communications courses become adept critical thinkers about communications, that is, skilled and active interpreters and evaluators of communications. Similarly, I expect that a minority (the better of the students) who major in, or take several courses in, biology become skilled and active interpreters of observations, particularly biological observations; that the better students who major or take several courses in political science become skilled, active interpreters of information, especially public policy information; and so on. But it does not necessarily follow that these students think critically about matters not specific to their domains of competence, or that they apply what can be generalized about their particular domains, or transfer their critical thinking skills to applications beyond their disciplines. For the bottom two-thirds or three-quarters of the class—the majority of graduating undergraduates—the prospects are even dimmer.

Should we believe that the situation changes as a result of the year of training that students receive at faculties of education while completing their qualifications to become K–12 teachers? I do not know the answer. Familiarity with the current theoretical literature on the teaching of critical thinking and practical experience in teaching critical thinking are not requirements for instructors in faculties of education, and the presence of critical thinking experts in these faculties is a matter of happenstance. Some faculties of education have several faculty members with these credentials and backgrounds, but others have few or none.

A more compelling factor than the absence of qualified faculty of education instructors is the extremely heavy curriculum burden facing would-be K–12 teachers, not to mention their instructors. There is so much other essential material, or so it is perceived, to be conveyed in such a short time in a one-year education program that it is doubtful that there is room for critical thinking instruction that could possibly make up for the shortfalls and defects of the student teachers in this context.

In sum, there is every reason to expect that the quality of critical thinking among K–12 teachers is, at best, uneven when they begin their careers, and not at a level that properly qualifies the majority of them to teach critical thinking. In the context of calls to improve students' critical thinking abilities, this raises some serious questions about our ability to provide the instructors required to teach critical thinking in K–12 in the absence of a dedicated component of theoretically sound instruction in critical thinking and its teaching as part of teacher training.

All of these considerations raise doubts about the ability of K–12 teachers to provide (without further training) critical thinking instruction to their students. These doubts suggest that teachers' critical thinking skills should be evaluated to discover whether the hypothesis that they do not have the necessary skills is supported by evidence as well as by speculation. My first point, then, is that we need to think about testing the critical thinking competence of K–12 teachers in tandem with testing that would test the critical thinking competence of K–12 students.

Let us suppose that my hypothesis about K–12 teachers can be supported by valid and reliable testing. Does that imply that we should abandon the notion that critical thinking instruction should be included in the K–12 curriculum, given the absence of sufficiently qualified instructors? I don't think so. It would indicate a problem, but one that can be solved, provided that there is some way for teachers to acquire the competence they need to teach critical thinking to their students.

The need for such instruction might seem to be as much of a hurdle as teachers' initial lack of qualifications, but I would suggest otherwise. If testing shows that K–12 students need training in critical thinking, and if the resources are available to provide it, then the conditions needed to prepare K–12 teachers to be critical thinking instructors can be supplied.

In providing critical thinking instruction to K–12 students, it will be necessary to design instructional materials for stand-alone units on critical thinking and critical thinking add-ons that can infuse critical thinking across the present curriculum. These critical thinking instructional materials can do double duty; they can be used to train teachers as well as students. It should be possible for anyone motivated to teach critical thinking to master such materials. In thoroughly mastering the materials, teachers will acquire sufficient critical thinking competence to teach critical thinking skills. In this way, teachers can teach themselves the material that they are to teach to their students. This much is the bare minimum, but it can be done.

Better, and also within the realm of practicality, is the mastery of some background theoretical knowledge—something like the Norris and Ennis (1989) and the Fisher and Scriven (1997) monographs, and ideally an encyclopedia of critical thinking, containing short articles on its key terms and various elements. So the second point I would make is that, if K–12 teachers are to be entrusted with teaching critical thinking, it will be necessary to produce materials for stand-alone or across-the-curriculum instruction, and desirable to design a package of backup theoretical material as well. (In testing such teachers, one might use the same instruments one uses to test the critical thinking skills of higher-level students.[5])

Some might object to my pessimism and the proposed solution to the problem of qualified critical thinking instruction by suggesting that there are other ways to teach critical thinking. At least at the secondary level in Ontario one might point to the opportunities that the Grade 11 and Grade 12 philosophy curricula provide for teaching critical thinking in high school. Both course descriptions include significant references to critical thinking, and teachers who have some university training in philosophy would seem qualified to teach these courses. According to this objection to my proposals, critical thinking can readily be taught in Grades 11 and 12—within the high school philosophy courses present in the Ontario curriculum—and in similar courses, if they exist now or once they can be introduced, in other provincial or state jurisdictions (such as California).

In deciding whether this possibility is a real option, we might look more closely at the relevant curriculum documents. The Ontario Grade 11 philosophy course, "The Big Questions," lists a series of philosophical questions—such as "What is a person?", "What is a just society?", and "What is human knowledge?"—as its topics. The course description states that "students will learn critical thinking skills in evaluating philosophical arguments related to these questions" (*The Ontario Curriculum, 2000*; course description for Grade 11 philosophy).

The Ontario Grade 12 philosophy course, "Questions and Theories," states that it "addresses three (or more) of the main areas of philosophy: metaphysics, logic, epistemology, social and political philosophy, and aesthetics" (ibid., course description for Grade 12 philosophy). The course description advises that, among other things, "the students will learn critical thinking skills" (ibid.). So the Grade 11 course description promises critical thinking skills as they apply to a particular topic (the philosophical arguments that relate to the questions taken up in the course), whereas the Grade 12 course description promises learning critical thinking skills, *tout court*. In both cases, the critical thinking skills are not a topic or a unit of the course, but are to be learned in the process of learning how to think about philosophical issues.

Turning to the detailed descriptions of the curricula for the courses in question provides a clearer idea of the way in which the course developers conceive of critical thinking and critical thinking instruction. In the Grade 11 course, the aspects of the course that might reasonably be related to the promise to teach critical thinking skills are the following expectations of what students will be able to do by the end of the course: "summarize some arguments for and against answers to [some of] the big questions of philosophy," "describe the strengths and weaknesses of the main arguments used to defend answers to [some of] the big questions of philosophy," "describe important similarities and differences [of competing philosophical theories]," "describe the strengths and weaknesses of alternative responses to questions of applied philosophy," "apply philosophical skills such as precise writing and critical analysis to solve problems that arise in jobs and occupations," "identify philosophical positions presupposed in some other disciplines," "contrast alternative philosophical viewpoints presupposed in some other disciplines," and "identify examples of fallacies in reasoning in writings from other subjects" (*The Ontario Curriculum, Grades 11 and 12: Social Sciences and Humanities, 2000*, Philosophy: The Big Questions, Grade 11).

Being able to do all these things does demonstrate a degree of critical thinking skill as it relates to philosophical issues and their applications. But philosophical theories and arguments are *sui generis*. The argumentation involved is conceptual and normative, not empirical. So even though the curriculum clearly envisages relating philosophical questions and theories beyond philosophy, it is doubtful whether such a course will teach critical thinking skills that apply to other kinds of subject matter or general critical thinking skills (assuming there are such general skills).

In the Grade 12 philosophy curriculum, the units on metaphysics, epistemology, ethics, social and political philosophy, and aesthetics contain no explicit reference to teaching critical thinking. They say students will use critical thinking skills in their arguing and evaluation of arguments, but nothing is said about dedicated instruction in the development of such skills. The learning of critical thinking skills would, in these units, presumably occur to the extent that these skills are needed for the interpretation and evaluation of philosophical arguments—and in some cases for the application of philosophical issues and theories to other subjects or topics. Moreover, the assumption seems to be that all there is to critical thinking is the critical assessment of arguments. The curriculum exhibits no explicit appreciation that things other than arguments can be the objects of critical thinking, that instruction in critical thinking skills might require separate attention, or that skill in critically evaluating philosophical reasoning and arguments might not generalize.

The only explicit reference to critical thinking in the Grade 12 philosophy curriculum is found in the guidelines for the unit on logic and the philosophy of science. It is stated there that by the end of the course students will "apply logical and critical thinking skills in practical contexts, and in detecting logical fallacies" (*The Ontario Curriculum, Grades 11 and 12: Social Sciences and Humanities, 2000*, Philosophy: Questions and Theories, Grade 12—unit on Logic and the Philosophy of Science). But explicit reference to critical thinking disappears when these expectations are spelled out more specifically and are replaced by references to logic. Thus students will be expected to demonstrate an understanding of what a valid argument is and what a logical fallacy is; correctly use logical terms such as "logical consistency," "contradiction," "deduction," and "validity"; and distinguish valid from invalid arguments, and sound from unsound arguments (ibid.). Critical thinking skills, in short, are taken to consist of the skills entailed in using deductive logical norms. As valuable as such skills are, they by no means exhaust the skills entailed even in the use of arguments, let alone the other aspects of critical thinking such as evaluating arguments.

It seems to follow that the Ontario Grade 11 and Grade 12 philosophy curricula cannot be regarded as the equivalent of, or as substitutes for, a curriculum in critical thinking. The philosophy courses certainly aim to convey some of the elements of critical thinking abilities, but they are too narrow in three respects. First, they focus only on philosophical questions, theories, and arguments, and their applications—a rather specialized domain. Second, they focus primarily on the analysis and evaluation of arguments, which comprise only one of the components of critical thinking. Third, they focus on the deductive norms of arguments, which apply to most philosophical argumentation, but which are only one of a variety of norms that apply to arguments and argumentation in general. These considerations themselves make it doubtful that teachers with sufficient competence in philosophy to teach these courses would thereby have the competence to teach critical thinking skills in other areas. I conclude that we should reject the suggestion that the philosophy curricula solve the problem of where and how to teach critical thinking in K–12, or even 9–12.

I believe that the move to teach critical thinking in K–12 is a desirable development, but one that will require a great deal of work. We have good reason to believe that K–12 students' critical thinking skills (like those of university students) will be found wanting, and this suggests that there is a need for critical thinking instruction. There are similar reasons for predicting that requisite critical thinking skills of K–12 teachers also will be lacking, which suggests that teachers need training, even if it is only self-administered. And the teaching of critical thinking in K–12 cannot plausibly be left to the Grade 11 and 12 philosophy courses in the Ontario curriculum (or similar philosophy courses in other jurisdictions).

Quite apart from the daunting political effort required for curriculum change (whether in K–12 or in university faculties of education), valid and reliable testing instruments should inform attempts to make critical thinking a key component of K–12 education. The advanced or K–12 test should be administered to potential teachers as well as current teachers and students. At the same time, suitable curriculum materials for students, and instructional packages for teachers, need to be prepared. Such tasks will require a sustained, multi-year commitment by those well positioned to bring about change in our education systems (both in schools and in faculties of education). For many reasons, I believe this is a project that is worth the effort.

Notes

1. The "other things being equal" qualification I have inserted in this paragraph hides difficult decisions about time- and resource-allocation priorities. Many things are desirable in our society. It is desirable to teach more things in K–12 than time and other resources permit. So, solely from the fact that it would be a good thing for students to acquire critical thinking skills, it does not follow that they should be taught in K–12. Still, it is arguable that the ability to think critically ought to have a high priority. I will proceed on the assumption that the case can be made for including it in the K–12 curriculum.
2. Especially Ennis's (1990) very influential definition that critical thinking is "reasonable and reflective thinking about what to believe and do" (396).
3. Skills are conceptually distinct from the disposition to practise them, however much the acquisition of a skill can causally depend on an inclination to engage in the activity in question. Moreover, skills can be assessed independently of any disposition to practise them, which is convenient, since they are easier to assess than attitudes. Whether one ought to try to inculcate a disposition to engage in critical thinking at the same time one is teaching critical thinking skills is a matter of debate that does not have to be resolved for the purposes of the present discussion.
4. Teaching something improves one's understanding of it and one's skill in doing it, so teachers might become better critical thinkers about argument and argumentation as teachers of it than they were as students. This is an important point, to which I return below.
5. If mastery of the curriculum materials minimally qualifies someone to teach critical thinking, then a high score on a Grade 12 critical thinking

test should suffice to select instructors who are ready to work through the critical thinking curriculum materials on their own and prepare unit and lesson outlines for critical thinking instruction anywhere in the K–12 range.

References

Fisher, A., and M. Scriven. 1997. *Critical thinking, its definition and assessment.* Point Reyes, CA: Edgepress.

Kuhn, D. 1991. *The skills of argument.* Cambridge, NY: Cambridge University Press.

Norris, S., and R. Ennis. 1989. *Evaluating critical thinking.* Pacific Grove, CA: Midwest Publications.

The Ontario Curriculum, Grades 9 to 12, Course Descriptions and Prerequisites. 2000. Toronto: Ministry of Education, Government of Ontario. Online. Available at http://www.edu.gov.on.ca/eng/document/curricul/secondary/descript/descri9e.pdf.

The Ontario Curriculum, Grades 11 and 12: Social Sciences and Humanities, 2000. 2000. Toronto: Ministry of Education, Government of Ontario. Online. Available at http://www.edu.gov.on.ca/eng/document/curricul/secondary/grade1112/social/social.html#philosophy.

Chapter Fourteen

Accountability and Critical Thinking in K–12 Education: A Policy-Developer's Perspective

Linda Kaser

*I*n *The Educated Mind: How Cognitive Tools Shape Our Understanding,* Kieran Egan (1997) concludes with this perspective:

> Evolution has not equipped us ideally for the education-al tasks required by advanced literate societies. We are equipped intellectually for the condition of small nonliter-ate social groups sharing unquestioned ideologies and im-ages of the cosmos. Our preparation for such groups is only too evident despite our educational assaults on our young, and helps to explain why we have such difficulty and pain in expanding our understanding into and through adulthood. We have to adapt our undifferentiated learn-ing capacity to deal with much more complex and flexible learning than it has been evolutionarily shaped to handle. We cannot tinker with the "hardware" supplied to us by evolution, so we have to adapt the "software" of educa-tional programs in order to subvert the natural constraints on our intellectual flexibility. (278)

Policy-developers work with policy-"makers" (elected officials) in min-istries of education. They influence the "software" of K–12 education programs by helping to develop policies regarding assessment, account-ability, curriculum development and implementation, and teacher and principal leadership development.

Policy-developers want to create educated citizens as gradu-ates of their K–12 public learning systems. Policy-makers believe that parents, community members, business leaders, and citizens, as well as student leaders and educators, want to develop young people who are truth-seeking, open and curious, self-confident in their critical thinking skills, and thoughtfully mature in their judgments (Facione, Facione, and Giancarlo-Gittens 2000, 23). There is broad agreement that these are the dispositions needed for contemporary citizenship as well as for productive, civil communities and knowledge economies. In Canada and the United States, thinking skills and dispositions are crucial for students participating in modern multicultural and multilinguistic so-cieties where diversity of background, language, culture, and orienta-tion is a way of life.

But policy-makers face many challenges when they try to trans-late these—and other lofty thoughts—into action. One of the crucial challenges is described by Levin (2001b):

> Governments are particularly susceptible to issues that take on public salience through the media. As most people get their information about public events from the mass media, an issue that is played up in the media often be-comes something that a government must respond to, even if the issue was no part of the government's policy or plan. Media coverage is itself motivated by a number of consid-erations, but long-term importance to public welfare is not necessarily one of them. Indeed, novelty is an important requisite for the media in order to sustain reader or viewer interest, so that governments are likely to be faced with an ever-changing array of issues supposedly requiring imme-diate attention. (5)

Despite these pressures, Levin (2001b) is optimistic about policy-making, suggesting that the situation has improved because of "the changing nature of the political process....Three particularly important developments concern the growing importance of public debate, the growing importance of research and evidence, and the growing under-standing of the importance of implementation and adaptation" (8–9).

According to Levin, we can make better public education poli-cies by focusing on that which matters. We should avoid fads and pay attention to central issues that are well researched and sustained over time. We should share strong public-policy ideas through think tanks and the productive use of the media (to make sure that evidence and ideas get into the public arena). We should build links with users, politicians, civil servants, community organizations, professional orga-nizations, and foundations, at all stages of idea development. And we should ensure ongoing discussion about what research should be done, how it should be done, and its outcomes and conclusions.

> Some hardheaded realism on the part of researchers and analysts is required, including a willingness to understand and accept the realities of government. If we are to take se-riously the constraints and requirements of political action, we improve our chance to bring the increasing knowledge about better schooling to bear on policy. (Levin 2001b, 11)

If this hardheaded approach is kept in mind, policy-develop-ers and critical thinking researchers are well positioned to success-fully apply expanding knowledge about critical thinking theory and evidence-based thinking to all aspects of Canadian learning systems. Policy-developers see critical thinking as a cornerstone of our elemen-tary and secondary learning programs and of our development of an educated citizenry. They want to build learning systems that develop thoughtful democratic citizens. Critical thinking theorists and practi-tioners have created workable strategies for developing thinking and a useful research base from which developers can draw. But, in the pro-cess, one must heed Levin's points and recognize that the current era is one of citizen scrutiny, media desire for novelty, and taxpayer, citizen, and political demands for accountability.

The situation might be summarized as one which requires a reconciling of competing points of view. Policy-developers want to create an educated citizenry. They want to give the public information that demonstrates that the K–12 system is working well. The public wants to be sure that they are getting good value for their education tax dollars; that their young people are attending productive and caring public schools. Academics and teachers want to develop thoughtful, democratic learners who are able to think critically, creatively, and imaginatively.

The tension between these compelling but sometimes competing desires—accountability for investment, assurance of productive and caring schools, and development of critical thinkers—is played out in a North American landscape inundated by large-scale and increasingly high-stakes testing programs. In the minds of the public (and often the media), testing programs equate with accountability. Increasingly, some policy-developers fear this trend, believing that the testing drive is leading policy-makers away from a focus on a high-quality thinking curriculum and towards a narrower definition of excellence and accountability.

In an era of high accountability and a focus on test performance as a system measure of educational success, both policy-developers and educators must struggle to find ways for practitioners at the school level to strengthen their focus on thinking. If there is agreement that critical thinking is necessary for democratic societies and for the individuals who live in them, then the question becomes how education policy-developers can ensure that critical thinking is at the centre of all their work? Even more challenging is this question: How can policies, once developed, contribute in a culture characterized by intense media and public scrutiny, a national mood of searching for certainty and security, and a national demand for transparency in decision-making and accountability for the expenditure of public funds?

Such questions must be asked and answered in a manner which recognizes that the needs of *all* learners must be addressed. Accountability must mean accountability to all segments of society. Therefore, one must ask, "Are *all* the learners in the system acquiring the literacy, mathematical problem-solving and citizenship skills and commitments they need to engage in lifelong learning, thinking, and civic participation?" and, "Are *all* the learners in the system, regardless of geographic location, family background, gender, orientation, language or culture, acquiring the dispositions and skills of critical thinking at the highest possible levels?"

Accountability and Intelligent Assessment Practices: The British Columbia Approach

To answer questions of accountability and questions of assessment, one must recognize that they are deeply intertwined. The province of British Columbia's key policy-developers have adopted an approach to accountability which operates through the following five connected initiatives:

1. Some large-scale assessment for purposes of system account-ability.
2. A focus on intelligent classroom assessment.
3. An inquiry-based school and district review process that values evidence and critical thinking.
4. A reduction in the number of mandated curriculum outcomes and the development of a thinking-focused curriculum.
5. A focus on school improvement leadership that connects moti-vated teacher and principal leaders in an inquiry-based, active research community.

These five initiatives have been shaped by a distinction among three different kinds of assessment described by Earl and Katz (2006) in *Rethinking Classroom Assessment with Purpose in Mind: Assessment for Learning, Assessment as Learning and Assessment of Learning.* An over-all approach to evaluation and accountability must place a priority on all three forms of assessment: large-scale assessments *of* learning to ensure that all learners are obtaining the levels of foundational learn-ing success they need to participate in society; classroom-based assess-ments *for* learning with clear intellectual standards that help students and their teachers to see what constitutes clear, critical thinking and performance in the discipline being studied; and learner-based assess-ments *as* learning whereby individual learners are helped to reflect on their thinking processes in order to become more proficient and self-aware in their critical thinking.

Large-scale assessment

British Columbia policy-developers accept the importance of some large-scale assessments *of* learning. Provincial assessment leaders work collaboratively with academics and teams of teachers to ensure that the assessments used at Grades 4, 7, 10, 11, and 12 reflect the importance of thinking critically. At the same time, they are realistic about the constraints of time and format in capturing the richness and depth of student thinking. Consequently, the data provided by provincial assessments form some, but not the only or most important, pieces of the assessment puzzle.

With such limitations in mind, policy-developers and policy-makers agree that the results from large-scale assessment are useful in focusing attention on areas of system failure. In British Columbia such results have highlighted the failure to ensure that aboriginal learners succeed at high levels. Years of individual professional judgment and individualized classroom assessment have not drawn sufficient public attention to the significant problems of the province's aboriginal learners. One positive result of the evidence provided by provincial assessments in literacy and numeracy has been a growing collective demand for focused attention at all levels—province, district, school, and classroom—on the improvement of learning for aboriginal students and their families.

Classroom assessment

Creating the right classroom environment for developing young people with critical thinking dispositions requires the sustained effort of teachers and principals working together in thoughtful teams. Daily assessment, close observation, careful design of learning opportunities, and regular and thoughtful "close-to-the-action" descriptive feedback are school conditions needed to create strong thinkers. These are the *for* and *as* assessment practices that British Columbia has adopted in setting overall policy directions for accountability, assessment, and school improvement.

The emphasis on assessment *for* and *as* learning must be thoughtfully linked to students' self-assessments in classroom and school practice in order to help learners self-assess and avoid the difficulties Kruger and Dunning (1999) point to in their article "Unskilled and Unaware of It: How Difficulties in Recognizing One's Own Incompetence Lead to Inflated Self-Assessments." If the dangers for critical thinking inherent in inappropriately high self-assessments are to be avoided, it is crucial that high standards of thinking performance be taught explicitly. Once high intellectual standards have become a regular feature of the classroom environment, the metacognitive skill involved in thoughtful self-assessment can be applied from a strong base of understanding. As students develop as critical thinkers using the strengths of assessment *for* and *as* learning, they will become *self-critical*, which is one of the most important traits of the critical thinker (because it is the key to improvement).

Humanity needs all the metacognitive power that can be mustered and brought to bear on the decision-making and thinking tasks involved in addressing a host of serious global problems. Policy-developers in British Columbia believe that the daily use, in the classroom and out-of-school settings, of high intellectual standards built into criteria in thoughtfully constructed assessment *for* learning tools can play a significant role in keeping critical thinking at the centre of the learning enterprise.

The Accountability Model:
Encouraging Thinking Through Inquiry

Policy-developers and educational practitioners in British Columbia are in substantial agreement on the importance of all three forms of assessment in creating a framework for the development of thoughtful learners. In creating models of assessment, they have also addressed the question of how an accountability policy (designed to help government and the citizenry know what they are getting for their public investment) can be combined with an inquiry model of education designed to highlight the importance of critical thinking and evidence-based research for schools.

The argument for an inquiry-based approach is straightforward. There is a desire for educators to engage in the development of critical thinking for themselves and for their students. Assessing schools and districts, therefore, needs to be done in the context of a model that publicly values both inquiry and critical thinking as ways of assessing intelligent learning systems. A belief in the centrality of critical thinking, in the importance of evidence-based decision-making, and in the value of both quantitative and qualitative inquiry has produced an approach to accountability that is based on a district and school review. A "ten points of inquiry" model is used to assess effectiveness in focusing on the continuous improvement of learning (see

Appendix).

One key component of the "ten points of inquiry" model is its insistence that the evidence proffered for learning gains must include thoughtful, classroom-based assessment information. In this way, the review process actively discourages over-reliance on large-scale testing measures as the most important indicator of learning results. To ensure a broad appreciation of all the issues of assessment, a critical thinking disposition frames the development of the training of review team members. This model was developed as a genuine effort to point policy, political, and educational leaders at the provincial, district, and school levels in the direction of thinking critically *about* testing as a means of improving public education.

Right-sized assessment

In developing policies like those in British Columbia, policy-developers face a number of challenges. Developers of accountability systems, including those based on inquiry, need to be vigilant about issues of system flexibility. Analysis of global practices done by the BC network leaders found that politicians and policy-makers were unlikely to back away from the existing assessment approach after their jurisdictions made a sizeable investment in extensive amounts of annual, large-scale, standardized testing. Politicians, policy-developers, parents, communities, and educators are interested in trends-over-time data and this shared interest acts as an impediment to changes to the testing regime, even when these changes would make the testing more effective (see Kaser and Halbert 2004).

As new and better forms of large-scale and in-class assessment are created, it becomes difficult to add them into an already developed program of large-scale testing. This is all the more so because think tanks and the media enjoy using testing data to create lists of winners and losers among schools and districts. Despite their limitations, there is a public appetite for such rankings and politicians are pressed to act within the time frame of their electoral mandate. Critical thinking theorists, as many contributors to this volume have expressed, want time to develop stronger assessment measures that truly capture the development of thinking dispositions and skills, but this need and desire must compete for the interest of the public and policy-makers.

Policy-developers must keep in mind the public's appetite for information. It can create a very challenging context for policy-developers who want to ensure their system is an open-source one, where there is room in the overall assessment and evaluation systems for a critical thinking perspective as knowledge about cultivating thinking deepens. In circumstances like this, if one is to work persuasively it is important to keep any large-scale assessment program "right-sized." Such an approach provides enough large-scale assessment information to allow thoughtful decisions about the allocation of resources (to create high measures of equality and quality of outcomes), while ensuring at the same time that standardized testing is minimized so that there is enough time and energy for classroom assessment, and so that resistance to new assessment initiatives might be avoided.

In British Columbia, large-scale assessment is criteria-referenced and is intended to measure curriculum-based reading, writing, and mathematical problem-solving. Such assessment occurs in Grades 4, 7, 10, 11, and 12. Viewpoints will vary on the right amount of large-scale assessment, but the British Columbia program of testing, when judged by world standards, is relatively light.

Right-sized "stakes"

A second challenge for policy-makers is the need to keep the "stakes" for students and schools within a moderate range. Without enough consequences for individuals and schools, the public will not be confident that students are learning the key skills for participation in society. But governments must ensure that the consequences are not so heavy that they cause a learning system distortion by forcing an emphasis on test performances rather than "close-to-the-learner" thinking assessments.

The information that is provided from large-scale assessments must yield publicly a direction for the intelligent allocation of resources. In Canada, the policy support for allocation of resources to learners exhibiting vulnerability has been assisted by a community of researchers who have examined before-school indicators of child and family health and learning. Politicians of all stripes and at all levels of government have been informed of the resulting body of evidence, which shows that an early investment in supporting learners to assist them out of their vulnerability and into learning confidence is a wise investment for both social and economic policy reasons.

People working in school communities know first-hand that it is easier to teach thinking in classrooms when vulnerability issues have been addressed proactively and in a preventative manner. As a result of this growing and evidence-based understanding, investments are increasing in the development of high levels of early success—in oral language, in listening to understand, in writing, in quantitative understanding, in reading critically, and in social responsibility. This investment is a tangible recognition that the development of the intellect in preschool and primary years is a critically important part of the development of young thinkers and of successful critical thinking learning in the intermediate and secondary years.

Classroom-level assessment

Classroom-level assessment poses a third challenge for policy-developers in the evaluation arena. Systems that have attempted to "close learning gaps" in low-performing jurisdictions through high levels of system-wide testing and inspection have shown mixed learning results. Some systems with policies of high testing loads have also found disturbing side effects in the form of teacher discouragement leading to difficulties in teacher retention and recruitment (as Giancarlo-Gittens argues in this volume). A policy environment that reduces intellectual capital in schools is unlikely to sustain thinking for students.

The international evidence on school improvement suggests that policy-developers who want a healthier thinking culture should develop an intense and systemic focus on the principles of informative assessment—assessment *for* learning and assessment *as* learning. Fortunately, new and more powerful forms of assessing thinking are being developed. These forms build on the assessment insights of Black and William (1998) in the United Kingdom, Earl and Katz (2006) in Canada, and Stiggins (2002) in the United States.

As new areas of research knowledge and imaginative education develop, they provide powerful new teaching forms for educators. In such a context, it is critically important that assessment systems be flexible enough to capture the important new learning they create. This flexibility can be accomplished in two important ways: by making the large-scale system light enough so that there is room for emerging knowledge, and by making local system assessment at the classroom and school levels robust enough to capture the new learning in rigorous and compelling ways.

A broader challenge is to reinforce moves in this direction by ensuring that the larger community—the province, state, or country—responds quickly to intelligent, evidence-based work at the international level. This can prevent less-informed systems from becoming "laminated" or "hardwired" into the "brain" of a computerized information system that is integrated with the education system. Instead, the overall assessment system needs to have the qualities of a healthy and sustainable ecological system—with a lot of diversity and natural experimentation. Hardwired, large-scale, high-stakes assessments are problematic because they can work to lessen, or even prevent, diversity.

Overall, a too dominant test- and technology-dependent approach may diminish thinking capacity rather than build it. The "one best test" approach needs to be replaced with a powerful open-source assessment community with high standards of thinking at every level. British Columbia continues to explore the testing-assessment balance through open debate, review, and ongoing inquiry. The evidence from district review recommendations and follow-through as well as network growth in size and impact suggests that districts are beginning to move towards greater assessment balance. It will be important to sustain this encouraging direction.

Local review and assessment

If the need for an open-source, high-standards-of-thinking approach stands up to scrutiny, then it follows that policy-developers need to encourage the building of powerful models of local assessment as forms of distributed thinking in all parts of the learning system (schools, colleges, universities, institutes, districts, regions, and professional networks). These local implementation models can be seen as a series of natural experiments that can be critically evaluated. Technology can be used to bring the strongest models to professional and public awareness through video presentations and video journals that engage learners, teachers, and principals.

In British Columbia, standards of intellectual performance using criteria for high levels of thinking, writing, reading, math problem-solving, physical health decision-making, artistic inquiry, and citizenship/social responsibility are being developed by and with local teachers. The inquiry-based implementation of these standards is making its way into province-wide communities of professional practice. Case and his associates have been instrumental in building a thinking community though their work with "TC2"—a "Critical Thinking Cooperative" which includes educators from several school districts, faculties of education, and professional teacher associations.

A number of other local groups are also at work within the province. Active inquiry communities studying early and later literacy success have been established in every district. The Network of Performance-Based Schools is a geographically distributed group of schools committed to critical thinking, inquiry, research, and the publication of their findings. They have consciously been developed as a "third space" where teams of educators can think about making classroom assessment as thoughtful, reliable, and valid as possible. Like the other networked groups, they share the conviction that thinking criteria (such as the scoring guides embedded in the British Columbia performance standards for writing, mathematical problem-solving, and social responsibility, or in the Case and colleagues critical thinking scoring guides) must be shared with learners, their families, and their communities.

Curriculum Design and Implementation

There are many ways in which policies shaping provincial, regional, and national curriculum can play a key role in the development of critical thinking by all students. Many jurisdictions are seriously considering the importance of redesigning curriculum by reducing the number of outcomes in every grade and in every discipline. A "thoughtful outcomes" reduction process allows teachers and learners to shift the emphasis from a focus on covering a large number of knowledge outcomes toward more time for, and a greater emphasis on, thinking more deeply about key ideas and important questions. An "unstuffed" curriculum is important to young thinkers and their teachers.

The critical thinking curriculum must emphasize the development of dispositions as well as skills. As Facione (2000) points out,

> [s]kill and disposition are two separate things in people. Employers and educators prize both (Facione, Facione, & Giancarlo, 1996). A developmental perspective suggests

that skills and dispositions are mutually reinforcing; and, hence, should be explicitly taught and modeled together (Kitchener & King, 1995 [*sic*]). Common sense tells us that a strong overall disposition toward critical thinking is integral to insuring the use of critical thinking skills outside the narrow instructional setting. Motivational theory (Lewin, 1935) provides the theoretical grounds for the assumption that the disposition to value and utilize critical thinking would impel an individual to achieve mastery over critical thinking skills, being motivated to close the gap between what is valued and what is attained. (2000, 32–3)

A curriculum is more likely to build dispositions and skills if it emphasizes key questions, rich tasks, and assessment indicators that are built into it in each discipline. Implementation practices that actively encourage dialogue and debate through lesson study and the shared assessment of student work samples—including the use of photography and video clips to capture student dispositions, skills, and metacognitive language—form important aspects of a culture of critical thinking. Ensuring that every curriculum and assessment document is examined from a critical thinking perspective is vital if critical thinking standards are to become a way of life-long learning.

Effective curriculum development must be backed by staff development that values and models critical thinking. How staff development is conducted must demonstrate thinking dispositions and skills. If a learning system is to have a thinking disposition, then its staff-development models must value thinking. High levels of thinking cannot be expected of teachers who are restricted to scripted, directive staff development. Thoughtful staff development can be strengthened by linking professional school-level communities of practice with university-based researchers and educators.

Leadership as Distributed Critical Thinking

The leadership development of educators can contribute to a learning environment conducive to thinking skills and dispositions. One important aspect of this work is the selection, development, and supporting of new teacher and principal leaders. If the goal is thoughtful students who are disposed to using reasons and evidence and who can demonstrate maturity of judgment, then there is a need for teacher and principal leaders who can work cooperatively to turn their schools into thinking communities. Preparation of and ongoing support for school leaders need to be designed with this in mind. Leader teams working at the classroom and school levels need to be supported through reasonable investments of human and fiscal resources.

The model for these programs needs to be built on a strategy that applies research evidence to practice. As Spillane, Diamond, and Jita (2003) point out, most teachers will have to be introduced to instructional reforms and supported at the school level. Two challenges arise in such a context. The first is making sure that reforms are not seen only in a few pilot schools of enthusiasts for instructional innovation. The second is the challenge of ensuring substance and depth of thinking. Even with these challenges, all reforms must be enacted in ways consistent with the spirit and dispositions of critical thinking.

The research of Spillane and his colleagues (2003) examines how leadership thinking and acting are distributed across the learning community. In their model, a distributed practice of leadership is "stretched" over multiple leaders, knowledge sources, and activities over time, creating a leadership group which has "cognitive properties that exceed those of any one member" (5). This suggests that we need to understand leadership practice at the collective rather than just the individual level. An effective commitment to critical thinking education will need to have distributed critical thinking skills and dispositions.

To the extent that leadership extends beyond the mind of the individual, it is even more important that those in the leadership group demonstrate the highest levels of critical thinking. They must be able to distinguish among competing claims for attention and bring accuracy to their interpretation of evidence; identify a rationale for action; evaluate major alternative viewpoints; draw warranted and reasoned conclusions; justify key results and strategies; and fair-mindedly follow evidence and reasons where they lead. In demonstrating these traits, the leadership group must be able to exhibit mature professional judgment in a work environment characterized by intense time pressures and immediacy of action, as well as in a political environment characterized by a powerful desire for short-term, quickly achieved results.

Policy-developers need to ensure that the distributed leadership capacity, characterized by a thinking disposition and a powerful set of thinking tools, is supported through the development of a sustained leadership learning program. International research suggests that such a program can best be developed through multiple partnerships—with preservice, mentoring, and in-service programs that are linked and of the highest quality. Small group contact, technology-enhanced links, and ongoing study and practice are the best ways to develop thinking leadership with the highest standards of intellectual practice in action.

The development of a good leadership program requires cooperation from practitioners, universities, policy-developers, and governments. In British Columbia, the evidence suggests that this cooperative institutional teamwork is more likely to develop with a policy-based blend of incentives for connection and negative consequences for isolation. Both pressure and support are needed—support for communities of practice across institutional boundaries, and pressure for change for institutions that prefer to stay within their traditional territorial boundaries.

One example of this positive interdependency is found in the United Kingdom, through links between the National College for Leadership, the Higher Education Institutions, and the school-based Networked Learning Communities. International school improvement researchers suggest that other examples can be found, including in Finland and Taiwan, where there are university-practice communities which share a thinking-based teaching/learning worldview characterized by frequent and ongoing collaboration, and the study and refinement of practice. Strong evidence suggests that this is the kind of big system culture that needs to be developed if learning and thinking skills are to be instilled in all students.

The next step in British Columbia policy development is the study of successful examples of leadership development from the international learning community and the attempt to use those examples to shape a contextually appropriate teacher/principal leadership program. In keeping with the commitment to inquiry and critical thinking, it is critically important that policy-developers and policy-makers study the international evidence of thoughtful performance in cultures with high equality and quality outcomes and then bring the evidence to bear on their own decision-making.

Conclusion

I have tried to sketch a policy-developer's view of the issues that confront critical thinking initiatives in K–12 education. In British Columbia, the policy development community is committed to

- ❖ an interlocking set of policies that create a culture of intelligent classroom-based assessment of thinking in core disciplines;
- ❖ an accountability approach that relies on inquiry and critical examination of a range of evidence and improvement practices;
- ❖ an implementation approach that encourages the formation of face-to-face and virtual extended learning communities characterized by the qualities of critical thinking and a more focused and thoughtful curriculum; and
- ❖ a concentrated focus on developing and supporting critical thinking leadership, as the most promising way to create an environment for learners that encourages each one to think critically.

The province's aspiration is to have both its learners and its democracy become the beneficiaries of a systemic orientation to critical thinking as a way of life in schools.

References

Bailin, S., R. Case, J. Coombs, and L. Daniels. 1999. Common misconceptions of critical thinking. *Journal of Curriculum Studies* 31(3): 269–83.

Black, P., and D. William. 1998. Inside the black box: Raising standards through classroom assessment. *Phi Delta Kappan* 80(2): 139–49. Online. Available from http://www.pdkintl.org/kappan/kbla9810.htm.

Case, R., and L. Daniels. 1994–2004. *Critical challenges across the curriculum.* Vancouver, BC: Pacific Educational Press.

Earl, L. 2004. *Assessment as learning: Using classroom assessment to maximize student learning.* Thousand Oaks, CA: Corwin Press.

Earl, L., and S. Katz. 2006. *Rethinking classroom assessment with purpose in mind: Assessment for learning, assessment as learning and assessment of learn-*

ing. Western Northern Canadian Protocol. Online. Available from http://www.wncp.ca/.

Egan, K. 1997. *The educated mind: How cognitive tools shape our understanding.* Chicago, IL: University of Chicago Press.

Ennis, R. 2000. *An outline of goals for a critical thinking curriculum and its assessment.* Online. Available at http://www.criticalthinking.net/goals.html.

Facione, P., and N. Facione. 1994. *Holistic critical thinking scoring rubric.* Millbrae, CA: California Academic Press.

Facione, P., N. Facione, and C. Giancarlo-Gittens. 2000. The disposition toward critical thinking: Its character, measurement, and relationship to critical thinking skill. *Journal of Informal Logic* 20(1): 61–84.

Facione, P., Facione, N., and C. Giancarlo. 1996. The motivation to think in working and learning. In *Defining expectations for student learning*, ed. E. Jones. San Francisco, CA: Jossey-Bass.

Hautamaki, J. 2002. *Assessing learning-to-learn: A framework.* Helsinki: Centre for Educational Assessment.

Huber, G. 2004. *Preparing school leaders for the 21st century: An international comparison of development programs in 15 countries.* London: Routledge Falmer.

Kaser, L., and J. Halbert. 2004. *Networks of inquiry for school and district improvement.* Paper presented at the International Congress of School Improvement and Effectiveness, Rotterdam, The Netherlands.

King, P., and K. Kitchener. 1994. *Developing reflective judgment.* San Francisco, CA: Jossey-Bass.

Kruger, J., and D. Dunning. 1999. Unskilled and unaware of it: How difficulties in recognizing one's own incompetence lead to inflated self-assessments. *Journal of Personality and Social Psychology* 77(6): 1121–34.

Levin, B. 2001a. *Reforming education: From origins to outcomes.* London, UK: Routledge Falmer.

Levin, B. 2001b. Governments and school improvement. *International Electronic Journal for Leadership in Learning* 5(9): 1–13.

Lewin, K. 1935. *A dynamic theory of personality: Selected papers.* Translated by D. K. Adams and K. E. Zener. New York: McGraw Hill.

Mintzberg, H. 2004. *Managers, not MBAs: A hard look at the soft practice of managing and management development.* San Francisco, CA: Berrett-Koehler Publishers.

Reynolds, D., B. Creemers, S. Stringfield, C. Teddlie, and G. Schaffer. 2002. *World class schools: International perspectives on school effectiveness.* London, UK: Routledge Falmer.

Spillane, J., J. Diamond, and J. Jita. 2003. Leading instruction: The distribution of leadership for instruction. *Journal of Curriculum Studies* 36(1): 1–14.

Stiggins, R. 2002. Assessment crisis: The absence of assessment for learn-ing. *Phi Delta Kappan* 83(10): 758–65. Online. Available at http://www.pdkintl.org/kappan/k0206sti.htm.

Willms, J., ed. 2002. *Vulnerable children: Findings from Canada's national longitudinal survey of children and youth.* Edmonton: University of Alberta Press.

Appendix

British Columbia Ministry of Education District Review

The ten points of inquiry for use at the school and district levels are:

1.   What one or two important goals have you set for improving learning?
2.   What rationale have you used to set them—from evidence sources and your own critical thinking?
3.   What evidence have you used and will you use to guide your improvement work?
4.   What set of strategies are you using—strategies based on blending research evidence, emerging thoughtful practice, and innovative thinking?
5.   What organizational structures are you changing to make your improvement work more powerful?
6.   How are you making sure your work is coherent?
7.   How are you informing your community about your work?
8.   How are families and parents involved?
9.   What are you doing to share and develop leadership at all levels?
10. What important learning gains are you making?

(http://www.bced.gov.bc.ca/review/reviewguide.pdf)

Chapter Fifteen

The Role and Impact of Critical Thinking in Democratic Education: Challenges and Possibilities

Laura Elizabeth Pinto and John P. Portelli

*T*here appears to be a consensus that critical thinking is a necessary (though not sufficient) component for democracy. Education for democracy requires a commitment to cultivate critical thinking. In this chapter, we consider the current understanding and practice of critical thinking in K–12 education in the context of current political forces. We discuss the implications for education both in and for democracy. Finally, we highlight some challenges for critical thinking education and offer recommendations for policy and practice that would foster the integration of critical thinking into education in a way that strengthens the practice of democratic values in both schools and society.

The Current Context
We begin by recognizing that critical thinking is not value-neutral. Different conceptions of critical thinking reflect different values and the socio-political interests they support (Fernández-Balboa 1993). Consequently, we need to look at the political origins of educational policy trends if we wish to shed light on the dominant political forces that shape critical thinking and the extent to which it occurs in schools.

In the past decade, many jurisdictions (including parts of Canada, the United States, the United Kingdom, and Australia) have experienced significant, large-scale educational reform. All of these reform efforts have relied on centrally developed policy to define curriculum and shape classroom practice for a particular nation, state, or province. A number of theorists illustrate how "neo-conservative" ideologies have driven these recent reforms (Lankshear 1998; Levin 1998; Taylor 2001; Apple 2001, 2004; Wrigley 2003). This ideological impetus is reflected in the language that has characterized reform in recent years: competition, choice, excellence, standards, accountability, and "common sense" (Levin 1998; Apple 2004).

The resulting policies have been guided by two principles: (1) the priority of markets, which implies that government is part of the problem rather than the solution, and (2) the substitution of consumers for citizens—democracy is defined less by common public choice than by private market decisions. Central to these principles is a belief that democracy is the same thing as market democracy; this belief encourages the view that the spreading of markets and associated privatization constitutes spreading democracy (Beyer 1988; Barber 2004). Curriculum policy tied to notions of market democracy tends to emphasize academic achievement of students through uniform standards, outcomes-based education, and comparative testing structures (Portelli and Solomon 2001; Apple 2004).

These reforms have had significant implications for critical thinking education. There have been positive movements in the field of critical thinking education in universities and colleges, and in some K–12 programs (see, for example, the chapters by Groarke, Blair, Hatcher, Kaser, and Case in this volume). On the other hand, K–12 education policy based on the recent reforms tends to promote narrow conceptions of critical thinking. They are job-focused and serve the immediate interests of employers through "problem-solving" and "creative thinking" aimed at career preparation for corporate performance. Kenneth Sirotnik (1998) observes, "Rarely does the curriculum treat critical thinking as a dialectical process of reflective thought and communication, of competent discourse between people having both common and conflicting values, needs and human interests" (65). Instead, critical thinking is sometimes treated as an exercise of "problem-solving" within a narrow "cooperative learning" model that focuses on getting along without learning to address conflict constructively.[1]

There may be reasons why some stakeholders do not view critical thinking positively. One is the concern that critical thinking encourages the questioning of authority, and a second is the worry that it may disrupt the educational status quo. But should challenging authority and the status quo in education be a matter of concern in a society that values democratic principles? Without a doubt, critical thinkers will be compelled to challenge authority in various contexts—in schools, in government, and in the workplace (respectively: teachers/administrators, politicians, employers). We believe that such challenges foster democracy, but some in positions of authority may not relish engaging in discussion, or being accountable for responding to questions about their authority and its use (or abuse).

Indeed, a serious and full focus on critical thinking would suggest changes to many components of the educational system. Among other things, it would imply (as Blair argues in this volume) significant changes to teacher education, and changes to textbooks and other curriculum tools. An examination of curriculum policy documents in Ontario (Ministry of Education 1998, 2000) suggests that resistance to critical thinking in education may be tied to Canada's and Ontario's aim toward "economic prosperity" at the expense of other educational aims, such as the preparation of students for democratic citizenship and the inculcation of the values of deliberation and debate associated with such citizenry.

The narrow conceptions of critical thinking that seem to characterize curriculum minimize or wholly disregard some key intellectual and dispositional aspects of critical thinking that are required for active citizenry outside the economic sphere. If critical thinking is presented predominantly or exclusively as an "employability skill," its powerful role as an instrument for democratic life—and for the possible transformation of the state—may be lost and its moral empowerment undermined.

Challenges to Critical Thinking Policy and Practice

In a number of ways, the political environment we describe presents challenges for critical thinking education when it is conceived of as democracy in education.[2] We do not attempt to deal with theoretical challenges. Instead, we attempt to present the realities in which students, schools, and teachers are enmeshed. Only by addressing these challenges can the capacity for critical thinking be nourished and grow in a way that promotes democracy and an active citizenry.

Making "space" for critical thinking

Contemporary curriculum policies tend to be laden with learning expectations which rarely contain outcomes that foster critical thinking.[3] In addition, prescriptive and narrow state-mandated educational policies create further impediments to critical thinking. Teachers are pressured to ensure success on high-stakes tests which tend to focus on basic literacy and numeracy; and all educational workers are increasingly responsible for completing an excess of bureaucratic, accountability-related tasks. Collectively, these pressures create a situation in which accountability measures become the tail that wags the dog of learning—a phenomenon of "rationing education" (Gilborn and Youdell 2000). Giancarlo-Gittens (in this volume) uses data from several sources to show that literacy- and numeracy-focused high-stakes tests in the United States tend to drive instructional activity at the expense of the development of critical thinking activity in the classroom.

Given the pressure to ensure students are prepared for high-stakes tests, classroom time is spent on "the basics,"[4] in a manner that emphasizes "direct instructional techniques" rather than the possibilities of co-constructing knowledge, inquiry, and other activities that better foster critical thinking.[5] The consequent absence of the latter teaching methods compromises a crucial aspect of democracy in education. The direct instruction that is inspired by high-stakes testing might not promote critical thinking instruction to the extent that alternative views are not explored. Also, learning how to resolve conflict does not seem possible with the type of instruction that is intended to promote the basic learning solicited on these standardized tests.

If only one point of view on a particular issue is taken seriously in the classroom—because it is on "the test"—there is not likely to be a weighing of reasons for that point of view or a questioning of the information or process. In testing situations like those which Gilborn and Youdell (2000), Giancarlo-Gittens (this volume), and Groarke (this volume) describe,[6] students lack the opportunity to engage in inquiry that considers other perspectives. But when consciousness of alternatives to dominant views is suppressed or devalued, this is at the expense of a more holistic development that considers multiple perspectives in a manner that is required for democratic life. Democratic education needs to be education that "gives students access to social understanding developed by actually participating in a pluralistic community by talking and making decisions and coming to understand multiple perspectives" (Darling-Hammond 1996, 6).

Other voices, other positions

Struggles over meaning and values shape education policy. Critical thinkers should be wary of the possibility that only certain voices are reflected in curriculum policy. For instance, recent curricular reforms in many jurisdictions tend to be rooted in an ideology that emphasizes competition, education for economic prosperity, and standardization. In a democracy, exclusive ideological leanings such as these—conveyed overtly or through hidden and null curricula—should not shape the teaching of critical thinking. A focus on a narrow conception of critical thinking will not enhance democracy, especially if it is accompanied by an implicit or explicit emphasis on any one ideological perspective,[7] and therefore fails to address issues of diversity. For critical thinking to enhance open-mindedness, and not insulate students' beliefs or prejudices from challenge, there must be opportunities for students to explore a variety of positions.

In the context of critical thinking, it is especially notable that a variety of voices and positions have critiqued more traditional and narrower conceptions of critical thinking. We will briefly explore two voices that have contributed to reshaping the way critical thinking is viewed and taught: critical pedagogy and feminist pedagogy. Though these two positions are not identical, for the purpose of this discussion we will treat them as approaches that share a common perspective about critical thinking.[8]

Critical and feminist pedagogues challenge the common misconception that critical thinking is merely a set of skills that requires detachment between agent and object, and a disassociation between emotion and reason. Both argue against the limitations that result when critical thinking is constructed primarily or exclusively as logic and rationality. These stances do not deny the role of reason in critical thinking. Rather, feminist pedagogies seek to "integrate the inner voice (the subjective, intuitive, believing voice) and the voice of reason (the objective, critical, doubtful voice)" (Thayer-Bacon 1995, 56). However, as Nicholas Burbules and Rupert Berk (1999) remark, "critical thinking's claim is, at heart, to teach how to think critically, not how to think politically; for Critical Pedagogy, this is a false distinction" (53).

The critical thinker, as ordinarily conceived, is able to make informed and reasoned judgments, and come to understandings through a dialogical process, but does not *necessarily* apply the critical thinking process towards democratic (social and political) ends. Despite this difference of conception, we agree with Burbules and Berk's claim that critical thinking and critical pedagogy can co-exist since they share common ground. Combining the two can produce an alternative conception of critical thinking which has a social change focus while still drawing upon fundamental skills and dispositions commonly associated with critical thinking. In keeping with this, Mark Weinstein (1991) suggests that "critical thinking bridges critical theory and practice, offering a possible mechanism for education for democracy that speaks to deep motives that underlie democracy as an expansive ideal" (26). Consequently, the integration of critical pedagogy in critical thinking instruction and practice enhances the latter's capacity to strengthen democratic education.

This is not to say that a democratic vision of critical thinking in schools is a "free for all" in which the views of all individuals or groups are valued equally. On the contrary, dangers arise from excessive protection of the rights of every individual when attempts are made to avoid discomfort based on the preferences or beliefs of a particular individual or group. The critical spirit calls for respectful intervention or an attempt to increase awareness. Allowing an expression of differing views, respecting views, and accepting views are all different actions. The genuine critical spirit calls for proper interpretation of views expressed, and respecting others' rights to express them. Most importantly, and for the purposes of explaining our position here as critical thinking educators, the critical spirit must lead to engagement in fair evaluation of a variety of views in order to establish which fit best with our democratic ideals.

It is clear that a genuine critical spirit calls for a serious consideration of diverse views, even though it is "by no means clear that parents want such an education for their children" (Postman 2000, 160). Indeed, numerous situations have arisen in which parents have attempted to exercise their rights to restrict what information or ideas are available to their children in the school.[9] This practice is at odds with critical thinking and democratic education: if we keep differences out of school, then we deny children "the opportunity to consider freely various life options and to engage in the forms of dialogue that will develop their capacities to engage in democratic institutions" (Strike 1988, 260).

Welcoming Controversy and Risk

Democracies require citizens who are able to critically and openly discuss controversial issues without fear of penalty, and who are able to engage in meaningful and respectful dialogue about their differences. To think critically, in the fullest sense, in the classroom environment requires, at some point, that teachers and students address controversial issues. If students are to be taught the spirit of democratic life, they must be taught how to reason in light of moral and ethical choices. Such reasoning cannot be effectively introduced if it is disconnected from the ethical, social, and political controversies that may arise in all subject areas (Strike 1988; Dearden 2001, Winn 2004). Democratic education also requires controversy because democratic life requires tolerance and pluralism, and an ability to understand a variety of perspectives and viewpoints, some of which will inevitably cause controversy (e.g., issues of religion, sexual orientation, and lifestyle choices). A genuinely democratic way of life requires openness, including an openness to critical discussion of the thorniest of issues.

Dealing with controversy in the classroom raises a number of delicate issues. They include questions of whether teachers should reveal their views, how they should deal with disagreements, the danger of feeling insulted, and so forth. Teachers and their students must face the possibility that disagreement could be conflated with offence. In many instances, this conflation is evident in the misconception that disagreements are not desirable.

Some evidence suggests that cultural obstacles rooted in our current political climate deter the presentation of controversial issues in classrooms.[10] High profile cases involving creationism, children's literature that presents alternative lifestyles, and a host of other issues have often resulted in explicit and implicit school and board policies that compromise teacher autonomy. Such policies constrain the freedom of teachers to deal with controversial issues in classrooms as they see fit. For example, in November 2004, the Texas State Board of Education created national controversy when they required publishers to revise health textbooks to change the definition of marriage to the union of "a man and a woman," and excluded information on family planning and sexually transmitted diseases (Stutz 2004; Troppo 2004). Critics argue that the "hidden" curricula generated by these sorts of omissions will not serve the needs of students (Stutz 2004; Troppo 2004).

Another controversy—creationism versus evolutionism—has received considerable attention, particularly in the United States, although United States Supreme Court rulings have tended to uphold the right of teachers and students to discuss controversial issues (Cook 1984). That said, there are instances where the discussion of controversial issues is encouraged. The Toronto District School Board (TDSB) has taken a stance, resulting from its policies on equity, to encourage and support the discussion of controversial issues in the classroom. The board published a document titled "A Teaching Resource for Dealing with Controversial and Sensitive Issues in Toronto District School Board Classrooms" (TDSB 2003) with the intention of equipping teachers to address such issues.

Critical thinking requires an openness to controversy. It also requires a willingness to accept several forms of risk-taking on the part of teachers. Teachers must be prepared to accept that when students think critically, they will most probably disagree with and challenge the teachers' views. Though some teachers are no doubt comfortable with open discussion and disagreement in their classrooms, many may not feel comfortable taking this sort of risk.[11]

Another impediment to addressing controversy is the current accountability-driven educational culture. Critical thinking requires teachers to take risks by adopting practices that run counter to mainstream thinking. John Passmore (1967) discusses the need for courage among teachers to take on this difficult role, in the face of resistance from peers, students, parents, and administrators. In this volume, Giancarlo-Gittens suggests that as a result of accountability policy and overt pressure from administrators to boost test scores, teachers are placed in a difficult and conflicting position when it comes to taking risks and making critical thinking a central focus in their classrooms. The result is that teachers are encouraged or mandated to "teach to the test," rather than take risks related to addressing controversial issues. When "the test" does not include critical thinking—and that is almost always the case—then critical thinking is left out of the classroom in favour of rote knowledge exercises.

The ability and willingness to take risks in thinking and communication are another prerequisite for an educational experience in which students engage in critical thinking. Denise Clark Pope's (2001) ethnographic work suggests that systemic issues, evaluation procedures, and teacher characteristics often combine to prevent this from happening. As students, we have all wondered at one time or another, "Is this what the teacher is looking for?" But student reactions of this sort reflect poorly on school environments, suggesting a fear of poor test results or a narrow attitude developed over time in a rigid system. Pope has shown how extrinsic rewards and punishments (such as grades or test scores) can play an enormous role in students' school experiences, and can result in "safe" choices or highly calculated risks rather than critical thinking. Examples of these sorts of problems also appear in Megan Boler's work on democratic dialogue (Boler 2004).

Regardless of the reasons for it, the inability or unwillingness of students to speak freely is simply not consistent with a commitment to nurture critical thinking, nor is it conducive to democratic life. While critical thinking must encourage students to make judgments and act accordingly, many evaluation methods (particularly high-stakes tests) contradict such goals by creating fear and/or preventing students from expressing their views (for arguments regarding the latter issue see Sobocan, this volume). Students subjected to such evaluation methods may instead focus on providing what they believe to be the "right answer" in order to pass, and not take the risk associated with the attempt to express a view that might conflict with this perception of "right." This suggests that current evaluation practices need to be re-evaluated to make them more consistent with critical thinking content and pedagogy.

Accountability, Critical Thinking, and Democracy

Current educational policy is characterized by an emphasis on a particular notion of accountability (see Pratte 2001). This accountability is manifest in various policy instruments[12]—from formalized teacher performance appraisals to publicized high-stakes testing—whose results are used to make inferences about teacher performance, school performance, and school board excellence. Although these accountability instruments are a significant obstacle to critical thinking in the classroom, there are ways in which they could be reshaped to help cultivate an educational environment that promotes the development of students and teachers as critical thinkers.

Standardized teacher performance appraisals

In some jurisdictions, standardized teacher performance appraisals are used to evaluate the performance of individual teachers. Teacher appraisal has a significant influence on classroom practice given that teachers must meet minimum performance standards in order to continue teaching. In the present context, the important point is that performance appraisal criteria and performance expectations can be structured in ways that can encourage or discourage critical thinking in classrooms. Expectations for teacher performance are detailed in Ontario's *Manual for Appraisal of New Teachers* (Ministry of Education 2008).[13] The manual identifies a number of teaching competencies but fostering or encouraging critical thinking in teaching, or in student learning, is not among them. Moving to include critical thinking in teacher performance appraisal guidelines would be one important way to promote critical thinking in classroom practice. If teachers were accountable in this way for the cultivation of critical thinking in their classrooms, they would be more likely to take steps to encourage it among their students.

High-stakes tests and performance-based assessment

Many have argued that high-stakes testing is at odds with democratic education (Beyer and Pagano 1998; Caputo-Pearl 2001; Vinson, Gibson, and Ross 2001). According to Landon Beyer and Jo Anne Pagano (1998), evaluation in this context should not be a summary of performance, but an act that must be "part of an ensemble of educative practices that are democratic in character." A key characteristic of democratic evaluation, they suggest, is the inclusion of conversation and dialogue. In contrast to standardized tests—which tend to overlook complexity, reasoning, and context (see Groarke's critique of the *California Critical Thinking Skills Test* in this volume)—conversation allows contexts to be articulated and provides an opportunity for a whole-student assessment.[14] In their chapter in this volume, Ellett and Pitman discuss the role of moral, social, and political values in test validity, and make the point that a test cannot be separated from its socio-political context. Their position is that these values ought to be taken into account when designing evaluation methods.

Three brief, *prima facie* arguments illustrate how standardized, high-stakes testing is at odds with the ideal of democracy in education.

1. High-stakes standardized tests contain a hidden curriculum that legitimizes the knowledge and skills that are on those tests and marginalizes other kinds of skills and knowledge (see, for example, Dantley 2003).
2. High-stakes standardized tests make test preparation the primary focus of classroom activity, at the expense of other content and activity, and critical thinking in particular.[15]
3. High-stakes standardized testing sends strong messages about a conception of "accountability" that students experience through test-taking—including its (potentially negative) consequences for their teachers, schools, and communities.[16]

We have already presented variants of the first two arguments regarding the "basics" curriculum and the impact of high-stakes tests on classroom activity (see Giancarlo-Gittens, in this volume, for another variant of the second). The third reflects the emphasis that high-stakes testing places on an "external" authority, i.e., a body outside the school (and possibly outside the community) that makes crucial decisions about the nature and format of the test. The implied external account-abilities and extrinsic payoffs suggest that "authority" external to the immediate realities of students does not encourage the development of responsibilities and dispositions based on internal values.

High-stakes standardized testing has a number of negative implications for critical thinking. Evaluations that are democratic in nature do not lend themselves to rigid standardization. As Ellett and Pitman propose in this volume, we are more likely to create evaluation strategies that suit democracy by moving toward performance-based assessment. This is the most promising method for the effective assessment of critical thinking because it can incorporate elements of narrative and conversation and can better account for context (as suggested by Beyer and Pagano 1998). Because effective large-scale assessment and high-stakes testing require a more standardized approach to critical thinking, they are problematic. That said, performance-based assessments may not be sufficient for all purposes, because there may be situations in which the flexibility they allow promotes disputes over what constitutes satisfactory performance.

The problem with dispositions

One problem in testing is the complex role that dispositions play in democracy and critical thinking. Students cannot be good democratic citizens unless they have a disposition to think critically outside the classroom.[17] This suggests that the teaching of critical thinking is effective only to the extent that it creates this disposition. But how can this disposition be properly assessed (especially for accountability purposes) when teachers are limited to only those contexts in which they can encourage and see students' critical thinking—those being primarily classroom experiences? There seems no reasonable way to assess students' dispositional characteristics outside the boundaries of specific, "performance task" evaluations. In view of this, Ellett and Pitman's performance-based assessment allows for a slice of critical thinking evaluation, but it is one which may not assess the dispositions that present themselves in students' lives as citizens or community members outside of the school environment.

That which a student demonstrates during a performance-based assessment provides evidence only within the context of that activity—not evidence of how students would perform on a similar task in a different context, that is, outside the classroom. This is a deep problem with testing for critical thinking in democracy, because even if a valid and reliable test for measuring critical thinking skills and dispositions could be created, there is no guarantee that test-takers would act accordingly outside of the academic setting, and use critical thinking in a broader democratic context.

Towards a Democratic Approach to Critical Thinking

We have argued that current political trends (in particular, the rise of neo-conservativism and neo-liberalism) have driven educational reform in a variety of jurisdictions and that this has had a negative impact on critical thinking as a key component of democratic education. According to Aaron Wildavsky (1979), democratic education must promote an active and sustainable political arena which ensures that democratic principles (not politicization[18]) drive curriculum policy development. Such political arenas must promote continuous debate about values and feasibility, and reduce the politicization of the curriculum. This book provides just this sort of dialogue as it relates to critical thinking. Given the challenges that we have pointed out in this chapter, we offer six recommendations that aim to strengthen the role of critical thinking in democratic education.

1. We have emphasized the problems that attend functionally driven, narrow conceptions of critical thinking (as they currently appear in policies across many jurisdictions) that aim at outcomes tied to "economic prosperity." If critical thinking for democratic life is a desired curricular component, then an emphasis on democratic citizenship and choices, not a restrictive emphasis on career-focused educational goals, must be articulated in policy texts and embedded within all subject areas.

2. Democratic life and true critical thinking require an environment that allows students and teachers to take risks in their thinking and dialogue, and the ability to tackle controversial issues should they arise in the course of schooling (or life more broadly conceived). Educational policies must outline steps to create environments that allow such risk-taking. State- or board-level policy should, therefore, better support teacher autonomy and promote changes to teacher performance evaluation schema that would reward risk-taking or re-define professional standards in a way that welcomes risk-taking on the part of accreditation bodies (such as Colleges of Teachers).

3. Within a critical thinking education, the variety of voices and positions of individuals and groups in a democracy must be acknowledged and taken seriously. If a single conception of critical thinking is standardized through prescriptive policy, key aspects of critical thinking relevant to particular communities and groups may be lost. In a democracy, the understanding of "critical thinking" articulated in policy texts must be sufficiently broad and flexible to address different (and particularly marginalized) viewpoints.

4. Because what happens in classrooms tends to be driven by the

need to address prescribed, state-mandated learning expectations in education, critical thinking must have a prominent role in education policy if there is to be any hope for widespread critical thinking in classrooms.

5.   Although articulating critical thinking in policy texts is important, such policies must be enacted in schools. Enactment of critical thinking curriculum policy would require teacher education and development to ensure proper understanding of meanings and policy intents, as well as practical pedagogical recommendations aimed at the cultivation of critical thinking. As well, inclusion of critical thinking as a "look-for" in teacher performance appraisals might also contribute to widespread inclusion. This addresses the concerns raised by Blair in this volume concerning limited teacher capacity, and the issues raised around teacher performance appraisal.

6.   Given the recommendations above, the education system must make room for a variety of student assessments, which should include some broadly defined performance-based tasks. Democratic evaluation practices require more open-ended and flexible forms of evaluation instead of standardized tests. In developing new assessment tools, one must recognize that the assessment of critical thinking dispositions poses a special challenge in terms of reliability and validity. Although we suggest that it may be possible to create a democratic assessment and evaluation instrument for critical thinking, we do not believe that such an instrument has been developed.

Notes

1. For example, see the widely used Conference Board of Canada Employability Skills 2000+ inventory of skills.
2. Whereas "education for democracy" aims at fostering democratic citizenship, "democracy in education" focuses on creating a democratic learning environment (including curricula, pedagogies, and practices) that contributes to the aims of democratic citizenship through active participation.
3. For example, in Ontario, one-semester secondary school courses contain between 80 and 130 student learning expectations.
4. The notion of "the basics" is deemed uncontroversial within the neo-liberal and neo-conservative movements. However, this is a value-laden

concept at the centre of which are disagreements over what amounts to "basic." For elaboration, see Grumet (1993). It is important to note that even if we were to agree, for example, that literacy is a "basic," this in itself does not eliminate all the differing and competing notions of literacy.

5. Though Giancarlo-Gittens cites a number of other, negative outcomes related to standardized testing, we will focus only on the barriers standardized testing poses against critical thinking.

6. Giancarlo-Gittens provides a variety of empirical evidence which suggests that preparation for high-stakes standardized tests tends to drive classroom practice and content. She presents two scenarios that illustrate how teachers who are committed to constructivist pedagogies experience pressure from mentors and administrators to minimize or even abandon their preferred methods in order to focus on "the basics" required for standardized test performance.

7. If students, for example, are constantly introduced to a conservative position without consideration of counter-positions that are reasonable (there may, of course, be unreasonable alternatives that are examined and discharged), then open inquiry cannot occur. Given the tendencies expressed in K–12 educational policy towards neo-conservative ideas and values, we believe that students are not consistently exposed to a variety of viewpoints in mainstream education.

8. Critical pedagogues (e.g., Henry Giroux 1993, 2000; Juan-Miguel Fernández-Balboa 1993; Paulo Freire 1998a, 1998b) have addressed educational forms that explicitly aim at a more just society by addressing contestation and political struggle in the school/classroom environment. The views of feminist pedagogues (e.g., Jane Roland Martin 1992; Barbara Thayer-Bacon 1995, 1998; Carol Gilligan 1990) are rooted in the women's movement. They focus on social change as it relates to gender issues and the empowerment of women. More specifically, the feminist position holds that women have "ways of knowing" derived from the experiences that shape the way they see the world. It holds that these different ways of knowing are discounted by the dominant culture though they are potentially powerful for critique and transformation. Some other pedagogues explicitly combine the critical and feminist positions (e.g., bell hooks 1989).

9. For example, in November 2004, the Toronto District School Board introduced a video for students in Grades 3 through 7 that depicts children of same-sex families talking about how hurtful insensitive comments can be. In response, a group of Muslim parents at Market Lane Public School wanted their children excused from class when the issue of same-sex families came up on the grounds that their religious freedom was infringed.

The school board voted not to allow the children to leave, pointing out that it would violate the rights of the children the program is designed to protect (Benzie, Kalinowski, and Scrivener 2004).

10. Kincheloe (1999) asserts that the current political climate has resulted in "a false notion of neutrality" in schools (75). Evidence of barriers to dealing with controversial issues is presented in Evans, Avery, and Pederson (1999), Brandes and Kelly (2001), Lewison et al. (2002), Noddings (2004), and Winn (2004).

11. There are many reasons teachers experience discomfort, including, fear of loss of their authority; perceived or real pressure from students, parents or colleagues that they must be "experts" and "know the answers"; performance appraisal criteria; and the risk of being charged with unprofessional conduct. Some of these are discussed by Brandes and Kelly (2001) and Evans et al. (1999).

12. McDonnell and Elmore (1987) identify four categories of policy instruments that can be employed to ensure enactment of policy: mandates (negative consequences for noncompliance); inducements (rewards for compliance); capacity-building (providing training or resources to support enactment); and system changes (restructuring institutions in a way that incites enactment).

13. The *Manual for Appraisal of New Teachers* (2008) outlines 16 competency standards and a standard rubric to measure them.

14. Many high-stakes standardized tests tend to favour the regurgitation of facts over meaning, and selected-response-type items with narrow conceptions of "correct" answers (Sobocan, in this volume, argues this point with respect to the Ontario Secondary Schools Literacy Test's pass/fail evaluation rubric limiting the range of possible answers and what could be more detailed and creative critical thinking responses). This point has also been discussed by Vinson, Gibson, and Ross (2001), Caputo-Pearl (2001), Noddings (2004), and others.

15. Apple (2004) suggests that high-stakes testing "locks" curriculum in place such that it becomes teachers' dominant framework for classroom activity.

16. This may be referred to as the hidden curriculum of high-stakes testing.

17. Although Nosich (this volume) does not describe generalizability of the critical thinking skills fostered by his central reasoning assessment approach as "dispositions," he does propose one solution to the disposition problem we discuss here.

18. We are referring to the resolution of conflict through the use of power rather than consensus or negotiation.

References

Apple, M. 2004. Creating difference: Neo-liberalism and neo-conservatives and the politics of educational reform. *Educational Policy* 18(1): 12–44.

———. 2001. *Educating the 'right' way: Markets, standards, God and inequality.* New York: Routledge Falmer.

Bailin, S., R. Case, J. Coombs, and L. Daniels. 1999. Conceptualizing critical thinking. *Journal of Curriculum Studies* 31(3): 285–302.

Barber, B. 2004. Taking the public out of education. *School Administrator* 61(5): 10–13.

Benzie, R., T. Kalinowski, and L. Scrivener. 2004. Premier calls for "gay-ed" tolerance; School refuses to excuse Muslims. Teachers flocking to diversity class. *Toronto Star* [Ontario Edition], November 18, A1.

Beyer, L. 1988. Can schools further democratic practices? *Theory into Practice* 27(4): 262–9.

Beyer, L., and J. Pagano. 1998. Democratic evaluation: Aesthetic, ethical stories in schools. In *The curriculum: Problems, politics, and possibilities*, 2d ed., ed. L. Beyer and M. Apple, 380–98. Albany, NY: SUNY Press.

Boler, M. 2004. *Democratic dialogue in education: Troubling speech, disturbing silence.* New York: Peter Lang.

Brandes, G., and D. Kelly. 2001. Shifting out of "neutral": Beginning teachers' struggles with teaching for social justice. *Canadian Journal of Education* 26(3): 437–47.

Burbules, N., and R. Berk. 1999. Critical thinking and critical pedagogy: Relations, differences, and limits. In *Critical Theories in Education*, ed. T.S. Popkewitz and L. Fendler, 45–65. New York: Routledge.

Caputo-Pearl, A. 2001. Challenging high-stakes standardized testing: Working to build an anti-racist, progressive social movement in public education. *Taboo: The Journal of Culture and Education* 5(1): 87–121.

Cook, K. 1984. *Controversial issues: Concerns for policy makers.* Boulder, CO: ERIC Clearinghouse for Social Studies/Social Science Education.

Dantley, M. 2003. Purpose-driven leadership: The spiritual imperative to guiding schools beyond high-stakes testing and minimum proficiency. *Education and Urban Society* 35(3): 273–91.

Darling-Hammond, L. 1996. The right to learn and the advancement of teaching: Research, policy, and practice for democratic education. *Educational Researcher* 6(6): 5–17.

Dearden, R. 2001. Controversial issues and the curriculum. In *Philosophy of education*, ed. W. Hare and J. Portelli, 129–38. Calgary: Detselig.

Dewey, J. 1994 [1916]. *Democracy and education.* New York: Columbia University Institute for Learning Technologies. Online. Available at http://www.ilt.columbia.edu/publications/dewey.html (Last retrieved September 30, 2004).

Eisner, E. 1985. *The educational imagination*, 2d ed. New York: MacMillan.

Evans, R., P. Avery, and P. Pederson. 1999. Taboo topics: Cultural restraint on teaching social issues. *The Social Studies* 90(5): 218–24.

Fernández-Balboa, J. 1993. Critical pedagogy: Making critical thinking really critical. *Analytic Teaching* 13(2): 61–72.

Freire, P. 1998a. *Teachers as cultural workers: Letters to those who dare to teach.* Boulder, CO: Westview Press.

————. 1998b. *Pedagogy of freedom: Ethics, democracy and civic courage.* Lanham, MD: Rowman & Littlefield.

Gilborn, D., and D. Youdell. 2000. *Rationing education: Policy, practice, reform and equity.* Philadelphia: Open University Press.

Gilligan, C. 1990. Teaching Shakespeare's sister: Notes from the underground of female adolescence. In *Making Connections*, ed. C. Gilligan, N. Lyons, and T. Hanmer, 6–29. Cambridge: Harvard University Press.

Giroux, H. 2000. *Impure acts: The practical politics of cultural studies.* New York: Routledge.

————. 1993. *Theory and resistance in education.* South Hadley, MA: Bergin & Garvey Publishers.

Grumet, M. 1993. What are the basics and are we teaching them? In *Thirteen questions: Reframing education's conversation*, ed. J. Kincheloe and S. Steinberg, 33–57. New York: Peter Lang.

Gutmann, A. 1987. *Democratic education.* Princeton: Princeton University Press.

Hare, W., and J. Portelli. 2001. *Philosophy of education: Introductory readings*, 3d ed. Calgary: Detselig.

Haroutunian-Gordon, S. 1998. Some issues in the critical thinking debate: Dead horses and red herrings, anyone? *Educational Theory* 48(3): 411–25.

hooks, bell. 1989. Feminism and black women's studies. *SAGE* 6(1): 54–6.

Inglis, F. 1985. *The management of ignorance: A political theory of the curriculum.* Oxford: Basil Blackwell.

Kincheloe, J. 1999. Critical democracy and education. In *Understanding democratic curriculum leadership*, ed. J. Henderson and K. Kesson, 70–83. New York: Teachers College Press.

Lammi, W. 1997. The hermeneutics of ideological indoctrination. *Perspectives on Political Science* 26: 10–14.

Lankshear, C. 1998. Meanings of literacy in contemporary educational reform proposals. *Educational Theory* 48(3): 351–72.

Levin, B. 1998. The educational requirement for democracy. *Curriculum Inquiry* 28(1): 57–9.

————. 1994. Democracy and education, students and schools. Paper presented at the Under Scrutiny Again: What Kind of Secondary Schools Do We Need? Conference, Simon Fraser University, Burnaby, British Columbia, February 14.

Lewison, M., C. Leland, A. Flint, and K. Moller. 2002. Dangerous discourses: Using controversial books to support engagement, diversity, democracy. *New Advocate* 15(3): 215–26.

Martin, J. 1992. Critical thinking for a humane world. In *The generalizability of critical thinking: Multiple perspectives on an educational ideal*, ed. S. Norris, 163–80. New York: Teachers College Press.

McDonnell, L., and R. Elmore. 1987. Getting the job done: Alternative policy instruments. *Educational Evaluation and Policy Analysis* 9(2): 133–52.

Ministry of Education. 2008. *Manual for appraisal of new teachers.* Available at http://tpfr.edu.gov.on.ca/NTIP/NTIP-EngTeacherPerformanceAppraisalManual-May5-Final.pdf. (Last retrieved January 7, 2009)

———. 2000. *The Ontario curriculum, grades 11 and 12.* Toronto: Queen's Printer.

———. 1998. *The Ontario curriculum, grades 9 and 10.* Toronto: Queen's Printer.

Noddings, N. 2004. War, critical thinking and self-understanding. *Phi Delta Kappan* (March): 490–5.

O'Neill, S. 2000. The politics of inclusive agreements: Towards a critical discourse theory of democracy. *Political Studies* 48: 503–21.

Olssen, M., J. Codd, and A. O'Neill. 2004. *Education policy: Globalization, citizenship and democracy.* London: Sage.

Parker, W. 1996. *Educating the democratic mind.* Albany, NY: SUNY Press.

Passmore, J. 1967. On teaching to be critical. In *The concept of education*, ed. R. Peters, 192–212. London: Routledge & Kegan Paul.

Pithers, R., and R. Soren. 2000. Critical thinking in education: A review. *Educational Research* 42(3): 237–49.

Pope, D. 2001. *"Doing school": How we are creating a generation of stressed out, materialistic, and miseducated students.* New Haven: Yale University Press.

Portelli, J. 1996. The challenge of teaching for critical thinking. In *Philosophy of education: Introductory readings*, 2d ed., ed. J. Portelli and R. Solomon, 55–71. Calgary: Detselig.

Portelli, J., and R. Solomon. 2001. *The erosion of democracy in education.* Calgary: Detselig.

Postman, N. 2000. *Building a bridge to the 18th century: How our past can improve our future.* New York: First Vintage Books.

Pratte, R. 2001. Standards movement, accountability, and responsibility. *Journal of Thought* 36(3): 35–44.

Scheffler, I. 1973. Moral education and the democratic ideal. In *Reason and teaching*, ed. I Scheffler, 136–45. London: Routledge and Kegan.

Siegel, H. 1988. *Educating reason: Rationality, critical thinking, and education.* New York: Routledge.

Sirotnik, K. 1998. What goes on in classrooms? Is this the way we want it? In *The curriculum: Problems, politics, and possibilities*, 2d ed., ed. L. Beyer and M. Apple, 58–77. Albany, NY: SUNY Press.

Stein, J. 2001. *The cult of efficiency*. Toronto: Anansi House.

Strike, K. 1988. Democracy, civic education, and the problem of neutrality. *Theory into Practice* 27(4): 256–61.

Stutz, T. 2004. Texas picks textbooks that stress abstinence. *The Seattle Times* [online edition], November 6. Available at http://seattletimes.nwsource. com. (Last retrieved November 8, 2004).

Taylor, A. 2001. *The politics of educational reform in Alberta*. Toronto: University of Toronto Press.

Thayer-Bacon, B. 1998. Transforming and redescribing critical thinking: Constructive thinking. *Studies in Philosophy and Education* 17: 123–48.

———. 1995. Constructive thinking: Personal voice. *Journal of Thought* 30(1): 55–70.

The Toronto District School Board (TDSB). 2003. *A teaching resource for dealing with controversial and sensitive issues in TDSB classrooms*. Toronto: TDSB.

Troppo, G. 2004. Marriage will be spelled out in Texas textbooks. *USA Today* [online edition], November 7. Available at http://www.usatoday. com. (Last retrieved November 8, 2004).

Vinson, K., R. Gibson, and E. Ross. 2001. High-stakes testing and standardization: The threat to authenticity. *Progressive Perspectives* [2001 Monograph Series] 3(2). Online. Available at http://www.uvm.edu/~dewey/mono-graphs/ProPer3n2.html. (Last retrieved September 5, 2002).

Walsh, J. 1964. *Education and political power*. New York: Center for Research in Education, Inc.

Weinstein, M. 1991. Critical thinking and education for democracy. *Educational Philosophy and Theory* 23(1): 9–29.

Werner, W. 1991. Curriculum and uncertainty. *Social change and education in Canada*, 2d ed., ed. R. Ghosh and D. Ray, 105–13. Toronto: Harcourt Brace Jovanovich.

Whitson, J., and W. Stanley. 1996. "Re-minding" education for democracy. In *Educating the democratic mind*, ed. W. Parker, 309–36. Albany, NY: SUNY Press.

Wildavsky, A. 1979. *Speaking truth to power: The art and craft of policy analysis*. Boston: Little, Brown and Company.

Winn, I. 2004. The high cost of uncritical teaching. *Phi Delta Kappan* 85(7): 496–7.

Wrigley, T. 2003. Is "school effectiveness" anti-democratic? *British Journal of Educational Studies* 51(2): 89–112.

PART FIVE

Critical Thinking for the Future

Chapter Sixteen

Matters of Goodness: Knowing and Doing Well in the Assessment of Critical Thinking

Sharon Murphy

*T*o assess critical thinking is to comment on its goodness. Yet, as the chapters in this book reveal, the essential goodness of critical thinking is a complex and highly contentious matter. Engaging in the educational assessment of critical thinking compounds questions of goodness as it raises questions about not only the goodness of critical thinking, but also about the goodness of the assessment methodology one employs.

Given these challenges, how does one conduct oneself well in the assessment of critical thinking? In answering this question, I draw upon the philosophical exploration of "epistemic responsibility" articulated in Code (1987). For reasons I discuss, I believe it can help in the development of assessment strategies, tools, and practices that can inform the teaching of critical thinking.

Epistemic Responsibility, Assessment, and Critical Thinking

Code (1987) begins with the assumption that "most so-called knowledge is really well-warranted belief" (47). As Fleck (1979) and other philosophers of science note, yesterday's flat earth (a "fact" well warranted by the arguments during the time of that belief) is today's object of benevolent amusement and even ridicule. Situating knowledge claims in this way suggests that facts do not stand on their own and need to be understood within the context in which they occur.

The first step in justifying knowledge claims is to provide reasonable argumentation to sustain the believability, or goodness, of the claims made within a particular field. But it is a mistake to think that this is all there is to justification. According to Code, epistemic responsibility is tied to moral responsibility. As she puts it, "in some sense, ethical responsibility is founded upon epistemic responsibility, even if it is not identifiable with it" (5), and "one who has not been scrupulous in knowing cannot be scrupulous in doing" (95). It is reasonableness of conduct, not absolute rightness or wrongness, that is the central concern in ethical conduct, and it can be judged only by considering and understanding context. To discharge one's epistemic and moral responsibility, one must therefore not only be concerned with the usual matters of evidence and justification, but also be sensitive to context.

This means that when we argue about the goodness of our claims, we must simultaneously consider their goodness or lack of goodness in a particular situation in a particular community. In short, the epistemically responsible approach "denies the autonomy of the known, maintaining that the nature of the knower and of his or her environment and epistemic community are epistemologically relevant, for they act as enabling and/or constraining factors in the growth of knowledge" (Code 1987, 28).[1]

Against this background, one might ask what it would mean to engage in an epistemically responsible assessment of critical thinking. Following Code, this requires that three things be considered: (a) the knowledge claims made about assessment, critical thinking, or both; (b) the manner in which such claims are warranted; and (c) how such claims situate themselves in a particularity of context. One might compare these requirements for epistemic responsibility to the challenges that Messick (1989) offers. Writing in the field of educational and psychological assessment, he argues that consequential validity—the value implications and social consequences of assessment—need to be considered in validity arguments about the goodness of the assessment (see Ennis and Ellett and Pitman, this volume).

Conceptions of Critical Thinking?

Claims about critical thinking are not in short supply. One popular Internet search engine returned over fifteen million hits for "critical thinking." Some comments, such as the following from the actor, Alec Baldwin, bemoan a shortage of critical thinking:

> There's less critical thinking going on in this country on a Main Street level—forget about the media—than ever before. We've never needed people to think more critically than now, and they've taken a big nap. (Brainy Quote website)

Others offer seemingly seductive promises:

> A great way to get kids to think is with materials from *Critical Thinking* [Company]. Be amazed, as I was, at the number of quality thinking products. Great, great stuff— and the work is done for you! (Kidsdomain.com, as cited on the Critical Thinking Company website)

Although these short quotes indicate the ordinary person's understanding of the term "critical thinking," they, like the chapters in this volume, also illustrate the differences that characterize attempts to conceptualize critical thinking. In keeping with the requirements of epistemic responsibility, these differences suggest that such claims must be considered in a context that gives them meaning. Context is doubly important in the case of critical thinking because critical thinking is, by definition, relational—it is done in relation to an action, object, person, event, idea, or situation.

In her account of epistemic responsibility, Code argues that the process of determining the warrantability of any claim should include seeking advice from persons knowledgeable about the area in question. When a term like "critical thinking" is used, users have to consider whether the debates that characterize the term reflect different epistemologies or the effects of different contexts. An attempt to tease out the warrantability of each claim made about critical thinking would require a detailed analysis of each situational use—a task that lies beyond the scope of this discussion. However, it is possible to sketch inclusive and exclusive parameters that establish some criteria which are and are not constitutive of critical thinking. In this way a foundation can be created for the evaluation of claims that are made about critical thinking.

One exclusionary criterion for critical thinking that is implicit (and sometimes explicit) in the chapters in this volume holds that critical thinking must not be mistaken for critique. Johnson cautions that the "critical" in critical thinking is not tantamount to "criticism." A particular critique may be an example of critical thinking at work, but not all examples of critical thinking are examples of critique, and not all examples of critique are examples of critical thinking. Critique is not, therefore, a satisfactory criterion for critical thinking.

Similarly, the chapters on creativity (Hare, Hoogland, and Sobocan) suggest that although some examples of creative thought may be examples of critical thinking, not all examples of critical thinking are examples of creative thinking. Indeed, some instances of critical thinking may be achieved quite mechanically—as when one follows a set of prescriptive processes to think critically about something. So, again, creative thought is not a satisfactory criterion for determining critical thinking. Likewise, dispositions and commitments (see Giancarlo-Gittens and Case) are stances towards engaging in critical thinking but are not necessary or sufficient determinants of critical thinking.

Taken as a whole, the essays in this book suggest that the exclusionary boundaries for critical thinking are more easily drawn than the inclusionary ones. Nonetheless, two central themes permeate the inclusionary criteria that various authors suggest—argumentation[2] and judgment. These two themes work in tandem: critical thinkers must be familiar with the conceptual bases of a set of ideas, as well as the evidentiary basis behind the ideas so they may assess their merits and, as the situation demands, put forth credible ideas of their own. The demands on the critical thinker are, in essence, to *perceive* the essential points in a set of ideas, to *ideate* (categorize, conceptualize, hypothesize and think openly, analyze, generalize, think conditionally) in relation to that set of ideas, and to *re-present* or *present* (as the situation demands) a response within the same knowledge domain (Goodman, Smith, Meredith, and Goodman 1987, 15). Each of these actions demands incrementally more of the thinker engaged in critical thinking.

Though the experts in this volume generally hold that argumentation and judgment are central to critical thinking, they differ in their individual articulations of what counts as argumentation and what is involved in judgment. In describing the nature of argumentation, van Eemeren and Garssen use discourse analysis as a heuristic device. Johnson is particularly concerned with the dialectical tier—how a discourse may be structured in terms of the anticipatory moves one makes in relation to opposing points of view. Hare's interest is less in contestation and more in openness and analytical thinking. Nosich's emphasis on the fundamental and powerful concepts within disciplines highlights the particularity of argumentation within these disciplines (and, as such, amplifies its contextual elements).

Another central theme unifying the essays in this volume is that education in critical thinking skills is either explicitly (Kaser, Blair, Hatcher, and Pinto and Portelli) or implicitly both necessary and good. Although it does seem likely that better thinking should enhance one's quality of life and perhaps that of others, the necessity of instruction in critical thinking and the form that instruction should take are more contentious. Some authors endorse an extreme version of the need for instruction in critical thinking skills; Blair, for example, argues that critical thinking is not innate and must be acquired.[3] Others situate critical thinking in practices within specific social contexts such as a democracy (Pinto and Portelli), a discipline (Nosich), creative activity (Hare, Hoogland), or the application of deductive logic in writing (Hatcher). Although the thematic focus of the discussion naturally encourages an emphasis on education, non-school occasions that highlight the goodness of critical thinking warrant more attention. Few are likely to deny that there are non-school contexts in which critical thinking skills are alive and well. Even in pre-school years, children pragmatically negotiate their way toward increasing the number of toys they have, postponing their bedtimes, or extending the amount of play time they have by analyzing situations, anticipating the arguments offered by parents, and creating counter-arguments (based on their limited background knowledge and experience of the world) that "trump" the parents' arguments. It would be useful to study such examples.

Echoing Code's work on epistemic responsibility and Messick's (1989) work on consequential validity, a number of the contributors to this book argue that the goodness of critical thinking is tied not only to good argument and judgment but also to their consequences in particular contexts. The interest here is not merely in thinking but also in doing. Pinto and Portelli are concerned that the teaching of critical thinking has been tied in recent years to a utilitarian business interest in education—suggesting that critical thinking should be situated within the framework of larger social democratic ideals. It seems likely that all the contributors to this volume would agree that consequences are of great importance. Indeed, since its inception the critical thinking movement has been rooted in the conviction that critical thinking will positively affect our personal, social, and political lives.

One might readily compare the ideals of critical thinking to Code's account of wisdom, which she regards as virtually interchangeable with epistemic responsibility. Wisdom, she asserts, "involves knowing what cognitive ends are worth pursuing and understanding the value of seeing particular cognitive endeavors in context so as to achieve a just estimation of their significance" (53). This emphasis on context and consequences in wise thinking is also evident in Sternberg (2003), who characterizes a wise person[4] as someone with the following qualities:

(a)   reasoning ability (involving knowledge, logic, reasoning);
(b)   sagacity (being open to advice, being fair, acknowledging error, showing concern for others);
(c)   the ability to learn from ideas and the environment;
(d)   judgment (understanding self-limitations, undertaking thoughtful action, considering the long as well as the short view of things);
(e)   the ability to use information expeditiously; and
(f)   perspicacity (having intuition, reading between the lines, positing solutions on the side of rightness and truth). (178–9)

To act with wisdom is, arguably, the ultimate goal in critical thinking, because it integrates thinking and action within the context of a broader good. But even if there were general agreement about this claim (which there is not), it would still leave open the tasks of determining how critical thinking—broadly or situationally defined—might be assessed, and how the goodness of a particular critical thinking episode might be evaluated.

Epistemologies of Assessment?

Any assessment of critical thinking immediately intersects with explicitly or implicitly held knowledge claims about assessment in general. The expression of these claims in any particular assessment can be considered in terms of four components: (a) the architecture/technology undergirding the assessment, (b) how the goodness value-scale (the absence, presence, or abundance of knowledge or ability) is codified within the assessment, and (c) the contextual sensitivity of the assessment.

The architecture/technology of assessment

The architecture or technology[5] of an assessment is like the basic design of a building: it enables certain activities but not others. Assessment design in critical thinking, like assessment design elsewhere, invites and enables the scrutiny of some elements of the area being assessed and does not enable or invite the scrutiny of others (Murphy 2003a). Assessment design seems so fundamental that it is remarkable to find Snow lamenting, as recently as 1993, that "the field of educational and psychological testing suffers today because it never developed a psychology of test design" (45).[6] Mounting criticisms of multiple-choice testing and concern about the broader implications of assessment using constructed responses led Snow (1993) and Bennett (1993) to develop hierarchies of assessment design (see Table 1). In these hierarchies, multiple-choice assessment occupies the lowest level, whereas "presentation" or collection of different assessments occupies the highest.

Bennett's Hierarchy		Snow's Taxonomy	
Design Feature	*Design Description*	*Design Feature*	*Design Description*
Multiple choice	Choose from an array of options	Multiple choice	Choose from an array of options
Selection/ identification	Number of choices large enough to eliminate guessing (e.g., key lists)	Multiple choice with intervening construction	Retrieve, reconstruct, reason with knowledge
Reordering/ rearrangement	Place in correct or alternate sequence	Short-answer essay, complex construction	Generate sentence or paragraph
Substitution/ correction	Replace with alternative	Problem exercise	Generate/explain solution
Completion	Complete sentence, problem with single numerical response, etc.	Teach-back procedure	Explain concept, procedures, structure, system
Construction	Construction of unit such as graph, written explanation, drawing, proof	Long essay, demonstration, or project	Produce with or without topic constraint
Presentation	Physical presentation or performance using real or simulated conditions	Collections of above over time, portfolios, etc.	

Table 1: Proposed categorizations for assessment design. Adapted from Bennett (1993, 3–4) and Snow (1993, 48).

The hierarchies suggested by Snow and Bennett represent emergent possibilities of the relative goodness of assessment design types in a relatively under-theorized and under-investigated area in psychology. Given the lack of development in assessment design as a field,[7] we must not expect any assessment design to afford perfection in assessment. Just as building designers must face up to design trade-offs (because of costs, material availability, aesthetics, zoning regulations, etc.), assessment designers *and* users[8] must face up to the trade-offs and limitations inherent in any single assessment design. As Code (1987) asserts, the goodness of any assessment must be bounded by a recognition of its limitations within specific contexts

Consider, for example, multiple-choice assessments. Much has been written about the goodness of and the problems associated with standardized multiple-choice assessments (e.g., Ennis, Giancarlo-Gittens, Groarke, Pinto and Portelli, and Sobocan, this volume; Hill and Larsen 2000; Murphy 1994, 2001, 2003b; Murphy, Shannon, Johnston, and Hansen 1998). As is the case for most things, goodness in relation to these assessments can be judged on two levels. On one level, the issue of goodness is about the specific design genre incorporated in an assessment (see, e.g., Johnson, this volume). On the other level, the goodness at issue is whether the specific design genre was well implemented in a particular assessment tool. In the latter case, the question would be whether the tests were well designed in relation to the principles undergirding good multiple-choice test design (see Groarke, this volume; Hill and Larsen 2000; Murphy, Shannon, Johnston, and Hansen 1998).

Like multiple-choice assessments, other assessment designs must answer both of these goodness questions: (a) Is the design genre of the assessment a good one? and (b) Is the implementation of this specific assessment design genre well done? Much has been written recently about performance-based or "authentic" assessments that are typically intended as a counterpoint to the shortcomings of standardized multiple-choice tests, or as a way to offer more opportunities for more cognitively demanding responses (see Giancarlo-Gittens, Sobocan, and Ellett and Pitman, this volume). Although there may be something to these motivations, even performance-based or "authentic" assessments have some general shortcomings (Snow 1993; Murphy 1995), and are likely to have additional shortcomings when used in relation to specific contexts. It bears repeating that no assessment is perfect.

Goodness in any assessment design demands its own set of warrants which must be considered in relation to contexts of use. Perhaps because of a culture of assessment in the United States (Hanson 1993), and despite a relatively under-theorized design basis, the goodness of multiple-choice standardized assessment has been assumed by society at large. Such assumptions are ethically untenable and, like all assessments, multiple-choice standardized assessments must be judged in relation to specific contexts of use.

The codification of goodness

How an assessment is used in context is inevitably intertwined with how that assessment codifies the goodness factor. In the context of a critical thinking assessment, codification provides an answer to the question of how good an individual's critical thinking is.

Codification is an attempt to measure the relative degree of knowledge, skills, or ability. The codification of goodness in assessment has two basic facets: an encoding mechanism—that is, whether the summary statements describing the goodness are reported numerically or in words; and a comparison index—the thing to which any single performance on an assessment is being compared. Assessment design decisions about these two facets introduce assumptions about knowledge into assessment and thereby reveal goodness in particular ways. The different aspects of codification can be represented as in Table 2 below.

	Encoding Mechanism	
Comparison Index		
Relative to how others perform	Numbers	Words
Relative to descriptions of knowledge, skills, and concepts	Numbers	Words

Table 2: The coding of goodness in assessment

The numerical codification of goodness has been a common feature of schooling for the past century. Percentages, percentile ranks, and standard scores are among the many ways in which numbers are used to summarize a person's (or a school's) goodness on an assessment. Minimalism is both a strength and a weakness of this approach. Numerical codification is designed to distill down to a single number, or a series of numbers, the essence of a performance. Such numerical descriptions are often seen as more efficient than elaborate word-based codifications of assessment performance.

But fundamental questions have been raised about numerical codification. Hacking (1990) argues "that defining new classes of people for the purposes of statistics has consequences for the ways in which we conceive of others and think of our own possibilities and potentialities" (6). The statistical transformations that result play a central role in the "making up of people" (ibid.). In assessment, the numbers encoding the assessment are transformations of performance into some form of countable unit. This numerical distancing creates a veneer of mathematical precision replete with the social values accorded to such precision.

On top of this numerical transformation often comes another transformation whereby numbers are re-transformed into simple categories (e.g., above average, below average, gifted, and so on) which take on a special meaning and contribute to the "making up of people" that Hacking proposes. These categories of re-transformation go on to assume a consequential burden (through the social effects of labeling, access to selected types of education or goods, and so on) that extends far beyond the limited context of the assessment in which they were achieved (Murphy 2003b).

Beyond the categorical dilemmas associated with the numerical codification of goodness is a series of other mathematical issues. The first is one of language. To take but one instance, "percentage" and "percentile" represent quite different aspects of a data set despite the similarity of their names. A second issue arises when one considers what numbers are understood to represent. If a student receives 80 percent on an in-class test, for example, what does this number represent? A grade based on correct responses to weighted or unweighted questions? A grade based on a comparison with the performance of others? One based on the result of past performances of the person being tested? Or one of specific proportion of the knowledge presented in the class? Unless test designers and interpreters can provide reasonable responses to these types of questions, the assumptions underlying the numerical scale used are open to question.

Overarching both of these mathematical issues is the concern that numbers have very specific properties and are based on assumptions that should not be violated. When numbers are used in a categorical sense (as labels in rating scales, with, for example, 1 representing high and 5 representing low), they should not be treated as though they were pure numbers and added, subtracted, divided, and multiplied, because such operations further distort the results of the performance.[9] Mathematical operations result in, for instance, an overall score of average for someone who is rated low on 50 percent of the items and high on the remaining items. Yet, the fallacy of such mathematical manipulations becomes clear when the object of the rating is the bitterness or sweetness of a food. If half the items tasted are rated bitter and half sweet, it would be absurd to say that the food being tasted was neither bitter nor sweet but somewhere in the middle. Yet, these types of inferential leaps based on mathematical operations are routinely made when dealing with ratings involving abstract or difficult-to-pin-down concepts such as critical thinking.

The word-based codification of performance may not have mathematical issues to contend with, but it has issues of its own. First, the word-based encoding of assessment performance runs the gamut from lengthy verbal descriptions of performance to single-word descriptors of performance (poor, average, very good, etc.) that may or may not be based on a set of rubrics. In comparison with numerical codification, word-based codification may be more sensitive to the nuances and context of actual performance simply because numbers are tightly constrained by rules and assumptions whereas words may not be as constrained.

Lengthy descriptive word-based codifications tend to particularize the performance to an immediate context and the meaning of word-based codifications may be more transparent than the meaning of numerically based assessments. But single-word codifications offer a minimalist description which raises many of the same issues found in numerical codification. Such codifications may be based on rubrics or descriptions that are more elaborate word-based codifications of the knowledge, skills, or concepts at stake in the assessment, but the transformation to single-word descriptions raises many of the same issues as numerical codifications. As anyone who reads literature must confess, words offer their own challenges in terms of interpretation—defensibility or warrantability of interpretation is, therefore, a key component of word-based codifications of performance.

Whether numbers or words are used to codify performance, *codification is a relative task*. The encodings of performance depend upon that to which the performance is compared: the performance of other people (including oneself) performing the same set of tasks (e.g., norm-referenced assessment, classroom ranking of student performance); or an ideal description of the concepts and skills within a field of knowledge (e.g., criterion-referenced assessment, items on an in-class test). Any assessment statement must be understood in the context of the interaction between an encoding mechanism and a comparison index, and the possibilities and issues that this interaction raises.

Contextual sensitivity in assessment

For much of the past century, one dominant goal in assessment was the development of assessments that were thought to be impervious to context. Such assessments were designed in a standardized fashion, not unlike quasi-experimental research, whereby as many sources of extraneous influence (variance) as possible were controlled. The idea was that the resultant performance would reflect the residue of pure knowledge/skills/abilities that transcend the imagined bounds of specific contexts. This imagined state, in which standardized assessments have no context, allowed comparisons among individuals on a fixed set of tasks,[10] but these regulated standardized assessment contexts created contexts so unique that no analogous contexts existed elsewhere, raising the question of what the assessment showed about performance in non-assessment contexts.

Standardized, typically norm-referenced, assessments can be contrasted with assessments for which context is everything. Performance-based or "authentic" assessments that involve simulation or real-life assessment situations are about the here-and-now. Of course, the devilish question for these assessments is whether they can offer much of relevance beyond the immediate context. In situations such as the high schools of Central Park East, where a portfolio presentation/defence system is in place (see Darling-Hammond, Ancess, and Falk 1995), the generalizability of skill, knowledge, or ability is often captured because performance is interpreted as representative of the student's learning. The interpreter of the assessment "reads into" the assessment (Moss 1994) instead of having the assessment task "announce" its judgment via the process of numerical transformations. In this way, as Giancarlo-Gittens argues, performance-based or "authentic" assessments are more open ended than standardized multiple-choice tests.

In keeping with current theorizing about assessment and with conceptions of epistemically responsible action, the results of assessment must be interpreted in context. This means that warrantable claims about the critical thinking skills captured in a dormant assessment must work in tandem with warrantable claims about the use of the assessment for specific ends in specific contexts in order for the assessment to be considered valid (Messick 1989). This is an inherently reasonable stance but one need look no further than many governmental policies to see the damaging consequences of assessments that are not properly considered in relation to their contexts (Meier and Wood 2004).

Critical Thinking Assessment: The Epistemological Double Helix

Again, no assessment is perfect. In the context of critical thinking assessment, further issues are raised by the lack of a definitive description of critical thinking. The challenge that this places on designers and users of critical thinking assessments is to start from these premises, but not to make it impossible to say anything worthwhile about critical thinking. Rather, this double helix of imperfection can be the basis of a commitment to epistemic responsibility in this case—a commitment to consider carefully both the definition of critical thinking and the design of the assessment. Designers and users must be open to the possibility of enlarging, narrowing, refining, elaborating, or discarding definitions and assessments in relation to the particular contexts of use. This double helix of imperfection obligates them to continue to try to perfect concepts and design while simultaneously accepting that perfection is unattainable.

Once the imperfection of the concepts undergirding assessments of critical thinking is recognized, it seems imperative that all assessments must be viewed with a moderating eye in terms of the consequences they may have (for assessors and those who are assessed). To avoid acting in an epistemically irresponsible way, designers and assessors need to be somewhat circumspect; to consider how goodness is and is not instantiated in any one assessment activity; and to demand that multiple assessment artifacts of different types be assembled to warrant any claim of significant consequence. This epistemically and ethically driven conduct, with its obligation to be open and contextual, may in turn offer new routes in the development of both critical thinking and assessment. This book is a concerted and worthwhile effort in the direction of fulfilling such epistemic and ethical obligations in relation to the goodness of critical thinking assessment and evaluation.

Notes

1. When arguing for a knowledge claim, one is often arguing within an epistemic community—a community that shares in large part a similar knowledge base. In such a situation, a community's interest in consensus among its members (which represents a type of good—in the minds of community members, at least) may be taken to override the goodness of epistemic claims even when those claims are justified. One thinks of Galileo-like situations in which a lonely scientist who has made an innovative discovery is confronted by a community that refuses to consider what are much later considered to be well-warranted claims because they would shatter the grounds upon which that community is founded. In these and other cases, epistemic communities continually struggle with the tension between convention, which preserves communal knowledge, and invention, which challenges such knowledge but has the potential to move a community forward in its collective thinking.
2. Understood as a set of ideas or propositions that does not necessarily include a contestational stance.
3. This position fails to consider its inherent temporal paradox—simply put, how did the "first" critical thinker acquire his or her abilities?
4. Sternberg (2003) offers a theory that relates wisdom, intelligence, and creativity. The listing of some of the traits of wisdom does not do justice to the complexity of his theory but is offered here as a possible direction for the elaboration of theories of critical thinking.
5. Technology is used here in the sense that a technology invites particular uses. For instance, a pencil invites use as a tool for writing. Granted, the

pencil may be used for many other things, depending on context, but the principal invitation extended by the tool is to write.

6.   For instance, much emphasis has been placed on statistical aspects of multiple-choice tests, but only a handful of texts have been written on the design of multiple-choice test items despite the fact that they have been heavily used for much of the past century. Bormuth (1970) writes about controlling confounding sources of error in tests through highly controlling the language in the tests while Haladyna (1999) and Osterlind (1989) both focus on a range of multiple-choice test design issues.

7.   Although the overall field of assessment design is underdeveloped in psychology, it should be noted that some individual assessment types have been the focus of much attention. For instance, with the adoption of portfolio assessment within the field of education, numerous texts have been devoted to considering what the components of portfolio assessment ought to be and how portfolio assessment should be implemented (e.g., Belanoff and Dickson 1991; Underwood 1999; Case 2008).

8.   Designs are plans for anticipated uses. However, human beings, being social and inventive, often use things for purposes other than those anticipated by designers. Many examples of the unanticipated uses and stresses on buildings are documented in the text *Why Buildings Fall Down: How Structures Fail* (Levy and Salvadori 1992). For instance, an atrium bridge in a hotel lobby may well have met design specifications for large crowds but when the crowds unanticipatedly jump up and down to the beat of music, new and unanticipated stresses occur. In building design, the goal is to anticipate more and more uses and design assessments that take into account those uses. In assessment, designers place the burden of use on the users. For instance, in most large-scale standardized test manuals there are warnings about overreaching the meaning of the findings (see Murphy et al. 1998). Indeed, in individualized assessments, the same is true (ibid.). However, a look at press headlines, political statements, or the statements of many others (Murphy 1995, 2001; Pinto and Portelli, this volume) indicates that assessment results can be used well beyond the purposes for which they were intended (see Ennis, this volume, for a discussion of purposes of assessment). The consequential validity (Messick 1988) of these assessments is thus put in question. Unfortunately, however, some users treat assessment results as definitive rather than as the tentative and fragile (Murphy et al. 1998) pieces of documentation that they are.

9.   A good example of the inappropriateness of mathematical operations for the categorical use of numbers can be illustrated by an example relating to taste, where 1 is very sweet and 5 is very tart. If we have two very tart drinks and two very sweet drinks, would it be appropriate to say that on

average the drinks tasted medium—not too sweet and not too tart? Most people would agree that such labeling does not represent the tastes but would agree that a better representation would be to say that two drinks are very tart and two very sweet. Yet when the 1 is assigned the label "very good" and the 5 is assigned the label of "poor," many fail to see the fallacy in saying that the performance yielded from two scores of 5 and two scores of 1 is average.

10. Of course, there is also a fundamental assumption at work in standardized assessment design—the assessments have been very well designed. Yet, a variety of sources (e.g., Fillmore 1982; Filmore and Kay 1983; Murphy et al. 1998; Hill and Larsen 2000) suggest that fairly recent examples of such assessments reveal relatively poor design. Added to the poor design features are problems of use. For instance, there may be unmet assumptions that the characteristics of persons taking the assessment are similar to the characteristics of those upon whom the test was originally normed.

References

Belanoff, P., and M. Dickson, eds. 1991. *Portfolios: Process and product*. Portsmouth, NH: Boynton Cook Heinemann.

Bennett, R. 1993. On the meanings of constructed response. In *Construction versus choice in cognitive measurement: Issues in constructed response, performance testing, and portfolio assessment*, ed. R. Bennett and W. Ward, pp. 1–27. Hillsdale, NJ: Lawrence Erlbaum.

Bormuth, J. 1970. *On a theory of achievement test items*. Chicago: University of Chicago Press.

Brainy Quote. 2005. Alec Baldwin quotes. Online. Available at <http://www.brainyquote.com/quotes/quotes/a/alecbaldwi179389.html.

Case, R., and S. Stipp. 2008. Assessment strategies for secondary classrooms. In *The anthology of social studies*. Vol. 2, *Issues and strategies for secondary teachers*, ed. R. Case and P. Clark, 383–97. Vancouver: Pacific Educational Press.

Code, L. 1987. *Epistemic responsibility*. London: University Press of New England.

Critical Thinking Company. 2005. Online. Available at http://www.critical-thinking.com/index.jsp.

Darling-Hammond, L., J. Ancess, and B. Falk. 1995. *Authentic assessment in action: Studies of schools and students at work*. New York: Teachers College Press.

Fillmore, C. 1982. Ideal readers and real readers. In *Analyzing discourse:*

Text and talk, Georgetown University Roundtable on Languages and Linguistics—1981, ed. D. Tannen, 248–69. Washington, DC: Georgetown University Press.

Fillmore, C., and P. Kay. 1983. *Text semantic analysis of reading comprehension tests.* Berkeley, CA: Institute of Human Learning, University of California (ERIC Document Reproduction Service, ED 238 903).

Fleck, L. 1979. *Genesis and development of a scientific fact,* ed. T. Treun and R. Merton, trans. F. Bradley and T. Treun. Chicago: University of Chicago Press.

Goodman, K., E. Smith, R. Meredith, and Y. Goodman. 1987. *Language and thinking in school: A whole language curriculum,* 3d ed. New York: Richard Owen.

Hacking, I. 1990. *The taming of chance.* Cambridge: Cambridge University Press.

Haladyna, T. 1999. *Developing and validating multiple-choice test items.* Mahwah, NJ: Erlbaum.

Hanson, F. 1993. *Testing testing: Social consequences of the examined life.* Berkeley, CA: University of California Press.

Hill, C., and E. Larsen. 2000. *Children and reading tests.* Vol. 65 of *Advances in discourse processes.* Stamford, CT: Ablex.

Korsgaard, C. 2005. Theories of the good. In *The shorter Routledge encyclopedia of philosophy,* ed. E. Craig, 325. London: Routledge.

Levy, M., and M. Salvadori. 1992. *Why buildings fall down: How structures fail.* New York: Norton.

Meier, D., and G. Wood, eds. 2004. *Many children left behind: How the No Child Left Behind Act is damaging our children and our schools.* Boston: Beacon Press.

Messick, S. 1988. The once and future issues of validity: Assessing the meaning and consequences of measurement. In *Test validity,* ed. H. Wainer and H. Braum, 33–45. Hillsdale, NJ: Erlbaum.

Moss, P. 1994. Can there be validity without reliability? *Educational Researcher* 23(2): 5–12.

Murphy, S. 2003a. Finding literacy: A review of the research on literacy assessment in early childhood education. In *Handbook of early childhood literacy,* ed. N. Hall, J. Larson, and J. Marsh, 369–78. London: Sage.

———. 2003b. Literacy assessment and the politics of identities. In *Contextualising difficulties in literacy development: Exploring politics, culture, ethnicity and ethics,* ed. J. Soler, J. Wearmouth, and G. Reid, 87–101. London: Open University Press.

———. 2001. "No one has ever grown taller as a result of being measured" revisited: More educational measurement lessons for Canadians. In *The erosion of the democracy in education: Critique to possibilities,* ed. J. Portelli and P. Solomon, 145–67. Calgary, AB: Detselig/Temeron Books.

———. 1995. *Revisioning reading assessment: Remembering to learn from the legacy of reading tests.* Clearing House 68: 235–9.

———. 1994. "No one ever grew taller by being measured": Six educational measurement lessons for Canadians. In *Sociology of education in Canada,* ed. L. Erwin and D. MacLennan, 238–52. Toronto: Copp Clark.

Murphy, S., P. Shannon, P. Johnston, and J. Hansen. 1998. *Fragile evidence: A critique of reading assessment.* Mahwah, NJ: Erlbaum.

Osterlind, S. 1989. *Constructing test items.* Boston: Kluwer.

Snow, R. 1993. Construct validity and constructed response sets. In *Construction versus choice in cognitive measurement: Issues in constructed response, performance testing, and portfolio assessment,* ed. R. Bennett and W. Ward, 71–88. Hillsdale, NJ: Erlbaum.

Sternberg, R. 2003. *Wisdom, intelligence and creativity synthesized.* Cambridge, MA: Cambridge University Press.

Underwood, T. 1999. *The portfolio project: A study of assessment, instruction, and middle school reform.* Urbana, IL: National Council of Teachers of English.

Index